Advance Praise for *January 6*

"Julie Kelly is a singularly courageous journalist and indefatigable defender of truth. This is an eye-opening and breathtaking book that should be read by anyone who cares about justice, due process, and America's future."

—**Mark R. Levin**

JANUARY 6

HOW DEMOCRATS USED
THE CAPITOL PROTEST
TO LAUNCH A
WAR ON TERROR
AGAINST
THE POLITICAL RIGHT

JULIE KELLY

Foreword by Lee Smith, author of *The Permanent Coup*

BOMBARDIER
BOOKS

Published by Bombardier Books
An Imprint of Post Hill Press
ISBN: 978-1-63758-264-0
ISBN (eBook): 978-1-63758-265-7

January 6:
How Democrats Used the Capitol Protest to Launch a War on
Terror Against the Political Right
© 2022 by Julie Kelly
All Rights Reserved

Cover Design by Tiffani Shea

Post Hill Press
New York • Nashville
posthillpress.com

Published in the United States of America

Dedicated to everyone who still knows
America is worth fighting for.

And to the political prisoners.

TABLE OF CONTENTS

FOREWORD BY LEE SMITH xi

INTRODUCTION:
JANUARY 6 AND THE AMERICAN COGNITIVE DIVIDE 1

CHAPTER ONE:
WHAT REALLY HAPPENED ON JANUARY 6? 13

CHAPTER TWO:
THE MYTH OF AN ARMED INSURRECTION.. 51

CHAPTER THREE:
THE MYTH OF WHITE SUPREMACIST MILITIA GROUPS 79

CHAPTER FOUR:
LAUNCHING A NEW DOMESTIC WAR ON TERROR 105

CHAPTER FIVE:
WHAT KILLED BRIAN SICKNICK? 139

CHAPTER SIX:
WHOSE SIDE ARE THEY ON? THE ROLE OF THE CAPITOL POLICE...............................157

CHAPTER SEVEN:
DID ASHLI BABBITT HAVE TO DIE?..181

CHAPTER EIGHT:
WHAT WAS THE ROLE OF THE FBI? 199

CHAPTER NINE:
WHERE IS THE VIDEO FOOTAGE?.. 223

CHAPTER TEN:
INSIDE THE "DEPLORABLE" JAIL... 243

CHAPTER ELEVEN:
WILL THE CAPITOL DEFENDANTS GET A FAIR TRIAL? 265

CHAPTER TWELVE:
AMERICAN SHOW TRIALS: WHAT TO EXPECT IN 2022 283

ACKNOWLEDGMENTS **299**

ABOUT THE AUTHOR **305**

BY LEE SMITH

Author of *The Plot Against the President*

Julie Kelly's *January 6: How Democrats Used the Capitol Protest to Launch a War on Terror Against Their Political Enemies* is a blow-by-blow account from one of America's top investigative journalists detailing the lead-up to the January 6 protest, the march itself, and the aftermath, including the extraordinary repressive measures the federal government has taken against American citizens.

These measures include: the detention of nonviolent offenders for months on end without bail; postponement of their trials to give prosecutors more time to find evidence of the crimes they intend to accuse them of committing; physical abuse; psychological torture; and demands that the detainees recant their political convictions — that is, their support for the candidate from one of the country's two main political parties, Donald Trump.

In other words, the Biden administration is unlawfully violating the rights of American citizens simply for their political preferences. The 46th president of the United States has imprisoned supporters of his predecessor.

Thus, Kelly's book is also a political testament that documents how an oligarchic confederation comprising corporate and political elites, intelligence services, and the media are determined to transform a constitutional republic into a third-world-style security surveillance regime. With the publication of *January 6*, Julie Kelly becomes one of America's leading dissidents.

Even as the protest was underway, Kelly immediately saw through the media's real-time propaganda campaign. It was not, as they described it then and still do, an "insurrection." Rather, the live coverage showed that it was, or started as, a patriotic and at times raucous demonstration in support of a president that many millions of voters believed had been cheated at the polls. Crucially then the protestors — Americans from all walks of life, from Iraq and Afghanistan veterans to grandmothers, parents with preschoolers to truck drivers — were defending their right to elect the men and women who govern them, by *their* consent.

The protestors had good reason to question the legitimacy of the 2020 election. First, the press and social media tilted the scales on behalf of Trump's opponent by censoring information damaging to the Joe Biden campaign. Next was the Democratic Party's full-court press for mass mail-in voting. Prior to the 2020 election, Democrats and Republicans agreed that voting by mail was a recipe for fraud, but with the advent of COVID-19 Democratic strategists seized the opportunity by encouraging voters to stay home and overwhelm the system with votes by mail. Further, Democratic Party operatives unconstitutionally altered the voting procedures in various states throughout the country. Finally, on election night itself, in key swing states where Trump held large leads — Pennsylvania, Georgia, Michigan — election officials shut down and stopped counting votes. When the lights came back on next morning, Biden was in front in all.

Had any one of these "irregularities" occurred in a third-world country, the US Department of State would have declared the election illegitimate. Taken together, they gave evidence of systemic fraud. Americans were right to want answers and well within their rights to assemble peacefully and protest the election results. When the violence started in earnest on January 6, it was initiated, as Kelly reports in these pages, by law enforcement officers.

Police used teargas and flashbangs to frighten and disorient peaceful protestors. Demonstrators acting in self-defense were characterized by the press as aggressors. But it was law enforcement in riot gear that left death in its wake. Capitol Hill police officer Michael Byrd shot to death Ashli Babbitt, a 34-year-old Air Force veteran and Trump supporter. Byrd acknowledged on TV that he used lethal force without ascertaining whether Babbitt was holding a weapon. She was not. Biden's Justice Department declined to bring charges. As Kelly reports here, police used truncheons to beat a Trump supporter named Rosanne Boyland senseless, and thus her death at the Capitol building appears also to have been the result of police brutality.

Perhaps the most consequential aspect of Kelly's investigation takes up the story of the January 6 detainees. Dozens of Trump supporters held in a Washington, DC correctional facility have endured excruciating punishment at the hands of their jailers who refuse them medical treatment for the injuries they've caused them. Biden administration prosecutors petition to hold them indefinitely, even nonviolent offenders, and federal judges rubber stamp the Justice Department's draconian and unconstitutional demands to jail defendants who have not been convicted of any crime.

The self-described "liberal" media abets this madness by labeling Americans who exercised their rights to freedom of speech and assembly as "domestic terrorists." Accordingly, domestic US spy services like the Federal Bureau of Investigation and Department of Homeland Security demand more resources to wage a secret war against the half of the country that didn't vote for Biden. Only a handful of Republican officials have stood to say anything in support of their political base, US voters who have been hunted, penned, and beaten like savage beasts.

And yet the most astonishing thing about the treatment of January 6 detainees is that if it weren't for Julie Kelly, we wouldn't know the truth of what the American government is doing to the citizens it holds as political prisoners. She alone has been reporting these events as they've unfolded over the last year. She's spoken, corresponded, and met with detainees and their families, and those encounters with men and women broken physically, psychologically, and financially score the pages of this remarkable account with a steely-eyed passion. Kelly doesn't just demand justice; since she first started reporting the stories of the 1/6 detainees, she has fought for it day after day. And so this book, her report of an American nightmare designed by those who seek to crush the spirit of an independent, free and proud nation and revise the country in their ghoulish image, is a pillar of her campaign, on behalf of the detainees as well as the future of our great country.

History is not linear. Instead, it moves by a different logic, driven by those yearning for freedom, their respect for the sanctity of human life, and search for the eternal, God, in their brief walk on earth. Kelly's remarkable book reminds us of the inspiration that readers continue to draw from the works of dissidents who were imprisoned behind the Iron Curtain, writers like Aleksander Solzhenitsyn, Vaclav Havel, and Nadezhda Mandelstam. In spite of the dark and awesome hell that that threatened to extinguish light, the souls that illuminated those pages kindled hope, pride, and dignity. They broke the darkness, and truth won. Truth does not always win. Its success depends on our courage to escort it into the light.

And that is what you will find in the book you now hold in your hands, the testimony of a witness who brings us the voice of truth. And the voice you hear in these pages belongs to Americans who demand the rights granted by our maker and that no man has the right to deny us. Julie Kelly's essential story is about Americans who despite the physical, psychological, and political violence used against them, nonetheless profess an unshakeable faith in freedom. Every night before the lights go off, Kelly tells us, they raise their voice in song and sing the National Anthem. May God bless America and all those who fight for freedom.

JANUARY 6 AND THE AMERICAN COGNITIVE DIVIDE

"THERE WAS A CONSPIRACY** unfolding behind the scenes, one that both curtailed the protests and coordinated the resistance from CEOs," reporter Molly Ball explained in a lengthy *Time* magazine retrospective on the 2020 election published on February 4, 2021. [1] "For more than a year, a loosely organized coalition of operatives scrambled to shore up America's institutions as they came under simultaneous attack from a remorseless pandemic and an autocratically inclined President."

Ball's piece described the concerted efforts of a large array of civic-minded individuals and groups who had set out to "save democracy" from the threat posed by Donald J. Trump: "The handshake between business and labor was just one component of a vast, cross-partisan campaign to protect the election—an extraordinary shadow effort dedicated not to winning the vote but to ensuring it would be free and fair, credible and uncorrupted."

For Ball and her liberal readers, the 6,000-word piece was a congratulatory victory lap. But for conservatives, it seemingly verified everything that Trump, his legal team, and his supporters had been saying since the election in November. Voting laws

---

[1]   Molly Ball, *The Secret History of the Shadow Campaign That Saved the 2020 Election,* (Time 2021).

and voting systems had been changed to favor Democrats. They recruited election workers and exploited the pandemic to justify loose rules on absentee voting. Social media companies acted as the referee between "disinformation"—meaning anything critical of Joe Biden, his family, or absentee voting rules—and the "truth," meaning anything critical of Donald Trump, Republicans, or Trump voters.

In short, these shadowy interests leveraged every bit of power at their disposal to tip the scales in Biden's favor while fueling speculation Trump would use every bit of his power to stay in office. "Protecting the election would require an effort of unprecedented scale," Ball wrote. "As 2020 progressed, it stretched to Congress, Silicon Valley and the nation's statehouses. It drew energy from the summer's racial-justice protests, many of whose leaders were a key part of the liberal alliance." This admission alone was worth the price of the article.

Why did these brave defenders of democracy come forward in February 2021? They wanted their heroic story revealed to a grateful nation, Ball explained. "That's why the participants want the secret history of the 2020 election told, even though it sounds like a paranoid fever dream—a well-funded cabal of powerful people, ranging across industries and ideologies, working together behind the scenes to influence perceptions, change rules and laws, steer media coverage and control the flow of information. They were not rigging the election; they were fortifying it. And they believe the public needs to understand the system's fragility in order to ensure that democracy in America endures."

Ball was right about one thing: To Trump supporters, the article read like a shameless confession. "These people have to understand why ordinary people are completely gaslit by this stuff," Mollie Hemingway said in a podcast for The Federalist. "They cannot do this. They cannot, through their own warped politicized worldview, come out and say these things and, you know, at the same time shout down everyone that questions the way that corporate America is putting their thumb on the scale in our culture and in our politics as a crazy, deranged conspiracy theorist."

Writing for the *New York Post,* a newspaper accused of spreading "Russian disinformation" about Hunter Biden's laptop (later amply verified) and censored by social media giants right before Election Day, columnist Jonathan Tobin concluded, "There's nothing wrong with getting more people to vote, as long as the votes are legal. But there is something profoundly wrong with a system in which Silicon Valley oligarchs, big business, union bosses and lefty agitators can effectively shut down free discourse and freedom of the press during a presidential election in order to ensure their candidate wins."

Trump had warned repeatedly about Democrats' plans to hijack the election, just as they had attempted to sabotage his campaign in 2016 and derail his presidency in numerous ways for nearly four years, even before he was sworn into office. "We have to be very careful because they're trying it again with this whole 80 million mail-in ballots that they're working on, sending them out to people that didn't ask for them, they didn't ask, they just get them and it's not fair and it's not right and it's not going to be possible to tabulate in my opinion," Trump said during a speech on August 24, 2020, the first night of the Republican National Convention. The only way Joe Biden would win, Trump said, is by a "rigged election."

Trump obviously believed what he was saying—and so did many of his supporters. Why wouldn't they? After all, the country had been divided for decades over competing claims of voter fraud by Republicans and equally inflammatory claims of vote suppression by Democrats. Both sides embraced these conspiratorial claims as unshakeable articles of faith. Even today, many Democrats still confidently assert that the 2000 election was stolen from Al Gore by George W. Bush. Nor have they let go of their belief that Stacey Abrams lost the 2018 Georgia gubernatorial race due to GOP suppression of minority votes, even though minority turnout in that election was actually higher than normal.

In neither case have in-depth nonpartisan investigations finding no culpable evidence shaken these convictions.

In sum, we live in a country that is increasingly marked by a deep cognitive divide that tracks along partisan lines. The very different way Ball's article was read by people on both sides of this divide handily illustrates the problem.

In this case, it was obviously felt that no credence whatsoever could be granted by the victors to the losing side. To do so would call into question the legitimacy of Biden's narrow victory and plunge the nation into a profound political crisis. It was even feared that Trump would exploit the opportunity to suspend the constitution and declare martial law.

And so, four days later, despite widespread documented irregularities and flagrant violations of state election law; despite the fact that the validity of 70 million absentee ballots had not been thoroughly vetted by state officials; despite the filing of numerous lawsuits related to illegal ballot processing and counting; and despite the fact that recounts would undoubtedly be demanded in close swing states, the national news media unanimously declared Joe Biden the next president of the United States.[2]

That was supposed to be the end of it. The nearly 75 million Americans who voted for Donald Trump were supposed to sit down and shut up.

Trump, however, refused to accept it. So, too, did most of his voters and some who didn't vote for him. Surveys taken days after the election found the overwhelming majority of Republicans did not believe the election was "free and fair." A CNBC poll taken at the end of November showed only three percent of Trump voters considered the election legitimate; 73 percent said Trump won the election and one-third wanted him to fight the results in court. Two-thirds said the president should not concede the race.

Then there were all the anomalies.[3] Biden was the first president in decades to lose bellwether states such as Ohio (by a big margin)

---

2   Brian Slodysko, *Explaining Race Calls: How AP called the race for Biden,* (AP News 2020).

3   J.B. Shurk, *5 More Ways Joe Biden Magically Outperformed Election Norms,* (The Federalist, 2020).

and Florida and all but one bellwether county but still win the White House. Republicans flipped twenty-seven House seats deemed "toss-up" races. Democrats failed to win one state legislature.

Pennsylvania's results were the most dubious. Joe Torsella, the Democratic secretary of state, widely considered a 2022 gubernatorial candidate, lost to a Republican challenger by nearly 80,000 votes. "Torsella's loss marks the first time since 1994 that a Republican beat an incumbent Democratic statewide officeholder and caps a brutal election cycle for Pennsylvania Democrats in down-ballot races," the Pittsburgh Post-Gazette reported on November 11, 2020. A Republican won the state auditor's race by 200,000 votes. And the Democratic minority leader of the Pennsylvania state senate, a thirty-year incumbent, lost to a Republican.

A big red wave washed over the Keystone State in 2020. So how did Joe Biden end up winning the state by 80,000 votes?

Who was the public to believe? After four years of incessant attacks on Donald Trump from an overtly biased media, Trump voters did not trust them. As a result, the cognitive "reality gap" that had opened up between conservatives and liberals during the Trump years now became an unbridgeable chasm. And our national politics have been completely reoriented around it. Both sides are deeply entrenched in their views and neither side will budge.

Belief that the 2020 election had been stolen was branded Trump's "Big Lie." Anyone who doubted the outcome or questioned any aspect of the process was labeled a "conspiracy theorist." Efforts to expose unlawful ballot handling in states like Wisconsin and Pennsylvania, where election workers clearly broke the law by curing and counting absentee ballots before Election Day, were overshadowed by hard-to-prove claims of foreign servers and twitchy software.

Lawsuits were tossed out of court, including by Trump-appointed judges, most without even a hearing.

Texas Attorney General Ken Paxton on December 7, 2020 sued four states for violating the Elector's Clause and the 14th

Amendment. Unelected officials usurped both state election law and the Constitution, Paxton wrote: "[T]hese same government officials flooded the Defendants States with millions of ballots to be sent through the mails, or placed in drop boxes, with little or no chain of custody and, at the same time, weakened the strongest security measures protecting the integrity of the vote—signature verification and witness requirements."[4] Eighteen Republican attorney generals and more than one hundred Republican congressmen joined the suit. But the Supreme Court, including Justices Brett Kavanaugh and Amy Coney Barrett, denied Texas' standing to file the complaint.

By December 14, every state certified its election results, giving Joe Biden a clear path to the White House.

Trump voters, however, were not appeased. Polling continued to show that most Republicans did not trust the results. Voters were organizing "Stop the Steal" rallies across the country.

Presumably after getting an earful from constituents over the holidays, Republican senators, led by Senator Ted Cruz (R-Texas) announced they would ask for the creation of a special commission to conduct "an emergency 10-day audit" in the disputed states and said they would vote on January 6 "to reject the electors from disputed states…unless and until that emergency 10-day audit is completed."

A big protest was already scheduled for January 6, 2021 the day a Joint Session of Congress would meet to certify the 2020 Electoral College. Trump urged his supporters in a December 19 tweet to go to Washington, D.C. "Be there, will be wild!"

*   *   *   *

This book will explore the reasons why hundreds of thousands of Americans were in the nation's capital on January 6, what did and did not happen on that day, and the consequences for many of the individuals involved. Some showed up to cause trouble; others

---

4   Julie Kelly, Will This Texas Lawsuit Overturn the 2020 Election? (American Greatness, 2020).

would tell investigators they were caught up in the mob mentality. Most did not realize they had done anything wrong until the handcuffs were on.

But, just like the 2020 election itself, there are more lies than truth in the air. More coverup than transparency. Instead of trying to uncover the truth, the event and its aftermath are being used to advance the political agenda of Joe Biden and the Democratic Party.

Further, as many Trump supporters in the capital that day will attest, the chaotic protest and pockets of violence and death had the exact *reverse* effect of what they wanted: an audit of the 2020 presidential election. Quite to the contrary of the Democrats' narrative, the collective goal of hundreds of thousands of Trump supporters at the Ellipse and later on Capitol Hill was not to stop the democratic process but to encourage Republican legislators to approve a plan to examine the election in key states.

After the four-hour disturbance, some backed off, a proposal to audit voting in a few swing states did not advance, and Joe Biden and Kamala Harris were officially certified as president and vice president about twelve hours later than usual.

Not only did the wild protest defeat what President Trump, several Republican lawmakers, hundreds of thousands of demonstrators, and millions of Republican voters wanted to happen on January 6; the Capitol breach, as the U.S. Justice Department calls it, immediately became a pretext to turn the country's law enforcement, intelligence, and national security authority against Americans on the political Right. The United States now has its own set of political prisoners, with dozens held under harsh conditions in a jail set aside in Washington, D.C. just to detain January 6 defendants.

At the same time, the government is concealing evidence that would show the public exactly what happened that day. Federal prosecutors have sought protective orders on all video evidence used in court, even thirty-second clips. More than 14,000 hours of closed-circuit television footage is under the tight fist of the U.S. Justice Department and US Capitol Police.

It's still unclear how many undercover FBI agents or informants were involved, and we may never know. Requests for documents, videos, and email exchanges between top officials have been denied.

The news media has applied virtually no scrutiny to the abusive investigation into hundreds of Americans for mostly trespassing on January 6. Journalists show no interest in egregious constitutional violations, including First, Fourth, and Sixth Amendment protections, against Capitol defendants. News organizations use the words "insurrectionists," "rioters," and even "terrorists" without a second thought. Lives have been destroyed, families torn apart, finances bankrupted, reputations irreversibly tarnished.

I have been covering this story since it happened. As I watched the events unfold on January 6, I did not share the immediate reaction by most in the political punditry space. To me, hyperbolic claims of a "war" or "battleground" around the Capitol seemed decidedly overblown. Yes, events had clearly gotten out of hand; how much was organic and how much may have been planned and instigated by the U.S. government, Democratic Party leaders, and various political actors is still an open question. But it was far from clear that these events reflected an organized plot to overthrow the government. The vast majority of those who attended Trump's rally were there simply to support the President.

Most people who were in the capital on January 6 describe a much different atmosphere and sense of camaraderie than media portrayals suggest. Indeed, footage recorded by people on the ground shows a festive climate; Americans of all races, socioeconomic backgrounds, even political affiliations, traveled from across the country to join their likeminded countrymen to express grievances against the government—a Constitutionally protected right, or so the majority of Americans still believe. Folks I've spoken with and interviewed explained that their presence on January 6 was as much about defending the sanctity of their vote as it was a show of loyalty to Donald Trump.

Yes, there were violent clashes outside the building that apparently resulted in both police and demonstrators being injured. There were also several deaths reported in murky circumstances that would later be hotly debated. Meanwhile, videos posted in the wake of the protest showed hundreds of people being admitted into the Capitol by uniformed police and milling around the rotunda taking selfies like ordinary tourists.

Not for the first time, I was struck by how differently the same events can be viewed by people on different sides of our national political divide. Certainly claims of an armed coup attempt by organized white supremacists seeking to overturn the election seemed hysterical and purposely overblown for political effect.

Moreover, the moves made by Democrats and federal law enforcement in the immediate aftermath of the protest seemed highly sinister and dangerous to me.

Democrats and their allies, desperate to maintain power, have moved swiftly and cynically not just to stigmatize dissenting views of January 6, but actually to criminalize those who express any doubt or dissent about the outcome of the 2020 election. This kind of conduct does nothing to instill confidence in the Biden Administration and if anything fuels further doubt about its legitimacy and ultimate aims. Recent attempt to label agitated parents concerned about curriculum changes and transgender policies in schools across the country as "domestic terrorists" is a natural extension of this strategy to stigmatize and ultimately outlaw political dissent.

I have therefore for the past year devoted my journalistic efforts exclusively to covering these events and their aftermath, trying to distinguish fact and truth from myth and propaganda. The results have been, to say the least, profoundly disturbing, and are in many cases diametrically opposed to the narrative that has been pushed with remarkable unanimity since Day One by Democrats and their allies in government, media, law enforcement and big tech.

Here are the main findings of my year-long investigation:

The Capitol breach was not—repeat, not—an insurrection in any meaningful sense of the term. Apart from some improvised weapons brought largely for the purpose of resisting violent Antifa members, the crowd was not armed. Those who brought weapons, according to testimony and media accounts, took steps ahead of time to make sure they would not violate D.C.'s strict gun control laws.

The incursion into the Capitol itself was not organized and planned by highly trained white supremacist militia groups—it was largely a spontaneous event. Nor did the protesters intend or seek to overthrow the US government; to the contrary, Trump supporters later expressed sincere disappointment that the pockets of violence halted attempts to pursue an audit of the election.

Officer Brian Sicknick was not killed in the line of duty by murderous Trump supporters. Unarmed reservist Ashli Babbitt—the only shooting victim on that day—did not pose a threat of any kind to members of Congress and most certainly did not deserve to die.

Police acted as badly, if not worse, than the protesters and actually instigated much of the violence, counter to media claims. Though they may well have been frightened, the lives of lawmakers themselves were never in actual danger.

Outside of a few smashed windows and doors, physical damage to the Capitol was minimal, certainly not the $30 million worth later claimed by the Architect of the Capitol, much of it likely the fault of police themselves. No photographs exist showing fecal matter smeared on the walls of the Capitol, as alleged by numerous media reports.

Pipe bombs, found near the headquarters of both the Democratic and Republican National Committee headquarters, were inoperable—and it is still not clear who planted them. Ten months after the devices were located, prompting the first evacuation and intense media speculation, a suspect has yet to be identified and charged.

Meanwhile, it has since come to light that an unknown number of FBI informants were present in the crowd and may even have instigated the assault on the Capitol building.

As for Donald Trump, while he certainly did his part to stoke outrage and doubt about the election results, he did not incite violence and spoke repeatedly against it.

As I completed this manuscript in early November 2021, at least 650 Americans had been arrested. That number will rise as the FBI continues to arrest more people every week as part of its national dragnet. To date, not a single trial has been held. Roughly 120 defendants have entered plea agreements, of whom 105 have pleaded guilty to misdemeanors such as "parading" in the Capitol.

Meanwhile, numerous defendants languish in an improvised prison where they are subjected to abuse worthy of a Third World hellhole. Their treatment should inspire shame, alarm and justified outrage in every American citizen.

"Cancel culture" came fierce and swift for anyone involved with the protest, including those ultimately charged with low-level, nonviolent misdemeanors. People told me stories of being fired as they returned home from Washington, D.C., even though they did nothing wrong; neighbors, co-workers, and even relatives—at the behest of the FBI—ratted out Capitol demonstrators to law enforcement. Bank accounts were closed, service providers cancelled subscriptions, social media accounts were deplatformed. They were alienated by friends and family members, branded with a scarlet letter "I," for "insurrectionists." As one man tearfully explained to a federal judge, he was "radioactive."

Needless to say, Democrats are planning to exploit their narrative advantage to the hilt. Trials are scheduled to begin in mid-2022, in the heat of the midterm elections. House Speaker

Nancy Pelosi's select committee—the hastily-appointed January 6 Commission—is taking aim at Republican lawmakers and former Trump associates who supported the "insurrection."

This book undoubtedly will fail to cover everything that happened on January 6 and the months after. It is an ongoing story with new angles uncovered every day.

But the view from the wide-angle lens is crystal clear: What is emerging as I write is a shocking dual system of justice based on political differences and a thirst for power.

And this is only the beginning of the story.

CHAPTER ONE:

WHAT REALLY HAPPENED ON JANUARY 6?

THE PEOPLE WHO TRAVELED to Washington, D.C. on January 6, 2021 went for a variety of reasons, not least of which was to thank a flawed but effective president for taking so many blows on their behalf. They were small business owners and veterans, truck drivers and cops. Some came alone, others as married couples or entire families. Many would later tell federal prosecutors it was the first political rally they ever attended; they went because they believed one of the most cherished American rights, the right to vote, had been cancelled out by anti-Trump interests determined to remove him from the White House by any means necessary.

Despite the extensive news coverage about January 6, a comprehensive timeline that interweaves the goings-on both inside and outside the Capitol building throughout the day does not appear to exist. To the extent any timeline has been produced, contextual pieces of the puzzle, such as the involvement of individual protesters at any given time, largely are omitted.

This timeline attempts to fill that gap. Much of the blow-by-blow is drawn from media coverage including video compilations produced by the *New York Times* and ProPublica; official documents including congressional reports and testimony; open source video; footage sent to me by people in attendance; body camera footage from law enforcement; government charging documents; and court hearings.

Together, this presents a portrait of confusion with different things happening at different times, in different places, often unbeknownst to people inside and outside the unfolding chaos. While I have attempted to cover all the ground, undoubtedly, some details unintentionally will be overlooked.

Explaining the complexities of the day is critical; without a full portrayal of what happened, the American people cannot fairly assess what many political leaders and news organizations deemed the worst attack on our democracy since the Civil War. Like any battle scene, the facts that emerge after the dust settles often tell a more nuanced story—the line between bad guys and good guys can blur.

The timeline presented below is not intended to reach any foregone conclusion but instead to reveal, perhaps for the first time, the interconnected activity by lawmakers, police, and individual protesters on January 6.

*   *   *   *

People started pouring into the nation's capital the night before, on January 5. Buses filled with Trump fans from across the country unloaded passengers at downtown hotels and the surrounding suburbs. Some flew commercial planes and private jets. "Washington is being inundated with people who don't want to see an election victory stolen by emboldened Radical Left Democrats," Trump tweeted on January 5. "Our Country has had enough, they won't take it anymore! We hear you (and love you) from the Oval Office. MAKE AMERICA GREAT AGAIN!"

Large post-election rallies had been held across the county and in Washington in November and December. The "Million MAGA March" in the capital on November 14, 2020 drew a massive crowd. "Everyone was cheerful, smiling, laughing, and nodding to each other, giving one another thumbs up," one woman told a reporter. "All walks of life. All Americans that love their country. Hats were taken off and hands placed on hearts for the Pledge of Allegiance followed by the National Anthem." Ali Alexander, the self-proclaimed founder of the "Stop the Steal" coalition, Amy Kremer, head of Women for America First, and others tied to Trump organized the event.

Trump supporters leaving the rally later that day were attacked by Black Lives Matter and Antifa activists. Viral videos showed families, couples, and senior citizens being heckled and assaulted by leftwing agitators. "Trump supporters who approached the area were harassed, doused with water, and saw their MAGA hats and pro-Trump flags snatched and burned, while counter-protesters cheered," Fox News reported the next day.

Similar scenes played out during another "Stop the Steal" event the following month. After the December 12 rally in Washington, brawls broke out between Trump supporters, including the Proud Boys, and Black Lives Matter activists; a local news station reported that four people had been taken to the hospital and nearly two dozen arrested.

Based on social media posts, Trump supporters anticipated that leftist activists would again try to cause trouble on January 6. "Antifa is a Terrorist Organization, stay out of Washington," Trump tweeted January 5. "Law enforcement is watching you very closely!" Downtown businesses had been boarded up; on January 3, Mayor Muriel Bowser announced a long list of street closures, including Constitution Avenue and Pennsylvania Avenue, and parking restrictions. "I am asking Washingtonians and those who live in the region to stay out of the downtown area on Tuesday and Wednesday and not to engage with demonstrators who come to our city seeking confrontation, and we will do what we must to ensure all who attend remain peaceful."

The Associated Press reported that Bowser had called up 340 National Guard troops to help with traffic and crowd control. D.C.

Metropolitan Police, according to the agency's chief, "was fully deployed on 12-hour shifts the week of January 4, with days off and leave canceled." But Bowser also sent a letter on January 5 to the acting Attorney General, acting Secretary of Defense, and Secretary of the Army confirming that "the District of Columbia is not requesting other federal law enforcement personnel and discourages any additional deployment without immediate notification to, and consultation with, [D.C] MPD if such plans are underway." It was a move that earned widespread condemnation after the Capitol protest, raising questions as to why Bowser rejected additional security.

Members affiliated with the Proud Boys, Oath Keepers, and Three Percenters—groups the media and some federal agencies consider "domestic violent extremists"—were headed to the nation's capital. While it's hard to get an accurate count of how many individuals tied to the three groups were present—some news reports and video montages claim "hundreds" of Proud Boys descended on the Capitol on January 6—dozens would later be charged in the sweeping federal investigation.

Throughout Trump's presidency, the news media had portrayed these organizations as constituting the violent, armed white supremacist base of Trump's support. Whether these groups were in fact armed, or white supremacist, or had an actual plan to overthrow the government is very much in doubt. However, the prevailing media frame projected these assumptions on them in a way that was highly effective and hard to dislodge.

Officials later (i.e. not beforehand) learned of a threat alert from the FBI's field office in Norfolk, Virginia on January 5 about possible violence related to lockdown protests. The agency cited anonymous online chatter discussing calls to "fight" and "get violent." Posts warned that "Congress needs to hear glass breaking, doors being kicked in, and blood from their BLM and Pantifa [sic] slave soldiers being spilled. Go there ready for war. We get our President or we die. NOTHING else will achieve this goal."

For weeks before January 6, members of the Oath Keepers were making plans to travel to Virginia and stay at various hotels outside of D.C. Several Oath Keepers traveled from as far as Florida and Alabama; they arrived on January 5 so they could get to Trump's speech in the early hours of January 6. Members of the Proud Boys also arranged to come to Washington.

A handful of pro-Trump rallies were scheduled for the evening of January 5 featuring Roger Stone and Lt. General Michael Flynn among other Trump loyalists. Once again, clashes between Trump supporters and leftist protesters at the recently renamed Black Lives Matter Plaza led to the arrest of at least six people that night. Enrique Tarrio, a leader of the Proud Boys, had been arrested on January 4 on an outstanding warrant but other members of the group—Joseph Biggs, Ethan Nordean, and Charles Donohoe—were preparing to participate in the rally outside the Capitol building.

While the media and Democrats fueled speculation that the groups would be violent, the head of the FBI's field office in Washington later said the agency had no intelligence showing the event "would be anything more than a lawful demonstration." But between 7:30 p.m. and 8:30 p.m. on January 5, someone allegedly placed pipe bombs outside the D.C. headquarters of the Democratic National Committee and the Republican National Committee. News of the pipe bombs was reported by U.S. Capitol Police just before the joint session of Congress convened at 1:00 p.m. the next day.

Most of the people who traveled to D.C., however, were groups of friends and relatives unassociated with any particular group. Thomas Munn, his wife Dawn, and their three children drove from Texas to Washington, D.C. "We made it to our hotel just outside DC…1,600 miles in 24 hrs!," he posted on Facebook the night of January 5. The family of fervent Trump supporters wore Trump garb the following day. On January 2, Tom Munn posted a meme with a photo of Trump alongside a photo of Todd Beamer, the 9/11 victim who famously yelled "Let's roll" before attempting to overtake the hijackers on Flight 93. "The Time has come!" Munn wrote.

California resident Lois Lynn McNicoll, sixty-nine, arrived in Washington early. On January 4 and 5, she went sightseeing; McNicoll walked past the Capitol but did not get close to the building since barricades shut off access.

TIMELINE OF EVENTS

12:43 a.m.: President Trump posts his first tweet about the electoral college certification. "Get smart Republicans. FIGHT!"

1:00 a.m.: "If Vice President @Mike_Pence comes through for us, we will win the Presidency," he tweeted. "Many States want to decertify the mistake they made in certifying incorrect & even fraudulent numbers in a process NOT approved by their State Legislatures (which it must be). Mike can send it back!"

Trump and others close to him believed that Vice President Pence had the authority to reject Biden's electoral votes from states the president thought he had won. A lawsuit filed in December by Rep. Louie Gohmert argued that Pence has the sole discretion in determining which electoral votes to count for a given State, and must ignore and may not rely on any provisions of the Electoral Count Act that would limit his exclusive authority."

3:00 a.m.: People start to arrive at the ellipse, the fifty-two-acre park south of the White House, where the president is scheduled to speak.

6:15 a.m.: Thomas and Sharon Caldwell, who drove from their Virginia farm to stay at a nearby hotel the night before, arrive downtown. The line to get into the rally wraps around the Washington Monument several times. It is still dark.

7:00 a.m.: Doors to the "Save America March" officially open. Numerous lawmakers, Trump family members, and advisers are scheduled to speak. According to congressional testimony by Steven Sund, chief of the U.S. Capitol Police, a D.C. Metro Police investigator informed him at 7:15 that "there were already lines to get into the event, but that the crowd was compliant, and he did not observe any concerning issues."

The crowd participates in a prayer and the Pledge of Allegiance as speakers blare some of Trump's favored rally tunes including "Tiny Dancer" and "Gloria." The crowd is visibly cold; the day is overcast; temperatures are in the high 30s and low 40s with winds gusting between fourteen and eighteen miles per hour.

Despite the dreary weather, Trump supporters are in a festive mood. People are dancing and waving flags. "I've been to marches large and small, but I don't recall encountering such a polite, well-mannered crowd," a New York Trump supporter later wrote.

9:00 a.m.: The program officially begins "We are not going to let them continue to corrupt our election," Representative Mo Brooks tells the growing crowd.

According to an in-depth series by the *Washington Post* published in late October, Trump spent the morning with his family and reviewing his speech with aide Stephen Miller. The *Post* revealed that Trump and Pence had a "terse call" in which Pence reiterated his objection to disrupting the electoral college certification.

10:00 a.m.: Aerial shots show the grounds filled with Trump supporters wearing MAGA gear and waving flags. Attendees later describe the crowd size in the hundreds of thousands. Planes fly "Stop the Steal" and "Deplorable Lives Matter" banners in nearby Maryland.

Around 10:15 a.m.: Texas Attorney General Ken Paxton, who in December had filed a detailed election fraud lawsuit, takes the stage. The Supreme Court, with dissent by Justice Clarence Thomas and Samuel Alito, had refused to grant certiorari in Paxton's case. "We sued four states for not following the Constitution, not following state law, and we took it directly to the Supreme Court. They should have heard our case," Paxton says, at which point the crowd starts to boo.

Members of the Proud Boys, including Joe Biggs, meet near the Washington Monument around 10:00 a.m. Others, including Robert Gieswein, who are not official Proud Boys members, intersperse with the group. They aren't wearing the group's usual yellow and black gear; many, according to a *New York Times* montage of video taken that day; some inexplicably wear neon caps and armbands. Biggs is acting as the de facto leader of the group since Enrique Tarrio, its leader, could not enter D.C. following his arrest on January 4. At least sixty users had earlier participated in an encrypted chat titled "Boots on the Ground" to discuss plans for January 6.

Shortly after the group convenes, they start walking toward the Capitol grounds, chanting "Whose streets? Our streets!" At least one FBI informant was later revealed to have been in the group of Proud Boys. The informant would remain in constant contact with his FBI handler about the group's activity that day. Ethan Nordean, also known as Rufio Panman, is wearing all black, a pair of dark sunglasses, and using a bullhorn to corral the group behind him. "Proud Boys," Nordean randomly says into the bullhorn at one point.

While watching events on television, Maryland resident Robert Reeder, a driver for Federal Express, decides at the last minute to take the Metro into D.C. to watch Trump's speech. The fifty-five-year-old travels alone and arrives in the capital around 11:30 a.m. A registered Democrat, Reeder later said that he liked some of Trump's policies and his "patriotism."

10:30 a.m.: The president's family appears as a row of American flags whip behind them in the wind. "This is the greatest group of patriots ever put together," Eric Trump says. Pointing to the White House behind him, he reminds the crowd that his father "will never, ever stop fighting for you." His wife Lara declares, "This fight has only just begun." She then leads the crowd in singing "Happy Birthday" to her husband.

Donald Trump, Jr. compliments the crowd for protesting the election results "without burning down buildings...or ripping down churches," a reference to Black Lives Matter rioters who had set fire to St. John's church across from the White House in the summer of 2020. Don Jr. then takes aim at Republicans in Congress. "We are all watching," he warns. "This isn't their Republican Party any more. This is Donald Trump's Republican Party!" The crowd starts to chant, "Fight for Trump!"

10:50 a.m.: Rudy Giuliani and John Eastman, Trump's lawyers who had handled most of the campaign's election lawsuits, address the crowd. "We don't want to find out three weeks from now even more proof that this election was stolen, do we?" Giuliani asks. The crowd shouts, "No!" Giuliani endorses the plan to ask for a ten-day audit of the election results, which numerous Republican senators intended to do that day, calling the audit "perfectly reasonable and fair." They finish speaking around 11:00 a.m., the time Trump is scheduled to begin. But his speech is delayed an hour for unknown reasons; meanwhile the crowd continues to assemble as a mix of pop and country music blare from the speakers.

Noon: The House of Representatives is called to order by Speaker pro tempore Eric Swalwell. Lawmakers are led in prayer. "Defend us from those adversaries, both foreign and domestic, outside these walls and perhaps within these Chambers, who sow seeds of acrimony to divide colleagues and conspire to undermine trust," Reverend Margaret Grun Kibben says.

Down Constitution Avenue, "God Bless The U.S.A." plays as President Trump claps and waves at the sea of supporters. He marvels at the size of the crowd. "I've never seen anything like it. We have hundreds of thousands of people here and I want them to be recognized by the fake news media," Trump says.

While media accounts insisted the crowd was only in the thousands, photos taken that day seem to confirm Trump's assessment. Trump tells the press to turn their cameras and show the crowd behind the ellipse. "These people are not going to take it any longer."

For the next several minutes, Trump rails against the media, Big Tech, and the "rigged election"—his constant theme for many months. He recounts some of the apparent voting irregularities in swing states. "[U]sing the pretext of the China virus and the scam of mail-in ballots, Democrats attempted the most brazen and outrageous election theft and there's never been anything like this. So pure theft in American history. Everybody knows it. That election, our election, was over at 10 o'clock in the evening. We're leading Pennsylvania, Michigan, Georgia, by hundreds of thousands of votes. And then late in the evening, or early in the morning, boom, these explosions of bullshit. And all of a sudden. All of a sudden it started to happen."

Trump's view about the likelihood of election fraud is widely shared among those who showed up to the rally that day and they are angry and in many cases desperately alarmed by what they see as an assault on our democracy.

Could anything be done? According to Trump, the last best hope is vested in Vice President Mike Pence who as president of the Senate oversees the certification proceedings and had—theoretically—the power to send the delegate tallies back to the states for verification. Pence, Trump says repeatedly, had to "do the right thing." He blasts "weak Republicans" including Senate Majority Leader Mitch McConnell. "If this happened to the Democrats, there'd be hell all over the country going on. There'd be hell all over the country."

These statements were later cited during Trump's second impeachment trial as evidence that he had deliberately and knowingly incited a rebellion at the Capitol. This is far from clear since the idea of a planned insurrection is at odds with the notion of a spontaneous rebellion inspired by the president's inflammatory speech. Still, it is true that Trump at times unwisely chose to focus on farfetched, hard-to-prove election fraud claims rather than provable violations of election law in key states.

12:30 p.m.: As Trump continues to speak, the U.S. Senate is called to order. Right before he enters the Capitol, Senator Josh Hawley raises a fist in a sign of solidarity with the crowd. Hawley had announced on December 30, 2020 that he would object to the Electoral College certification. "He will call for Congress to launch a full investigation of potential fraud and election irregularities and enact election integrity measures," his office said in a statement. A few days later, seven incumbent Republican senators including Ted Cruz and three incoming Republican senators announced they would ask Congress for an emergency ten-day audit of the election returns in the disputed states.

Chaplain Barry Black opens the Senate session with a prayer: "As our lawmakers prepare to formally certify the votes cast by the electoral college, be present with them. Guide our legislators with Your wisdom and truth as they seek to meet the requirements of the U.S. Constitution. Lord, inspire them to seize this opportunity to demonstrate to the Nation and world how the democratic process can be done properly and in an orderly manner."

12:50 p.m.: Pence and members of the Senate prepare to walk to the House side of the Capitol building to commence the joint session of Congress to certify the results of the election. Nancy Pelosi, wearing a bright blue dress and patterned face mask, stands at the House podium waiting for Senate members to enter. "As the House comes to order for this important, historic meeting, let us be reminded that each side, House and Senate, Democrats and Republicans, each have 11 Members allowed to be present on the floor," Pelosi announces. "Others may be in the gallery. This is at the guidance of the Attending Physician and the Sergeant at Arms."

At the same time, Capitol Police receive word of a possible bomb threat outside the headquarters of the Republican National Committee, just a block or so south of the Cannon House Office building. An emergency management specialist working from home for the U.S. Commerce Department has noticed what she believed to be a bomb outside the RNC as she walked to do her laundry. "I saw a tangle of wires," Karlin Younger told reporters a few weeks later. "I looked closer and saw a six-inch pipe capped on both ends. Then I saw a timer that was stuck on the number 20. It was a radial dial." She notified a guard who contacted police.

The mayor of Madison, Wisconsin, Younger's hometown, later presented Younger with a special commendation, noting, "January 6th will live in infamy as a day in which an armed mobbed overran the U.S. Capitol and Ms. Younger's swift action prevented further injuries and deaths on that terrible day."

Another device is seized near the headquarters of the Democratic National Committee, a few blocks away. The Hazardous Materials Response Team of the USCP, according to a statement released the next day, determined both devices were "hazardous and could cause great harm to public safety." USCP disable the devices and reportedly give the materials to the FBI to investigate.

USCP Chief Steven Sund later testified to Congress what happened next. "At almost the exact same time [that they heard of the threat] we observed a large group of individuals approaching the West Front of the Capitol," Sund told the Senate Committee on Rules and Administration and the Senate Homeland Security and Government Affairs Committee on February 23. "As soon as this group arrived at our perimeter, they immediately began to fight violently with the officers and to tear apart the steel crowd control barriers, using them to assault the officers. It was immediately clear that their primary goal was to defeat our perimeter as quickly as possible and to get past the police line."

"This mob was like nothing I have seen in my law enforcement career," Sund continued. "The group consisted of thousands of well-coordinated, well-equipped violent criminals. They had weapons, chemical munitions, protective equipment, explosives, and climbing gear. A number of them were wearing radio ear pieces indicating a high level of coordination."

Sund's description was shocking and extreme, but so far it has not been substantiated by evidence. No guns were recovered inside the building nor were any explosive devices. The only chemical munitions recovered at the scene were cans of pepper spray and bear repellent. It is also not clear how he knew with such assurance that the crowd contained "thousands of violent criminals." No evidence has since been presented to show that it did.

What we do know is that a group of a few hundred protesters, including Joe Biggs and several Proud Boy members, faced off with a thin row of police officers on the west side of the Capitol right before 1:00 p.m. The entire grounds of the Capitol complex had been closed to the public for January 6, something without recent precedent. Designating a huge swath of outdoor public property—the nearly sixty-acre site is considered a public park—off-limits when hundreds of thousands of Americans planned to be in the capital that day seems highly unusual. Many who set foot on the property, even those unaware the outdoor space was closed to the public, were later arrested and charged with trespassing.

The building itself, which covers nearly four acres and 1.5 million square feet with nearly 600 offices, is sparsely protected with lightweight bike racks, some temporary fencing, and a limited number of officers.

12:53 p.m.: The first set of protesters, including Biggs, an unknown number of self-identified Proud Boys and others unaffiliated with the group have taken a position outside the fencing on the west side near Peace Circle at a pedestrian entrance. Scaffolding for the inauguration stage had been erected outside the building in advance of Biden's swearing-in ceremony on January 20. Several staircases and terraces provide access to the building's entrances.

Biggs rallies the group with a bullhorn. "We love Trump! We love Trump!" Ryan Samsel, a Pennsylvania resident on parole with a history of assault convictions, briefly speaks to Biggs. As he walks toward a line of people standing in front of five ill-equipped Capitol Police officers he is approached by another man, subsequently identified as Ray Epps, who whispers into Samsel's ear.

Epps is later heard on tape repeatedly telling groups of Trump supporters the night before to go inside the Capitol on January 6. As people leave Trump's speech that afternoon, Epps, wearing a Trump hat, is again seen on video shouting orders to passersby: "We are going to the Capitol where our problems are," Epps yells. Pointing toward the building, he shouts, "It's that direction."

After Epps speaks to him, Samsel confronts police, compelling several individuals to help him overrun a barricade of bike racks and light fencing; video shows one officer knocked to the ground. "We don't have to hurt you, why are you standing in our way?" Samsel asks one officer.

Others join in, pushing police backwards and tossing aside temporary metal barriers. Two men on top of the steps furiously wave people in the direction of the building. Biggs and others "shook the metal fence until it broke apart and toppled at their feet," prosecutors wrote in a criminal complaint filed against Biggs in March. They then stomped over the racks and headed toward the building.

Samsel, wearing a "Make America Great Again" hat turned backwards, jogs up the steps to the west side of the Capitol building, followed by other protesters who overwhelm the handful of officers stationed at the pedestrian entrance.

This first mob, numbering roughly two hundred, makes its way to the west side of the building. Physical brawls break out between protesters and police; dozens push past police attempting to guard a set of stairs that leads to an upper terrace on the west side near the inauguration set-up. No one yet has breached the building.

Some carry flags bearing Trump's name or the "Don't Tread on Me" symbol. A few men start climbing the scaffolding erected for Biden's inauguration. Cops tackle a man scaling the top of the apparatus; the crowd starts to boo. Chants of "USA! USA" and "This is our house" can be heard.

Shortly before 1 p.m., a man rips away temporary fencing. Another woman, fully masked, removes a few metal racks preventing access to the building.

1:00 p.m.: Pence and the members of the U.S. Senate enter the House chamber. They seem unaware of the disturbances outside; video taken of the Senators as they walked through Statuary Hall to the House chamber indicate no concern about any possible threat. No additional security is present in their vicinity.

Pence takes his seat alongside House Speaker Nancy Pelosi. As for the hope that Pence would send the disputed tallies back to the states, the president would receive very bad news. Before he began officiating the proceedings, Pence had delivered a three-page letter to Congress explaining why he would not object to certification. While acknowledging "numerous instances of officials setting aside state election law," a clear violation of the Constitution, Pence insisted he did not have any authority to address the unlawful conduct. "It is my considered judgment that my oath to support and defend the Constitution constrains me from claiming unilateral authority to determine which electoral votes should be counted and which should not," he wrote. The letter was made public about a half-hour later.

Senators are seated on the right side of the chamber. The joint session begins with an alphabetical roll call of every state beginning with Alabama. When any House member, with the support of a U.S. Senator, objects, members retreat to their respective chambers to deliberate and report back to the joint session.

With no objections to the counting of Alabama and Alaska, Rep. Paul Gosar rises to state his objection to certifying Arizona's electoral votes, supported in writing by Senator Cruz. Senators go back to their chamber to deliberate while debate begins in the House.

Meanwhile, as the president's speech wraps up, tens of thousands of Trump supporters begin walking toward Capitol Hill—a distance of about 1.7 miles and a roughly thirty-minute walk in a heavy crowd.

1:13 p.m.: D.C. Metro Police Commander Robert Glover calls for officers in riot gear. "Hard gear at the Capitol! Hard gear at the Capitol!" he yells into his radio. About three dozen D.C. Metro officers are stationed on the west side of the Capitol where the first breach would occur.

1:15 p.m.: Trump finishes his speech. "But we're going to try and give our Republicans, the weak ones because the strong ones don't need any of our help. We're going to try and give them the kind of pride and boldness that they need to take back our country. So let's walk down Pennsylvania Avenue."

Robert Reeder leaves the ellipse. He later told investigators he planned to visit some museums and monuments but instead followed the crowd to the Capitol grounds. Trump-supporting California resident Lois McNicoll also leaves the ellipse and walks toward Capitol Hill.

In the House chamber, Rep. Steve Scalise, seriously wounded by a Bernie Sanders supporter in a 2017 shooting, takes the floor. "I rise today to object to a number of states that did not follow the constitutional requirement for selecting electors," Scalise explains. "Madame Speaker, in a number of those states, that constitutional process was not followed, and that is why we are here to object."

On the Senate side, outgoing Senate Majority Leader Mitch McConnell, in an evident rebuke to the President, condemns efforts to halt the certification process, insisting the election results had been thoroughly vetted at every level. "Dozens of lawsuits received hearings in courtrooms all across our country, but over and over, courts rejected these claims, including all-star judges whom the President himself nominated," McConnell tells his Senate colleagues. Noting that Democrats "spent four years" questioning the validity of Trump's election in 2016, McConnell warns, "We must not imitate and escalate what we repudiate." He announces he will vote in favor of certification.

Outside, the atmosphere around the building turns more tense. According to several open source, time-stamped videos, DC Metropolitan Police officers start throwing explosive devices known as "flashbangs" into a large crowd outside the building on the west side. The crowd, which is not at this time attempting to breach the barriers, includes young children and senior citizens, according to witnesses.

What happens next by all accounts is unprovoked and leads to a sharp escalation of anger and violence. Trump supporters uninvolved with the initial breach or skirmishes with police are shocked to find themselves assaulted by law enforcement.

Unlike the mild-mannered officers seen on the perimeter of the grounds or inside, US Capitol and D.C. Metro police guarding the building are covered head to toe in helmets, gas masks, and boots. Michael Bolton, the USCP inspector general, later confirmed that D.C. Metro officers used sting balls.

"They're very painful, these types of munitions," Bolton told Congress in April. A sting ball is a hand-held grenade that produces a loud sound, a bright flash of light, and a blast of approximately 180 rubber pellets with a radius of up to fifty feet. Police also used what one judge later described as "super soakers" filled with tear gas.

J. Michael Waller, a senior analyst for the Center of Security Studies, explained in a column for *The Federalist* a few days later what he saw around 1:17 p.m.:

> A contingent of perhaps 30 to 50 Capitol Police emerged at the top of the inaugural platform above the VIP section and worked their way down to the spot where Biden will take his oath of office. They were armed with paintball-type long guns that fired capsules of pepper irritant, teargas launchers, and long guns that I could not identify from my position. One fired a teargas canister—not at the plainclothes militants at the front line, but into the crowd itself. Then another. Flash grenades went off in the middle of the crowd. The tear gas caused pandemonium. But there was still no stampede,

and people helped create or widen paths to allow others to leave the area. Some, seeing frail
or elderly people who had a hard time standing,
broke into a pallet of black folding chairs for
the inauguration and distributed them. But the
mood had gone from patriotic—although con-
temptuous of Congress—to furious.[1]

This unexpected assault on protesters agitates the crowd.
Many confront police, shouting and raising their middle finger
toward the line of officers. After a year of expressing support for
law enforcement amid calls for defunding police by Democrats,
Trump supporters express shock that police officers are attacking
them. "This is straight-up bullshit…they've been throwing flashbangs, shooting people with bullets, look at that shit," Kash Kelly,
a well-known supporter of Donald Trump, tells a friend recording
the attack outside the building. The sound of explosive devices
and screams can be heard on the video. "These are American citizens standing out here protesting the right way…and we're getting
treated like we're not citizens."

In a separate video included in the criminal complaint
against Micah Jackson, a blogger charged with four misdemeanors, the crowd turns on the police. "Fuck you! Fuck you!" several
protesters start to scream. Two men are heard complaining rubber
bullets hit their legs and their "ass."[2]

Protesters swarm the west side of the building, climbing on
scaffolding erected for the inauguration. Some unfurl Trump banners and flags. Trump supporters and police continue to clash. At
one point, a line of D.C. Metro Police officers in full riot gear
walk through the crowd as protesters scream, "We've always had
your back!"

Samsel is seen in a video produced by an independent blogger pouring water into the eyes of a person who was sprayed by
police.[3] Someone else is bleeding on the ground. Samsel and a

1   J. Michael Waller, *I Saw Provocateurs At The Capitol Riot On Jan. 6* (The Federalist, 2021).
2   Glenn Hudson, *Stop the steal protest Washington D.C Jan.6th 2021* (YouTube, 2021).
3   Status Coup News, *ARREST Donald Trump* (YouTube, 2021).

few others confront police again. A physical altercation ensues between several USCP officers, Samsel, and the protesters. "USCP officers attempt to hold back the rioters with chemical munitions, such as oleoresin capsicum ("OC") spray, more commonly known as 'pepper spray,'" a Senate report later confirmed.[4]

1:20 p.m.: Trump returns to the White House.

1:25 p.m.: Law enforcement continue to launch explosives, about every thirty seconds. "Keep it coming, motherfucker!" one man yells as the device explodes on the ground and people turn away in self-defense. Someone is on a bullhorn behind the crowd yelling, "Keep pushing, patriots!" Others start to chant, "Hands up, don't shoot!"

1:30 p.m.: USCP orders the evacuation of the House Cannon Office Building and the Library of Congress in part because of the suspected pipe bombs near the RNC. Law enforcement later say the packages were detonated.

A wall-to-wall crowd of Trump supporters continues to walk down Constitution Avenue toward the Capitol. Many carry flags and chant "USA! USA!" as they trek eastward.

1:45 p.m.: Rep. Elaine Luria (D-Va.) announces she has been told to leave her office. "I just had to evacuate my office because of a pipe bomb reported outside," she tweets. "Supporters of the President are trying to force their way into the Capitol and I can hear what sounds like multiple gunshots." (There were no reports of gunfire; it's likely the noise from flashbangs being thrown at protesters.) As of October 1, 2021, the suspect who planted the alleged pipe bombs had not been caught.

1:50 p.m.: Sund and Bowser call for extra police support. D.C. Metropolitan Police declare a riot at the Capitol and the complex is put on lockdown. Capitol Police announce that another pipe bomb

---

4   United States Senate Staff Report, *Examining the U.S. Capitol Attack* (United States Senate, 2021).

has been recovered outside the headquarters of the Democratic National Committee.

Meanwhile, deliberations continue during the joint session. Rep. Paul Gosar (R-Ariz.) argues against the counting of Arizona's electoral votes. "Madame Speaker, I filed my challenge on the slate of electors from the state of Arizona that was actually put forward by Governor Ducey of Arizona. My ask to you, the Speaker, through the Vice President, is simple. Do not count these electors until and unless the secretary of state allows a forensic audit of the election, a request she has denied repeatedly.

2:00 p.m.: Pelosi hands off the gavel to Rep. Jim McGovern to act as Speaker Pro Tempore. She later said on *60 Minutes* that Capitol Police "pulled her from the podium" after protesters smashed a window on the south side and started to enter the building. Hundreds of protesters overrun police, some assaulting the officers, and go inside chanting, "Stop the steal."

2:05 p.m.: Kevin Greeson, fifty-five, of Alabama, dies of an apparent heart attack outside the Capitol building; he is the first official fatality of the day. An anonymous witness later told National File that Greeson was hit in the eye by a projectile from an explosive device thrown into the crowd by police. "[H]e couldn't start breathing [sic], he collapsed, and that's when we [were] just like, 'Paramedic, paramedic!' We had to make a hole and try to drag him out. Some other paramedics went in, the DC police were firing on them, and anybody else who was in the area. Flash bangs were going off, a minimum of 30 flash bangs, and people were getting hit," the witness told a reporter for *National File* in February 2021.[5] National news outlets ignored Greeson's death.

2:06 p.m.: Police standing on the upper entrance of the east side of the Capitol retreat; one officer runs to the doors and goes inside. A group of at least one hundred people push to the top of the stairs.

---

5   Gabriel Keane, *EXCLUSIVE: Witness Says Man Who Died of Heart Attack on Jan 6 Was Shot In Face By Capitol Police Projectile* (National File, 2021).

2:08 p.m.: An unidentified man who has been pushed off an elevated railing by a Capitol Police officer is carried away on a bike rack used as a stretcher.

2:13 p.m.: Dominic Pezzola, an alleged member of the Proud Boys, uses a riot shield to smash a window on the east side of the building. This creates the first violent entry point. "Shortly after the glass in the window is broken, an unidentified individual can be heard yelling words to the effect of, 'Go, Go, Go!" a government charging document alleged. Video later posted online shows protesters surging up the steps of the Capitol, urged on by this unknown individual shouting, "Go, go, go! It's now or never!" "Several individuals enter the building through the broken window, including Pezzola. A nearby door was opened and a crowd of people began to enter the U.S. Capitol."

As Gosar continues speaking, there is visible commotion in the House chamber as members realize protesters have entered the building. The House is recessed at 2:18 p.m., and members are evacuated.

Michael Byrd, a U.S. Capitol Police officer, instructs members on the House side to look under their seats for a packaged gas mask. "Please grab a mask and place it on your lap," Byrd said. "And be prepared to don your mask in the event we have a breach." It is unclear why gas masks were placed ahead of time in the Chamber.

This is about the time Robert Reeder and the Munn family of Texas arrive at the Capitol complex. Trump supporters who have taken the long walk from the Ellipse are largely unaware of the clashes between police and protesters that began an hour earlier.

According to a report by CNN, Senator Mitt Romney receives a text from an aide warning that protesters have breached the building; Romney leaves the Senate chamber to find a "hideaway." While walking through an empty hallway, he is met by Officer Eugene Goodman, who instructs Romney to go back to the chamber where it is safe. Romney is seen on surveillance video turning around and running back to the Senate.

There, Senator James Lankford (R-Okl.) is voicing support for the election audit. "The constitutional crisis in our country right now is that millions of Americans are being told to sit down and shut up," Lankford says. "Their opinions matter. Pause the count. Get more facts to the States before January the 20th. We proposed a 15-member commission, just like what was done after the failed election of 1876. We are encouraging people to spend 10 days going through all the issues so States can have one last opportunity to address any challenges." Lankford's speech is interrupted, and senators are told to leave immediately. The Senate calls a recess at 2:13 p.m. and is also evacuated.

2:14 p.m.: Officer Eugene Goodman, after rescuing Romney, is confronted by numerous protesters on the first floor. Goodman backs away from the group, who are shouting at him, and picks up a baton. Douglas Jensen leads the pack; Goodman hustles up a set of stairs and is followed by dozens of protesters. Goodman and Jensen, a Trump supporter from Iowa later indicted on several counts, spar back and forth. Goodman leads the group to another area of the building away from the Senate chambers where they are confronted by other Capitol police officers.

2:20 p.m.: Officer Brian Sicknick allegedly is sprayed with a chemical irritant on the west side of the building. Video later shows Sicknick, patrolling an area where police were using tear gas against protesters, attempting to wash his eyes with water.

Protesters swarm the west side of the building, climbing on scaffolding erected for the inauguration. Some unfurl Trump banners and flags. Trump supporters and police continue to clash as cops continue to attack the crowds. At one point, a line of D.C. Metro Police officers in full riot gear walk through the crowd as protesters scream, "We've always had your back!"

2:24 p.m.: Apparently in receipt of Pence's letter defying his request to stop the certification from moving forward, Trump tweets in rage: "Mike Pence didn't have the courage to do what should have been done to protect our Country and our Constitution, giving States a chance to certify a corrected set of facts, not the fraudulent or inaccurate ones which they were asked to previously certify. USA demands the truth!"

2:25 p.m.: Hundreds have entered the building. Video shows Jacob Chansley, the so-called "QAnon shaman," and a few protesters talking calmly with Capitol Police officers.[6] Rather than telling them to leave, the officers tell Chansley's group they must behave. Officer Keith Robishaw tells Chansley's group they won't stop them from entering. "We're not against . . . you need to show us . . . no attacking, no assault, remain calm," Robishaw can be heard saying in an open-source video.

Chansley agrees. "This has to be peaceful," Chansley yells to the others. "We have the right to peacefully assemble." Shirtless and clad in a furry animal headdress with horns and wearing red, white, and blue face paint, Chansley is recorded almost nonstop during the protest, including a photo with Nancy Pelosi's son-in-law, who is on the scene as a correspondent for a Dutch television station.

Robert Reeder, meanwhile, is outside the building. and takes a selfie video. "We've been getting tear gassed…thousands of people," Reeder tells the camera. He approaches an open door at the Capitol to look for water to rinse out his eyes. A line of officers is inside; he asks one where he can find water. They tell him to go outside and look, but he walks past them and enters the Rotunda.

Fumes from more than an hour of law enforcement dousing Trump supporters with chemical gas can be seen enveloping the outside of the building.

Around this time, Thomas Munn and his family crawl through an open window and wander through the building taking pictures and posting videos on social media. At one point, they enter an unidentified Senate office on the first floor. "We stormed in went in and out broken window!!" Dawn Munn later wrote in

---

6   Julie Kelly, *Video Shows U.S. Capitol Police Gave Protestors OK to Enter* (American Greatness, 2021).

a Facebook conversation. "They barricaded the door so they took out window…climbed in!!!"

Also at 2:25 p.m., according to a motion filed by his defense attorney, Glenn Croy, a Trump supporter from Colorado, is shocked to see police assault a protester. "[He] watched in amazement as the police attacked a protestor for what seemed to be no apparent reason," his attorney wrote in an October filing prior to his plea sentence. "He found it shocking how hard they beat down this person as everyone watched. He grabbed his cell phone to capture the incident but only managed to get the aftermath. Mr. Croy believed he was bearing witness to an unprovoked attack by law enforcement on a citizen for no reason and that the use of force was excessive given the situation." He later tells the FBI that the only violence he witnessed on January 6 was D.C. Metro police officers "attacking this protestor."

2:26 p.m.: Trump accidentally calls Senator Mike Lee–the president is actually trying to reach Senator Tommy Tuberville. Lee hands his phone to Tuberville. They speak for about five minutes before Capitol Police announce the building is being evacuated. "I don't want to interrupt your call with the president, but we're being evacuated and I need my phone," Lee says to Tuberville. "OK, Mr. President. I gotta go," Tuberville says as he ends the call.

Thomas Webster, a retired New York Police Department officer who once provided security detail at Gracie's Mansion, the mayor's official residence, runs up to a police line and screams at D.C. and Capitol cops who are attacking the crowd with chemical gas and explosives.[7] "You fucking piece of shit. You fucking commie motherfuckers, man. You wanna attack Americans? No, fuck that!" He and an officer get into a physical brawl. His defense lawyer later described the altercation in a court filing. "Officer N.R. can be seen reaching over the metal barrier and pushing a female protester holding a flag to the ground on two separate occasions.

---

7   Marshall Cohen, Katelyn Polantz, *Justice Department Releases Harrowing New Bodycam Footage from January 6 Attack* (CNN Politics, 2021).

The protesters . . . were by and large peaceful. It was only after tear gas and pepper spray were deployed by police upon this group of peaceful protesters that the crowds changed.

"Officer N.R. [the cop Webster allegedly assaulted] was equipped with a helmet, a shield, a gas mask, and a full complement of body armor. [P]rotesters—who did not attend the protest with a mask or face shield—are observed suffering the effects of being gassed and pepper sprayed by police. Officer N.R. can also be observed mocking several protesters who were complaining about this Officer's excessive use of force."

2:27 p.m.: CNN reporter Wolf Blitzer describes the scene at the Capitol. As the camera shows a line of protesters calmly walking through Statuary Hall, honoring rope lines, Blitzer is outraged at their presence. "This is a moment I never saw before in my life, these individuals just rushed through security, they are inside Statuary Hall, this is a legendary, a legendary place where all of us who covered Capitol Hill, it's hard to believe what we're seeing right there. They're just walking through. It's a strange, it's an awful situation. They're having a good time in Statuary Hall." Speaking to Jake Tapper, Blitzer frets it is a "dangerous situation unfolding here in the United States."

2:30 p.m.: Security camera video shows senators hustling down a flight of stairs to a secure location on a lower floor.

2:31 p.m.: D.C. Mayor Muriel Bowser declares a curfew from 6:00 p.m. that night until 6:00 a.m. on January 7: "President Trump continues to fan rage and violence by contending that the Presidential election was invalid." Virginia Governor Ralph Northam also issues curfew orders for Arlington and Alexandria counties as well as a state of emergency in the commonwealth.

2:33 p.m.: In a forty-minute clip released in October over the objection of Biden's Justice Department, hundreds of protesters are seen walking through open doors on the upper west terrace of the building. Several Capitol police officers are positioned between the exterior door and an interior door that leads to the Rotunda. Officers do not attempt to stop people from entering; the door has been left ajar by unidentified people exiting the building as a Capitol cop watches them leave. Those entering the building are not aggressive or hostile to police. Many seem confused as to where they are headed and just follow the person in front of them into the inner part of the Capitol. Senator Ron Johnson, in a letter to the acting chief of the Capitol Police department months later, estimated at least 300 people went into the building at that access point.

2:35 p.m.: A group of Oath Keepers on the east side of the Capitol begin to move through the crowd in a military-style "stack formation." They eventually enter the building; none are carrying a firearm or other deadly weapon.

2:37 p.m.: Surveillance video shows Ethan Nordean entering the building peacefully on the upper west terrace, allowed by Capitol police to go inside. No weapon on his person.

2:38 p.m.: Trump, perhaps prompted by White House advisors, urges calm. "Please support our Capitol Police and Law Enforcement," he tweets. "They are truly on the side of our Country. Stay peaceful!"

2:43 p.m.: Officer Byrd, who had earlier instructed House members to grab their gas masks, shoots and kills Ashli Babbitt, an unarmed veteran and Trump supporter, as she attempts to crawl through a broken window into the Speaker's lobby, a long hallway adorned with paintings of past House Speakers located outside the House chamber. John Sullivan, a self-described independent journalist and supporter of Black Lives Matter, is on the scene to record the moment. He has been filming the chaos inside and outside for hours. (Sullivan was also seen near Ray Epps, the suspected FBI asset, on the night of January 5.) News of Babbitt's shooting quickly reaches protesters inside and outside the building.

2:47 p.m.: House Speaker Nancy Pelosi asks the National Guard to secure the Capitol building.

2:50 p.m.: On the Senate side, a New Yorker magazine videographer is recording Chansley, eighteen-year old Bruno Cua, Florida resident Paul Hodgkins and others inside the Senate chamber. One unidentified man is sitting on the floor, bleeding from getting "shot," he says—presumably hit with a rubber bullet before entering the building. Some protesters are recorded as they rummage through materials on the desks of U.S. Senators.

Chansley takes the podium and sits in the same chair Vice President Pence had occupied earlier. He leaves a note for Pence: "It's only a matter of time, justice is coming."

Hodgkins hoists a Trump flag, perhaps for the photographers inside the chamber. Bruno Cua, a high school senior from Georgia who had traveled to Washington with his parents, wanders around the room. Chansley offers a prayer through a bullhorn. "Let's all say a prayer in this sacred place," Chansley yells and removes his horned hat. "Thanks to our Heavenly Father for giving us this opportunity to stand up for our unalienable God-given rights." Several protesters kneel before the podium as Chansley continues his prayer.

U.S. Capitol police officers finally ask them to leave. The officers speak to them politely. None of the protesters seem to have any intention of hanging Mike Pence or violently overthrowing the government.

2:55 p.m.: Lois McNicoll enters the Capitol through the Senate West wing door wearing a Trump hat and draped in a California state flag with the words "California Republic" replaced by "Trump Country." She walks through the area known as the Crypt and exits about thirty minutes later after police usher her out of the building.

Hundreds of protesters continue to roam the halls, offices, and open spaces of the massive building. Some are heard shouting, "Treason! Treason! Treason!" or "We Want Trump!" Police and protesters spar in a few locations.

Broadcast and cable news start wall-to-wall coverage of the chaos.

3:04 p.m.: Christopher Miller, the acting Secretary of Defense, authorizes the use of National Guard. "[Joint Chiefs of Staff] Chairman Milley and I just spoke separately with the Vice President and with Speaker Pelosi, Leader McConnell, Senator Schumer and Representative Hoyer about the situation at the U.S. Capitol," Miller says in a statement. "We have fully activated the D.C. National Guard to assist federal and local law enforcement as they work to peacefully address the situation. We are prepared to provide additional support as necessary and appropriate as requested by local authorities. Our people are sworn to defend the constitution and our democratic form of government and they will act accordingly."[8] This order moves about 1,100 guardsmen to the Capitol complex.

3:05 p.m.: Body cam footage released on October shows D.C. and Capitol police brawling with protesters inside the Rotunda.[9] Some had been allowed in by Capitol police in the upper west terrace. "Move back! Move back!" one D.C. officer is heard shouting at the crowd, which is not engaged in any violence. Officers are clad in full riot gear, some wearing gas masks with their identity completely obscured. A few shove protesters and hit them with their fists and batons. "Are you guys proud of yourselves?" one protester yells. Other start to chant, "USA! USA!" It's unclear whether this crowd has heard of Babbitt's killing at this point. One man screams at a cop that he's an Iraq War veteran; the offi-

---

8   Kate Brannen, Ryan Goodman, *The Official and Unofficial Timeline of Defense Department Actions on January 6* (Just Security, 2021).

9   Ryan J. Reilly, *Body-Worn Camera Footage Shows Part of the Battle for the Capitol Rotunda on Jan. 6. Released in Connection With the Case Against James Mcgrew, Who Has a Distinctive Belly Tattoo* (Twitter, 2021).

cer tells him to leave. "*You* leave!" he responds. Another woman calls the police "traitors to the country." An unidentified D.C. cop punches one man in the head.

3:13 p.m.: Trump again asks for calm from the White House. "I am asking for everyone at the U.S. Capitol to remain peaceful. No violence! Remember, WE are the Party of Law & Order—respect the Law and our great men and women in Blue. Thank you!"

More law enforcement officers start to arrive, including personnel from the FBI, ATF, Department of Homeland Security, Arlington County Police, Fairfax County Police, and Virginia State Police. But violence escalates between protesters and police at the lower west terrace. D.C. Metro Police continue to throw explosives and spray tear gas into the crowd as protesters chant, "Traitors!" and "I can't breathe!" at the officers.

3:20 p.m.: D.C. Metro police officer Michael Fanone, who had arrived at the building around 3:00 p.m., is dragged out of the lower west terrace tunnel. He clearly is struggling from the effects of chemical gas; Trump supporters see his distress and attempt to rescue him from the mob of people. One man tases Fanone in the neck, and another rips his badge from his uniform, later insisting it was an accident as he was attempting to assist Fanone. "I've got kids," Fanone says, asking people to bring him back into the tunnel. He is carried back to the building.

4:00 p.m.: An entrance tunnel to the Capitol has become a battle scene. D.C. and Capitol police, clad in riot gear with shields and batons, form a human barrier. "Officers...rushed to the tunnel from within the building while rioters outside of the tunnel continued to summon more men to push their way through the tunnel," according to one criminal complaint. "The tunnel became the point of an intense and prolonged clash between rioters and law enforcement."

One man attempts to break another window near the tunnel. Police use a noxious gas inside the tight space causing people to vomit and pass out. Protesters are later seen on video pushing back with riot shields either taken or dropped by law enforcement as police beat people with batons. The crowd begins to chant, "I can't breathe! I can't breathe!" Rosanne Boyland, a Trump supporter from Georgia, is trapped in the melee.

4:05 p.m.: Joe Biden gives prepared remarks from his home in Delaware: "At this hour, our democracy is under unprecedented assault, unlike anything we've seen in modern times, an assault the Citadel of Liberty. The scenes of chaos at the Capitol do not reflect a true America, do not represent who we are. What we're seeing are a small number of extremists dedicated to lawlessness. This is not the dissent. It's disorder. It's chaos. It borders on sedition, and it must end now."

4:17 p.m.: Trump tweets out a video message to his supporters. "I know your pain. I know you're hurt. We had an election that was stolen from us. It was a landslide election and everyone knows it, especially the other side. But you have to go home now. We have to have peace."

4:26 p.m.: People attempt to perform CPR on Boyland while begging Capitol Police and D.C. Metro Police to stop attacking the crowd and help her. "The woman had fallen on the step and was being crushed as officers pushed protesters back away from the doors of the tunnel entrance," a District Court judge confirmed during a March pre-trial detention hearing for Michael Foy. Foy, a Marine who drove alone from Michigan to Washington D.C. in the early hours of January 6, armed with a hockey stick, attempts to help Boyland outside the tunnel. He swings the stick at police who do not relent, yelling, "She's being crushed... she's dead, she's hurt."

Sergeant Aquilino Gonell later tells the January 6 select committee he administered "CPR to one of the rioters who breached the Capitol in an effort to save her life" at that exact time. An officer starts to drag Boyland's lifeless body, face up, into the building. Officer Harry Dunn, according to his congressional testimony, brings her body to the office of the House Majority Leader until paramedics arrive. She is taken to a local hospital.[10]

4:30 p.m.: Robert Reeder, who previously exited the building but could not find another way off the grounds, re-enters the Capitol to look for a way to exit. "I'm leaving now...I got tear gassed at least four times inside the Capitol. I saw the lady they say got shot, I walked right past her in a pool of blood. And it's just... completely crazy in there. I was one of the last people out. I was in there for over half an hour. I got gassed several times inside the Capitol, many times outside the Capitol. Got shot with pepper balls. It was fucking nuts. We had to do...ah...battle with the police inside. It was crazy...absolutely insane."

4:30-6:00 p.m.: Law enforcement secures both chambers, the basement, and hallways. Protesters clear out. Tom Munn posts an update on Facebook: "WOW!!! Made it back to the hotel about an hour ago...couldn't post in DC, no cell service? Have lots of pics and videos to follow as soon as we can get them downloaded," he wrote at around 5:30.

Munn's comments directly contradict what will later be said by Chief Sund. "I need to tell you all that the media is LYING TO YOU...the DC police opened up on a small group climbing the scaffolding, with gas grenades...the concussions rippled through the crowd...which only ignited the crowd and patriots began chanting 'they are stealing our country' and 'press forward' as they were carrying the wounded out through us. The only damage to the capital [sic] building was several windows and sets of doors. Nothing inside the capital was damaged. As for the shooting, I did not see it but I can tell you, patriots NEVER made it to the chamber. There was no violence in the capital building, the crowd was NOT out of control...they were ANGRY!!! The media wasn't even there, never saw any media or

10   Julie Kelly, *What Did the Capitol Celebrity Cops Do to Roseanne Boyland?* (American Greatness, 2021)

police…the vast majority of the crowd was heading back down Constitution and Pennsylvania avenues by 5pm, with virtually no police presence, as Antifa began marching through the middle of us towards the capital. They are now calling this and [sic] insurrection…?"

5:45 p.m.: Paramedics arrive to retrieve Rosanne Boyland's body.

6:01 p.m.: "These are the things and events that happen when a sacred landslide election victory is so unceremoniously & viciously stripped away from great patriots who have been badly & unfairly treated for so long," Trump tweets. "Go home with love & in peace. Remember this day forever!"

6:09 p.m.: Rosanne Boyland, thirty-four, is pronounced dead.

6:15 p.m.: A security perimeter is established on the west side of the building.

By the end of the day, another man, Benjamin Phillips, a Trump supporter from Pennsylvania, will also be dead. His location at the time of his death is unclear; the D.C. Medical Examiner's office concluded Phillips died of a stroke on January 6.

8:00 p.m.: The Capitol is declared secure. The Senate reconvenes a few minutes later. Vice President Pence takes the floor, lamenting a "dark day" in the Capitol's history. "We grieve the loss of life that took place in these hallowed Halls, as well as the injuries suffered by those who defended our Capitol today. To those who wreaked havoc in our Capitol today, you did not win. Violence never wins. Freedom wins. And this is still the People's House."

*   *   *   *

The term "insurrection" was used almost immediately to describe the chaotic event. McConnell condemned the "failed insurrection." Chuck Schumer blasted the "rioters and insurrectionists, goons and thugs, domestic terrorists," who tried to "take over the Capitol."

Senators abandoned their plans to object to the certification. The chaos, to the dismay of the hundreds of thousands of Trump supporters in the capital that day, prompted the reverse of what they had wanted.

Republican Senator James Lankford, who was speaking in support of a commission to audit the 2020 election when the Senate was evacuated, returned to his seat and promptly folded. "Rioters and thugs don't run the Capitol. We're the United States of America," Lankford said later that evening to cameras in a nearly empty chamber. "Obviously the commission we asked for is not going to happen at this point, and I understand that. And we are headed tonight…toward the certification of Joe Biden as president of the United States." (Lankford was swiftly censured by Oklahoma county Republican organizations and now has a Republican primary challenger.)

Others caved, too. Senator Kelly Loeffler, who learned of her own defeat that day in a runoff election in Georgia, joined Lankford. "[W]hen I arrived in Washington this morning, I fully intended to object to the certification of the electoral votes," Loeffler said. "However, the events that have transpired today have forced me to reconsider, and I cannot now, in good conscious [sic] object to the certification of these electors. I believe that there were last minute changes to the November 2020 election process and serious irregularities that resulted in too many Americans losing confidence, not only in the integrity of our elections, but in the power of the ballot as a tool of democracy. Too many Americans are frustrated at what they see as an unfair system. Nevertheless, there is no excuse for the events that took place in these chambers today. And I pray that America never suffers such a dark day again." She was applauded by her colleagues and by Vice President Pence.

Objections to the electoral vote count for Arizona and Pennsylvania were also rejected and at 3:42 a.m. on January 7, less than fifteen hours after the uproar began, the Joint Session of Congress affirmed the results of the 2020 Electoral College vote. Joe Biden and Kamala Harris were sworn into office two weeks later.

But the trouble for those involved in the Capitol protest had only begun. Democrats would control the White House, the Senate, and the House of Representatives; they planned to make the most of their unchecked power.

The entire Munn family would be arrested in July, each charged with four misdemeanors including "violent entry and disorderly conduct on Capitol grounds." A relative of the fiancée of one of the Munn daughters tipped off the FBI about the family's trip to Washington and provided screenshots of her Facebook posts.

Robert Reeder turned himself in to law enforcement a few days after the protest and was fired from his job as a FedEx truck driver even though he, too, was charged with four misdemeanors. He pleaded guilty to one count of "parading" in the Capitol. Before Judge Thomas Hogan sentenced him to three months in prison for the low level offense, Reeder explained that his life had been ruined. He told the judge he lost his family, including his teen son who shares the same name, his friends, and his neighbors. Reeder said his church asked him to stop attending. "That's tough because it is my support group," Reeder told the court through tears. "I'm radioactive."

Lois McNicoll's co-workers at the Los Angeles Department of Public Social Services notified the FBI about her presence in the Capitol. Hundreds of protesters themselves, at the urging of the FBI and Attorney General, would turn in colleagues, neighbors, friends, and family members over the course of the next several months. In May, without a lawyer present, an FBI agent interrogated McNicoll at her place of work. She was arrested on June 28 and charged with four misdemeanors, including "violent entry and disorderly conduct on Capitol grounds." In August, she pleaded guilty to all charges.

Dozens of protesters including Jacob Chansley, Michael Foy, and Ryan Samsel would be held for months in solitary confinement under pre-trial detention orders sought by the government and approved by federal judges. Samsel would be assaulted by prison guards in a D.C. jail and seriously injured.

The Biden regime would make avenging the Capitol protest a top priority. On his first day in office, Joe Biden ordered an assessment of the "domestic terror" threat. Hundreds of Americans, along with Republican lawmakers who had planned to object to certifying the Electoral College, would end up in the crosshairs. The FBI Twitter account routinely posted photos of January 6 "Most Wanted," asking Americans to call the agency's tip line to help nab suspected insurrectionists.

Names of the accused were dragged through the mud by the news media. Anyone caught up in the Capitol breach probe would be described as a rioter, an insurrectionist, a traitor, a racist, a terrorist. The public humiliation, for many defendants, would be worse than their legal woes.

January 6 would occupy the attention of official Washington and the media for months. No one could escape the nonstop drama over America's alleged "insurrection."

But the early portrayal of what happened on January 6— that thousands of armed white supremacist militia members loyal to Donald Trump planned in advance to overthrow the government and were further "incited" by the president's speech that day, resulting in the killing of police officers and massive damage to the U.S. Capitol—and the foundations of our democracy itself—slowly crumbled under the pressure of mounting facts and evidence.

This book exposes the myths, lies, and partisan spin about the events of January 6. Who, actually, was involved in the Capitol breach? Who were the good guys, and more importantly, who were the bad guys? Was it an act of domestic terrorism, or a spontaneous demonstration that turned ugly, or as some have speculated, a riot provoked by police overreaction and shadowy FBI informants in the crowd? How did the media dangerously spin so many false accounts and slanted storylines with virtual impunity?

What happened to Officer Brian Sicknick? What happened to Ashli Babbitt and Rosanne Boyland, two female Trump supporters who died that day? How many protesters did the Biden Justice Department seek to keep behind bars, denied bail, pending trial?

Why are Biden's Justice Department and the Capitol Police keeping thousands of hours of video footage concealed not just from the public but defendants as well, in violation of their constitutional rights? Why is the government slow-walking discovery and withholding potential Brady material? Why, nearly a year later, is the Justice Department unprepared to go to trial against people arrested in January 2021? These are just a few of the questions this book attempts to answer.

It is indisputable that some police officers sustained grave injuries and numerous people committed serious crimes. Protesters who attacked police officers attempting to do their job should and will be held accountable. As of November 1, 2021 roughly 110 defendants had been charged with either attacking or "impeding" law enforcement.

But the overwhelming number of people involved in January 6 do not fit the media's narrative of treasonous insurrectionists who wanted to hang Mike Pence or kidnap Democratic lawmakers with zip ties. FBI Director Christopher Wray, in congressional testimony two months after the protest, described it this way:

> "[T]he largest group, the group we need to spend the least time talking about is peaceful, maybe rowdy protestors, but who weren't violating the law. Then there's the second group, think of a reverse pyramid. The second group that is people who may have come intending to just be part of peaceful protest, but either swept up in the motives, or emotion, or whatever, engaged in kind of low-level criminal behavior. Trespassed, say on the Capitol grounds, but not breaching the building. Still criminal

conduct, still needs to be addressed, but more on the fly, in the moment, opportunistic. The third group, the smallest group numerically, but by far and away, the most serious group are those who breached the Capitol grounds, who engaged in violence against law enforcement, who attempted to disrupt the members of Congress in the conduct of their constitutional responsibilities. And of those, some of those people clearly came to Washington, we now know, with plans and intentions to engage in the worst kind of violence we would consider domestic terrorism."[11]

As many have suggested, January 6, 2021 will be remembered as one of the darkest days in America's history. I agree—but not for the reasons given by Joe Biden, the Democrats, the news media, and NeverTrump Republicans. It will be a dark day because it swiftly became a pretext for the accelerated weaponization of the federal government to target U.S. citizens on the political Right.

---

11   FBI Director Christopher Wray, *FBI Director Christopher Wray Testifies on January 6 Capitol Attack* (C-Span, 2021)

CHAPTER TWO:

THE MYTH OF AN ARMED INSURRECTION

THE DESIGNATION OF THE CAPITOL BREACH as an "insurrection" took hold even as the chaos unfolded on January 6. Congressmen still inside the building plastered the term across social media, immediately establishing the narrative that would frame the events for the public.

"This is a violent insurrection. An attempted coup by Trump supporters at his encouragement," Rep. Ted Deutch tweeted at 3:40 p.m. "They're attacking the building that represents our democracy and threatening those who work in it. History will remember this dark day as a seditious attack by Americans against America."

Rep. Debbie Wasserman Schultz, former head of the Democratic National Committee, followed suit. Tagging Trump's now deplatformed Twitter handle, Schultz asked, "This is how we make America great? Violence, storming the Capitol, attempting to block your duly elected successor by encouraging armed insurrection? The blood spilled today is on your hands." Her tweet was posted at 4:09 p.m.

Rep. Bobby Rush (D-Ill.), a founding member of the violent Illinois Black Panther Party who served jail time decades ago for weapons possession, somehow prepared and released a statement from what he described as a "secure bunker" in a House office building. "Today's actions are nothing short of a murderous insurrection and armed coup incited by Donald Trump and executed by his diehard supporters," Rush pronounced. "These terrorist acts will not silence the voice of the people."

Establishment Republicans also weighed in. "The violent assault on the Capitol—and disruption of a Constitutionally-mandated meeting of Congress—was undertaken by people whose passions have been inflamed by falsehoods and false hopes. Insurrection could do grave damage to our Nation and reputation," George and Laura Bush wrote in a joint statement released that afternoon under the headline "Statement by President George W. Bush on Insurrection at the Capitol."

Bush's brother Jeb, the Florida governor whom Trump vanquished early in the 2016 Republican primary, opined that Trump "has gone from creating chaos to inciting insurrection."

Barack Obama didn't use the word insurrection but condemned Trump in typically sonorous terms for whipping up a "violent crescendo" that resulted in the "desecrated chambers of democracy." In a statement released that evening, Bill Clinton mourned "an unprecedented assault on our Capitol, our Constitution, and our country."

Former GOP presidential candidate Mitt Romney wasted no time blasting the man who had snubbed him for a cabinet position. "What happened here today was an insurrection, incited by the President of the United States," Romney said in a statement. He urged his colleagues to "unanimously affirm the legitimacy of the presidential election." He later made the same remarks on the Senate floor.

From his home in Delaware, Joe Biden gave an eight-minute televised speech shortly after 4 p.m. on January 6. "This is not dissent, it's disorder. It borders on sedition. It's not protest. It's insurrection."

Business leaders piled on. "Today marks a sad and shameful chapter in our nation's history. Those responsible for this insurrection should be held to account, and we must complete the transition to President-elect Biden's administration," Apple CEO Tim Cook tweeted on January 6.

The president of the National Association of Manufacturers slammed the president, referred to the day as "sedition," and said Vice President Mike Pence should work with Trump's cabinet to invoke the 25th Amendment. "Throughout this whole disgusting episode, Trump has been cheered on by members of his own party, adding fuel to the distrust that has enflamed [sic] violent anger," Jay Timmons, the group's leader, ranted in a statement released at 3:37 p.m. on January 6.

Jamie Dimon, head of JP Morgan Chase, had been photographed taking a knee in a Chase bank branch office in New York in June 2020 and told BLM activists that "we are watching, listening and want every single one of you to know we are committed to fighting against racism and discrimination wherever and however it exists." Seven months later, Dimon denounced the Capitol protesters and insisted elected officials "have a responsibility to call for an end to the violence." (The violence had long since ended.) Google CEO Sundar Pichai also objected to "lawlessness and violence" at the Capitol seven months after advising Google employees to "show solidarity" with BLM protesters destroying businesses and assaulting police.

When the Joint Session of Congress reconvened that night, numerous lawmakers reinforced this description. Rep. Greg Stanton, the former mayor of Phoenix who had just been re-elected to a second term in Congress, twice referred to the "armed insurrection" during a speech on the House floor at 9:30 p.m. "Never did I expect to see our Capitol overrun by armed insurrectionists intent on disrupting our government at the urging of the President," Rep. Mary Gay Scanlon (D-Penn.) said. "What happened here today has made me heart-sick for our country."

Senator Ed Markey (D-Mass.) berated his Republican colleagues who had planned to request an audit of some election results. Allegation of voter fraud "is dangerous, anti-democratic, treasonous fiction," Markey said on the Senate floor. "There is a word for this. It is called 'sedition.' All of these unfounded objections to State electors are seditious. They are nothing short of an insurrection against the established order of the U.S. Constitution and our democratic Republic."

Donald Trump himself clearly bears some responsibility for fueling unsatisfied outrage about the 2020 election. He warned for months that the election would be stolen yet his legal teams seemed unprepared to handle the onslaught of election irregularities and outright unlawfulness detailed in Texas Attorney General Ken Paxton's lawsuit.

Moreover, rather than focus on clear instances of illegal voting—absentee ballots and mailing envelopes "fixed" by election workers before the legal deadline and outside the view of election observers; ballot harvesting; extended deadlines in violation of state law; the use of untested digital voting machines—all of which deserved investigation, Trump loyalists and attorneys distracted attention away from those valid concerns by pushing hard-to-prove accusations that would take too much time, if ever, to substantiate.

Calls by Sidney Powell, the lawyer who succeeded in forcing the Justice Department to drop the case against Lt. General Michael Flynn, to "release the Kraken"—referring to supposed information about rigged software in electronic voting machines—appeared as a comical sideshow rather than a serious legal challenge. Without providing evidence to back up her claims, she suggested that top Republican officeholders in Georgia received kickbacks after purchasing machines from Dominion Voting Systems, a program used in thirty states in 2020. Powell also claimed there was a "massive influence of communist money through Venezuela, Cuba, and likely China and the interference with our elections here in the United States."

Rudy Giuliani, Trump's personal attorney, announced by late November that the campaign team had cut ties with Powell to focus on voting illegalities in six states. But he seemed overwhelmed by the immense task of litigating election fraud under a tight deadline; his efforts not only fell flat but lent more ammunition to those insisting the election was completely on the up-and-up with no irregularities whatsoever. On November 8, 2020, Guiliani held a press conference outside a landscaping company in Philadelphia, hardly the sort of venue to inspire confidence that the president's legal challenges were in capable hands. An unfortunate incident during a November 20 press conference, during which Giuliani's hair dye dripped on to his face, prompted more mockery.

Meanwhile, most election lawsuits were rejected before the plaintiffs, either the Trump campaign or Republican Party state officials, could get an initial hearing. Lawsuits filed before Election Day were deemed too premature; those filed after Election Day were deemed too late.

A March 2021 analysis in The Federalist detailed the various reasons why numerous courts denied lawsuits out of the gate. "We needed the steady hand of impartial jurists. Most of all, the losing side needed to know that a fair shake was given, and that justice prevailed, even if it wasn't the outcome they wanted. That did not happen after Nov. 3," Bob Anderson wrote. Judges, Anderson explained, resorted to "Clintonian wordsmithing" as an excuse to dismiss cases. For example, the Pennsylvania Supreme Court, with a 5–2 Democratic majority, argued the word "shall" in a statue pertaining to absentee ballot declarations did not mean the process was "mandatory," legal hair-splitting at its best.

Regardless of the lame excuses, the media described every dismissal based on technicalities and not the merits of the lawsuits as a "loss" for Donald Trump. The American public, however, was led to believe that the lawsuits had failed to prove voting fraud and that judges of both political parties agreed nothing illegal happened in the 2020 election.

These failures in turn fed the liberal/media narrative that Trump was cynically peddling lies and conspiracy theories to rile up his credulous base and move them to violent action. This "Big Lie" theory was crucial to invalidating all dissenting views of any kind concerning the election, marginalizing and potentially criminalizing any person, including elected GOP officials, who dared to suggest there might be something—anything—that was worth looking into in order to restore confidence in the US electoral system. The uniformity and passion of mainstream liberal opinion on this subject was truly impressive.

The president's team, it must be said, faced a nearly insurmountable challenge from the start, both in terms of fair treatment by the media and in the court system. Every mistake, gaffe, or other unfortunate moment was amplified to drown out Republicans' justified concerns about the legitimacy of the election. Meanwhile blanket statements from the press and elected officials to the effect that this had been "the fairest and most transparent election in US history," obviously aimed at marginalizing and suppressing dissenting views, only fueled more skepticism among many Trump supporters.

In short, the refusal of the courts, the mainstream press, and establishment politicians to take their concerns seriously, coupled with the manifest and incontestable suppression of dissenting political views by major media and big tech platforms, inflamed their sense that some kind of grand conspiracy was taking place.

So, it's no wonder that so many of the president's supporters turned out to show their solidarity with him, and that many of them believed a literal coup had occurred and that Biden was an illegitimate president.

To people in this state of mind, rebellious actions are not only permitted, but may be required. The same logic had earlier applied to the anti-Trump resistance, and to the violent aspects of the George Floyd protests that summer.

Reasonable people can agree that the events of January 6 should not have taken place. Things got out of hand, and those who intentionally broke the law clearly deserve to be punished.

That is not the question. The question is whether these events amounted to an act of insurrection in terms that can be prosecuted legally. At this point it is increasingly clear that they did not.

Indeed, the idea that a brief disturbance at the Capitol—a chaotic political protest that had pockets of violence and featured more clownish behavior than criminal misconduct—rose to the level of an "insurrection" or attempted coup d'état was absurd and overblown from the start. To be considered an insurrection or attempted coup as opposed to a spontaneous riot, a violent attack upon the seat of government needs to meet certain basic criteria. It must be organized and coordinated; it must be armed; above all, it must have a plan of action once it seizes the reins of power.

Ultimately none of the conditions necessary to meet either the legal definition or the popular understanding of an "insurrection" have been shown to exist in this case. Federal prosecutors clearly have their work cut out for them making such a charge stand up in court—which may explain why so few have been charged with serious crimes amounting to armed conspiracy, and why the cases of so many still detained have not been brought to trial.

*   *   *   *

Historical definitions of the word "insurrection" compare the act to treason. "A rising against civil or political authority; the open and active opposition of a number of persons to the execution of a law in a city or state," Noah Webster explained in his 1828 dictionary.[1] "It is equivalent to sedition, except that sedition expresses a less extensive rising of citizens. It differs from rebellion, for the latter expresses a revolt, or an attempt to overthrow the government, to establish a different one or to place the country under another jurisdiction. It differs from mutiny, as it respects the civil or political government; whereas a mutiny is an open opposition to law in the army or navy. Insurrection is however used with such latitude as to comprehend either sedition or rebellion."

---

1   American Dictionary of the English Language, *Insurrection* (Webster Dictionary, 1828).

The U.S. Code is more vague in its legal description. "Whoever incites, sets on foot, assists, or engages in any rebellion or insurrection against the authority of the United States or the laws thereof, or gives aid or comfort thereto, shall be fined under this title or imprisoned not more than ten years, or both; and shall be incapable of holding any office under the United States."[2]

This provision is precisely why Trump's foes were so intent on pinning the crime not just on Trump himself but on his Republican supporters in Congress.

If the letter of the law is unclear, the public's understanding is not. "Insurrection" is a loaded word that should only apply to a coordinated, violent effort to subvert or overthrow the laws of the land. The largely spontaneous and scattered events of January 6 were far from an attempt to seize or overthrow the U.S. government; in fact, law enforcement had to erect "restricted" areas outside the building the day before in order to criminalize the act of simply walking around the grounds on January 6.

There's no proof that the Capitol building or the adjacent property were closed to the public on January 6, 2017, or at any other time when the electoral college was being certified. Explanations as to why the entire complex was considered off limits on January 6, 2021 remain unclear.

Further, only a few—exactly how many is still not clear—were arrested that day for any crime. If in fact thousands of people descended on the Capitol, battling police in an attempt to violently take over Congress, wouldn't more than a few be handcuffed and hauled to the local lock-up? Instead, most of those arrested either dutifully turned themselves in or were ratted out weeks later by colleagues, friends and neighbors at the instigation of federal authorities.

But none of that mattered. Instead the inflammatory word "insurrection" was splashed across the front pages of every news and political website. And it stuck.

---

2   U.S. Code §2383, *Rebellion or Insurrection.*

John Cassidy, a writer for *The New Yorker*, which had a videographer at the scene all day, opined that "this violent insurrection is what Trump wanted" in a column posted in the late afternoon of January 6.

"This is literally an insurrection," Scott Jennings, a former George W. Bush aide, wrote for CNN's website on January 6. "President Donald Trump caused this insurrection with his lies and conspiracy theories about the election process being rigged against him."

CNN chyrons throughout the afternoon referred to the events as an "insurrection." The network's hyperbolic coverage paid off: January 6, 2021 was CNN's most watched day ever with nearly 9 million viewers, even beating the three major broadcast news stations.

In a blow-by-blow account, the *Washington Post* published an online story headlined, "From historic day to 'insurrection,' how the mob takeover of the Capitol unfolded in news coverage."[3] The article explained how coverage became more inflated as the day wore on, including descriptions of the protesters as "anarchists" and "terrorists" by leading media figures.

Before Congress reconvened at around 8:00 p.m., an MSNBC reporter explained to anchor Brian Williams "what it was like being inside the Capitol when a violent pro-Trump mob waged an insurrection." Congressional reporter Garrett Haake assured Williams everyone was "powering through" after lawmakers were confined in "not very large rooms all together" for about six hours.

How exactly did so many influential people—from former presidents and Big Tech titans to the entire national news media—synchronize their messaging so perfectly in just a few hours?

Ironically it may have been Donald Trump himself who first suggested the idea a few months earlier.

---

3   Jeremy Barr, Paul Farhi, *From Historic Day to 'Insurrection,' How The Mob Takeover of the Capitol Unfolded in News Coverage* (*Washington Post*, 2021).

*   *   *   *

Memorial Day weekend of 2020 will long be remembered as one of the most chaotic in the nation's history. Violent protests erupted across the country in reaction to the death of George Floyd, a convicted felon and drug addict killed on May 25 in Minneapolis during his arrest for attempting to use counterfeit money at an area convenience store.

Looters and rioters took to the streets of major cities including Washington, D.C. Seven months before the Capitol breach, destructive political uprisings were viewed quite differently by the ruling class even when those protests threatened the safety of elected officials. The nation's capital was under attack for days on end; police were assaulted, businesses looted, and fires set throughout town.

There were similarities between what happened for days in late May and early June in Washington and what happened for several hours on January 6—except the "summer of love" protests were far more violent and dangerous, especially for the president and his family. Protesters and police clashed all weekend right outside the White House, which went on lockdown beginning May 29.

WTOP reporter Alejandro Alvarez covered the mayhem on Twitter. "Insanity outside the White House. Barricades have fallen to the west of the White House and the crowd is surging forward, once again coming face-to-face with Secret Service who've moved into formation and raised their riot shields—a few stained yellow from eggs just thrown," Alvarez tweeted on May 30.[4] An SUV and a dumpster were set on fire across from the White House; protesters threw fireworks at police.

"It's chaos out here," Alvarez posted late on May 31. "There's a towering inferno in the middle of H Street near the episcopal church. That supply shed in Lafayette is up in flames. I'm hearing booms from all around downtown."

---

4   Alejandro Alvarez, *Insanity outside the White House* (Twitter, 2020).

Alvarez reported that the AFL-CIO headquarters, just a block from the White House, had been "ransacked." Protesters were "setting off fireworks" and "lobbing gas canisters back at police."

That same day, the president was taken to a safe location in the White House. "Hundreds of protesters were gathering outside the gates, shouting curses at President Trump and in some cases throwing bricks and bottles," the *New York Times* reported on May 31. "Nervous for his safety, Secret Service agents abruptly rushed the president to the underground bunker used in the past during terrorist attacks."

An inspector general report issued a year later detailed the toll of the violence. Mark Lee Greenblat, the IG for the Interior Department tasked with investigating the use of force against protesters in Lafayette Square on June 1, 2020, confirmed that "some protesters threw projectiles, such as bricks, rocks, caustic liquids, frozen water bottles, glass bottles, lit flares, rental scooters, and fireworks, at law enforcement officials. Overall, 49 USPP officers were injured during the protests from May 29 to May 31, including one who underwent surgery for his injuries. Damage to both Federal and private property also occurred during the protests. With respect to Lafayette Park, historic statues were vandalized with graffiti, and on May 31, the park's comfort station was set on fire."[5]

Enraged by the deadly violence—and the refusal of state and local leaders to stop it—Trump reportedly floated the idea of sending U.S. soldiers to the most ravaged areas. He met with Defense Secretary Mark Esper, Attorney General William Barr, and Joint Chiefs of Staff Mark Milley in the Oval Office on June 1, 2020.

The president considered sending upwards of 10,000 active-duty troops to besieged cities under the purview of the Insurrection Act, which permits the president to use the armed forces "to suppress, in a State, any insurrection, domestic violence, unlawful combination, or conspiracy." Americans across the country, even those sympathetic to the cause, were not just horrified at

---

5   Mark Lee Greenblatt, Inspector General, *Review of U.S. Park Police Actions at Lafayette Park* (Office of Inspector General, U.S. Dept. of the Interior, 2021).

the looting, vandalism, and assaults against law enforcement and innocents but by political leaders who countenanced and even justified such criminal behavior. According to anonymous administration officials, White House advisors had already drafted a proclamation to invoke the Insurrection Act that week.

Trump, as usual, wanted swift action. "If a city or state refuses to take the actions that are necessary to defend the life and property of their residents, then I will deploy the United States military and quickly solve the problem for them," Trump warned in a Rose Garden speech on June 1.

But Barr, Esper, and Milley pushed back on the president's plan. The trio insisted enough law enforcement officials were on the ground in major hot spots to contain further destruction. Barr told *CBS News* that the chiefs were "on the same page" in advising the president against the use of American troops. (Over a ten-day period, at least a dozen people, including a seventy-seven-year-old retired police captain in St. Louis, were killed in the riots.[6])

"I do not support invoking the Insurrection Act," Esper said in a press conference on June 3. For his part, Milley later apologized for accompanying Trump to a photo op at St. John's Church, a landmark set on fire by rioters on June 1. Milley, appointed by Trump in 2018, reiterated his support for the Floyd protesters and opposition to using troops to stop the violence. At the time, his associates later told the *New York Times*, Milley considered resigning. Several months later, Milley and the seven chiefs of staff sent a letter to all U.S. military personnel calling January 6 a "violent riot" and reminding Americans that "the rights of freedom of speech and assembly do not give anyone the right to resort to violence, sedition, and insurrection."

Eighty-nine "former Defense officials" signed a letter published in the *Washington Post* on June 5, 2020 that condemned the president's plans. "While the Insurrection Act gives the president the legal authority to do so, this authority has been invoked

---

6   Robert Gearty, *Deadly Unrest: Here Are the People Who Have Died Amid George Floyd Protests Across US* (Fox News, 2020).

only in the most extreme conditions when state or local authorities were overwhelmed and were unable to safeguard the rule of
law," they wrote. "Historically, as Secretary Esper has pointed out,
it has rightly been seen as a tool of last resort."

Thus if anyone put the term "insurrection" into currency, it
may have been Trump himself. More importantly, however, the
idea fit seamlessly into liberal fever-dreams of Trump as a fascist
dictator huddled like Hitler in his bunker giving scorched-earth
instructions to his fanatical supporters.

Even before the election, Trump's enemies were floating the
idea that the president would use the military to keep him in the
Oval Office if he lost. Tabletop exercises conducted by influential Democrats and NeverTrump Republicans in the summer of
2020 gamed out every post-November scenario; in one scenario,
after he lost, Trump "encouraged provocateurs to incite violence,
then used the resulting chaos to justify sending federalized Guard
units or active-duty military personnel into American cities to
'restore order.'"[7]

January 6 gave Democrats the perfect opportunity to foment
claims of a Trump-directed coup. It was a clear and compelling
narrative. The question was whether the Democrats and the Biden
Administration would be able to make it stick. In order to do so,
both legally and in the court of public opinion, they would have
to show that the events of January 6 conformed to the model of an
insurrection: planned, armed, organized, and with a clear intent
to overthrow or subvert the US government.

In the days after the event, Democrats worked feverishly
to foster the impression that the nation's capital could be "attacked" again by gun-toting domestic terrorists. Fencing was
erected around the Capitol within days; streets were closed and
National Guardsmen were positioned throughout the downtown
area. The capital of the world's most revered democracy looked
like a militarized zone. The entire Capitol complex was closed
to the public.

---

7   Bendik Kaltenborn, *What's the Worst That Could Happen?* (*Washington Post*, 2020).

Nancy Pelosi held an overwrought press conference on January 7 spelling it all out and making clear who the ultimate target was. "[T]he President of the United States incited an armed insurrection against America, the gleeful desecration of the US Capitol, which is the temple of our American democracy, and the violence targeting Congress are horrors that will forever stay in our nation's history, instigated by the President of the United States," Pelosi said. "In calling for this seditious act, the President has committed an unspeakable assault on our nation and our people."

Pelosi's claim that the protesters were "armed" and ready to hurt or even kill lawmakers planning to certify the election results was another descriptor unquestioned by the media and most of the public.

Muriel Bowser, the Democratic mayor of Washington, D.C., had set the scene a few days before the event when she issued a statement reminding Americans planning to travel to the nation's capital that "District law prohibits anyone from carrying a firearm within 1,000 feet of any First Amendment activity." Firearms are not allowed on the grounds of the U.S. Capitol complex, any national park, or on the Mall, Bowser warned. "Additionally, members of the public are reminded that the District of Columbia does not have reciprocity with other states' concealed pistol licenses; unless a person has been issued a concealed pistol license by the District of Columbia, they cannot conceal carry a firearm in the city," Bowser wrote in a January 4 bulletin. "Finally, it is illegal to open carry firearms in the District."

In other words, the narrative frame was already in place. Deplorable hillbillies from flyover country were planning to invade Washington, D.C., bringing loads of rifles, ammunition, and other dangerous weapons with the intent to overthrow the government. A video clip produced for Bowser's Twitter account showed D.C. police officers affixing flyers with the same information about prohibited firearms on traffic lights and utility poles throughout the downtown area.[8]

---

8   Mayor Muriel Bowser, *I Am Asking Washingtonians and Those Who Live in the Region to Stay Out of the Downtown Area* (Twitter, 2021).

Robert Contee, the acting chief of the D.C. Metropolitan Police department, told reporters on January 4 that "there are people intent on coming to our city armed."

On the day of the protest itself, the news media widely reported that Trump loyalists with guns were trying to take over Congress. "The attempted coup by armed Trump supporters at the US Capitol on Wednesday marked the most significant breach of the building since 1814 during the War of 1812," wrote John Haltiwanger at *Business Insider* on January 6. No evidence was offered—it was simply assumed to be true.

Motivated by Trump's election "conspiracies," concluded *The New Republic*'s Melissa Gira Grant on January 6, a mob of his supporters had launched an "armed insurrection" at the Capitol. A January 6 headline on *Vanity Fair*'s website described the protest as an "active shooter drill."

Mayor Bowser reinforced this lie in an order declaring a curfew from January 6 to January 7. "First Amendment protests have turned violent," she wrote. "Many persons came to the District armed and for the purpose of engaging in violence and destruction, and have engaged in violence and destruction."

The notion that the Capitol building sustained massive damage was another lie that would eventually come to light. Meanwhile, members of Congress played their part to hype the events of the January 6 as a violent insurrection.

During the breach, Rep. Alexandria Ocasio-Cortez had been holed up in her office in the Cannon House Office building—not inside the Capitol itself. She later complained that a USCP officer, attempting to clear the building, looked at her "aggressively" when he tried to convince her to shelter with Rep. Katie Porter in the Longworth building. Cortez complied; she told Porter she wanted to live long enough to become a mother and looked for a closet to hide in.

Subsequently the self-dramatizing New York congresswoman told reporters that she needed therapy to deal with the lingering trauma. According to the *Washington Examiner*, "In mid-January, Ocasio-Cortez hosted an event in Congress in which representatives recounted their experiences during the riot. The New York Democrat…remarked that she almost died. "I can tell you that I had a very close encounter where I thought I was going to die," she said at the time. "I did not know if I was going to make it to the end of that day alive."

After she had partially recovered from her trauma, Ocasio-Cortez accused Republican lawmakers of knowingly trying to harm her on January 6. "I am happy to work with Republicans on this issue where there's common ground, but you almost had me murdered 3 weeks ago so you can sit this one out," the New York Democrat tweeted at Texas Republican Senator Ted Cruz on January 28, 2021. "Happy to work w/ almost any other GOP that aren't trying to get me killed." She later told CNN's Dana Bash in August that she feared she would be sexually assaulted on January 6:

> Cortez: "White supremacy and patriarchy are very linked in a lot of ways. There's a lot of sexualizing of that violence. And I didn't think that I was just going to be killed. I thought other things were going to happen to me as well.
>
> Bash: So it sounds like what you are telling me right now is that you didn't only think that you were going to die. You thought you were going to be raped.
>
> Cortez: Yeah. Yeah, I thought I was."

*   *   *   *

Unfortunately for the Democrat-media narrative about an "armed and deadly" insurrection, no one was arrested on January 6 for bringing a firearm into the Capitol. Protesters who did carry some sort of weapon told investigators they did so in order to protect themselves against anticipated attacks by leftwing protesters. After the Million MAGA March in November, Black Lives Matter and Antifa activists harassed and, in some cases, assaulted people as they left the event, throwing bottles and other projectiles at them. A black Trump supporter with her children, including one in a stroller, was encircled by BLM activists, which resulted in a few other children being knocked down. A man wearing a Trump t-shirt was knocked off his bicycle, pushed, and pelted with water.

Five weeks into the investigation, I personally reviewed all the criminal complaints filed by the Justice Department.[9] At that time only two men had been charged with possessing firearms at the protest that day; the government still cannot prove if either man was inside the building or intended to enter it on January 6. (A top FBI official told Senator Ron Johnson (R-Wisc.) during a Senate hearing in March that no one had been arrested for carrying a loaded firearm into the Capitol.)

Police did find several weapons along with rounds of ammunition and materials to make Molotov cocktails in a pickup truck belonging to one Lonnie Coffman, a seventy-year old Vietnam War veteran who had driven up from Alabama. Law enforcement found the stash while tracking down the person who had allegedly placed pipe bombs near the headquarters for both the Republican and Democratic National Committees earlier that day. He also had two loaded pistols in his possession.

Coffman was arrested upon returning to his truck around 6:30 p.m. and detained in a parking lot near the Capitol grounds. Prosecutors included in their criminal complaint filed the next day a photo of Coffman outside the Capitol; but they provided no

---

9   Julie Kelly, *No Proof January 6 Was An 'Armed Insurrection'* (American Greatness, 2021).

evidence that he went inside with the weapons or that he threatened to use them against anyone.

The grand jury, convened on January 8, quickly indicted Coffman on eleven counts including unlawful possession of guns and ammunition.[10] He was detained, denied bail, transferred to the D.C. jail, where he remained for months. In September, he finally agreed to a plea arrangement.

Christopher Alberts of Maryland was arrested around the same time on the evening of January 6. Alberts was on Capitol grounds near the visitor's center when a Metropolitan Police officer found a 9mm handgun in his pocket while searching people in violation of Bowser's curfew. He originally was indicted on three weapons charges and one count of trespassing.[11] In May, after law enforcement officials publicly admitted no firearms were recovered in the building during the protest, Alberts was hit with a superseding indictment, which added six more counts including civil disorders. The filing generated a new round of headlines even though Alberts' gun possession charge was old news.

In November, I again examined updated court documents to see whether anyone had been charged with carrying a gun into the building on January 6 and what weapons violations, four months later, had been filed. Sixty-five defendants faced charges of either possessing or using a deadly or dangerous weapon.

Here is the breakdown of weapons-related charges as of October 1. (Some defendants were charged with possessing more than one weapon and some were used by different people, such as the crutch and the axe.)

- Poles or flagpoles: 15 charges

- Chemical spray: 12 charges

- Batons: 9 charges

---

10   Grand Jury, *Indictment* (United States District Court, 2021).
11   Grand Jury, *Indictment* (United States District Court, 2021).

- Sticks: 5 charges

- Pocket knife/knife: 5 charges

- Baseball bats: 4 charges

- Fire extinguisher: 4 charges

- Crutch: 4 charges

- Temporary police barrier: 2 charges

- Metal sign; 2 charges

- Taser: 2 charges

- Tomahawk axe: 2 charges

- Stun gun/walking stick: 1 charge

- Tabletop: 1 charge

- Police helmet: 1 charge

- Firecracker: 1 charge

- Hockey stick: 1 charge

- Ice pick: 1 charge

- Firecracker: 1 charge

- Crowbar: 1 charge

- Skateboard: 1 charge

Clearly, attacking police using dangerous weapons cannot be tolerated for any reason. But since when is a skateboard or a crutch legally considered a "deadly or dangerous" weapon? (Ironically, in the November 2021 trial of Kyle Rittenhouse, government prosecutors mocked the idea that a skateboard could be considered a deadly weapon after a Kenosha rioter used it to attack the Illinois teenager.)

Contrast this with the weapons used during the 2020 summer riots. A report issued by the Major Cities Chiefs Association in October 2020 contained a comprehensive list of the weapons the rioters deployed, usually against law enforcement, during hundreds of violent protests that besieged U.S. cities for weeks:

> There were a variety of weapons used by protesters during acts of civil disobedience or violence. The most common weapons were improvised or weapons of opportunity such as rocks, bricks, pieces of landscape, and bottles (including frozen water bottles and glass bottles). Another common violent tactic used by protesters involved throwing "Molotov cocktails" at officers. Other items used as weapons or projectiles against officers included fire extinguishers, hammers, wood, cinderblocks, rocks, frozen fruit, and suspected bodily fluids. Law enforcement officers were also attacked with weapons and tactics that had rarely been seen before, such as the use of lasers to target the eyes of officers, which 41% of agencies reported. Approximately 63% of major city law enforcement agencies reported fireworks being launched or thrown at officers. Other protesters showed up with more traditional weapons, indicating that these individuals likely came prepared for, or looking to engage in, violence. These weapons included items like bats and poles…and shields. A slight majority of agencies (51%) were also confronted with firearms, most of which were legally carried based on open carry laws. In these instances, protesters often carried semi-automatic assault rifles such as

AR-15s, shotguns, and handguns. Five agencies reported police officers being shot or critically injured during protests. One agency reported four of their officers being shot and a retired police captain killed by protesters using firearms. Another agency reported protesters discharging their firearms from vehicle caravans and two agencies reported protesters being shot and killed by other protesters.[12]

The only person shot and killed on January 6 was Ashli Babbitt—by a federal police officer. One can only imagine what would happen if an unarmed BLM protestor had been killed by police during the summer of 2020.

The final blow to the "armed insurrection" narrative came when FBI Director Wray admitted to a House committee on June 10, 2021 that "he could think of at least one instance where there was an individual with a gun inside the Capitol," but that most of the weapons were items "other than firearms."

At the time of Wray's remarks, none of the 500 defendants was formally accused of having a gun inside the building. Then, as if by magic, the government handed down a superseding indictment against a man who had been arrested on January 19 on two counts of obstruction and one count of trespassing.

Guy Reffitt, a Texas man arrested January 19, had been charged with civil disorder and two obstruction offenses. He was ordered detained, denied bail, and has been housed in the D.C. jail since early February. Five months after his arrest, Reffitt suddenly faced new charges of entering the Capitol with a semiautomatic firearm. The government did not provide evidence in the indictment to support the charge.

Clearly the government is having a hard time sustaining the idea that the January 6 demonstration was some kind of armed insurrection. But as the months wore on, this wasn't the only claim

---

12   Major Cities Chiefs Association, *Report on the 2020 Protests* (MCCA, 2020).

falling apart. So was the entire premise that the protest amounted to an "insurrection," at least in actionable legal terms.

*   *   *   *

In the immediate aftermath of the Capitol breach, Democrats notched all sorts of political victories. Trump's Twitter and Facebook accounts were suspended—a longtime goal of the president's enemies. Among the incriminating tweets the company cited as evidence that Trump had violated their policies was his innocuous January 8 tweet promising that "75,000,000 great American Patriots who voted for me, AMERICA FIRST, and MAKE AMERICA GREAT AGAIN, will have a GIANT VOICE long into the future. They will not be disrespected or treated unfairly in any way, shape or form!!!" His last tweet confirmed he would not attend Biden's swearing-in ceremony. "To all of those who have asked, I will not be going to the Inauguration on January 20th."

It is something of a stretch to claim that such statements constitute incitement to break the law, let alone violently overthrow the US government.

Twitter also banned more than 70,000 accounts allegedly associated with the conspiratorial QAnon movement; influential users including Lt. General Michael Flynn and his (and Trump's) lawyer Sidney Powell were also removed from the site.

Several Trump cabinet members and advisors quit in the wake of the protest including Education Secretary Betsy DeVos; Transportation Secretary Elaine Chao (who is the wife of Mitch McConnell); acting secretary of Homeland Security Chad Wolf, and Stephanie Grisham, Trump's former press secretary and Melania Trump's chief of staff. "I can't stay here," Mick Mulvaney, Trump's one-time acting chief of staff and special envoy to Ireland, told Secretary of State Mike Pompeo on January 7. "Not after yesterday."

Ex-Trump officials urged their former colleagues to invoke the 25th Amendment to immediately remove Trump from office—as though he had refused to step down on the constitutionally appointed date. "The cabinet should meet and have a discussion," retired General John Kelly, Trump's former chief of staff, told CNNs Jake Tapper on January 7. "I don't think it will happen but the cabinet should meet and discuss this because the behavior yesterday and the weeks and months before that has just been outrageous from the president. What happened yesterday…is a direct result of his poisoning people with the lies and the frauds."

Mulvaney told CNBC on January 7 that talk of the 25th Amendment "does not surprise me at all. When the president of the United States encourages the people to interrupt a constitutional process and violently have an insurrection against the government of the United States, nothing is off the table."

A few weeks after the protest, Senate Minority Leader Mitch McConnell said the "mob was fed lies" by Donald Trump. "They were provoked by the president and other powerful people. And they tried to use fear and violence to stop a specific proceeding… but we pressed on," McConnell lamented on the Senate floor.

Amazon Web Services on January 10 deplatformed Parler, accusing Twitter's rival social media platform—used by many conservatives—of acting as a conduit for the "insurrection" plans. (Most of the social media evidence later collected against January 6 defendants, however, came from Facebook and Twitter posts.) "On January 6, 2021, rioters supporting President Trump's efforts to overturn President Elect Biden's victory stormed the U.S. Capitol," Amazon's lawyers claimed in response to a lawsuit brought by Parler. "Five people died, including a police officer. [T]his case is about Parler's demonstrated unwillingness and inability to remove from the servers of Amazon Web Services ("AWS") content that threatens the public safety, such as by inciting and planning the rape, torture, and assassination of named public officials and private citizens."

Amazon listed at least one hundred posts that the company flagged to Parler officials prior to January 6. "We are coming with our list we know where you live we know who you are and we are coming for you and it starts on the 6th civil war...Lol if you will think it's a joke...Enjoy your last few days you have," one user wrote.

Others made threats against Jack Dorsey, the founder of Twitter, and several Democratic politicians. "After the firing squads are done with the politicians the teachers are next," another user warned. (While highly inflammatory and vile, similar posts could be found on Twitter on any given day about the president, his family, his advisors, and his supporters.)

Trump would not be the only politician in the crosshairs. Republican senators and representatives who planned to object to certification on January 6 were branded the "Sedition Caucus" and a fundraising site was established to raise money for their Democratic opponents. Companies including Blue Cross Blue Shield and Marriott vowed not to donate to the so-called seditionists.

Pelosi naturally made the most of the crisis. She swiftly announced the appointment of Lt. General Russel Honore, a retired Army lieutenant general who managed the military's response to Hurricane Katrina in 2005, to lead a security review of the Capitol. In a tweet late January 6, Honore accused Capitol Police of doing a poor job that day: "I generally know how this shit is supposed to happen today secure the Capital (sic). This was a shit show today the @CapitalpoliceLS were on their Ass." (He later posted a tweet about Senator Josh Hawley: "This little piece of s--- with his @Yale law degree should be run out of DC and Disbarred ASAP." Honore subsequently deleted the tweet.)

Thousands of National Guardsmen patrolled the capital; by Inauguration Day, roughly 25,000 guardsmen were on duty to ostensibly protect Washington from more would-be insurrectionists. The capital of the world's most revered democracy looked like a militarized zone. The entire Capitol complex was closed to the public.[13]

Then, in a hasty proceeding, unprecedented in American history, the House of Representatives voted on January 13 to impeach Trump a second time, accusing the ex-president of "incitement

---

13   United States Capitol Police, *Enhanced Security Measures Throughout Capitol Complex* (USCP, 2021).

of insurrection." House Democrats used the word "insurrection" or "insurrectionists" more than sixty times in their eighty-page impeachment memo. "Provoked and incited by President Trump, who told them to 'fight like hell,' hundreds of insurrectionists arrived at the Capitol and launched an assault on the building—a seditious, deadly attack against the Legislative Branch and the Vice President without parallel in American history," impeachment managers wrote. "Once inside, insurrectionists desecrated and vandalized the Capitol."[14]

Kevin McCarthy, the Republican House leader, supported censuring Trump and insisted "the president bears responsibility for Wednesday's attack on Congress by mob rioters." McCarthy also said Republicans should be the first to denounce suggestions that Antifa played a role in the events of the day.

Ten Republican House members, including Rep. Adam Kinzinger (R-Ill.), Liz Cheney (R-Wyo.), and Pete Meijer (R-Mich.), heir to the eponymous supermarket chain, voted to impeach Trump.

In the immediate aftermath of the melee, Americans—based on saturation coverage of the "armed insurrection"—were deeply shocked. But polls taken within weeks of the protest showed a difference in how the event was viewed. An NPR/PBS NewsHour/Marist survey taken the week of January 11 showed while 58 percent of Americans thought Trump was to blame for "what happened at the U.S. Capitol," another 40 percent did not, including 82 percent of Republicans. A Harvard/Harris poll taken in February found that 65 percent of Americans believed the January 6 protesters would be "prosecuted to the fullest extent of the law." The same poll also concluded the majority of respondents wanted the 2020 summer riots fully investigated while fewer wanted the Capitol protest investigated. Two-thirds believed "the events at the U.S. Capitol are being used by politicians to suppress legitimate political movements" and 58 percent agreed that the "Capitol riots are being used as an excuse to silence political voices on the right."

---

14   House of Representatives, *Trial Memorandum of the United States House of Representatives in the Impeachment Trial of President Donald J. Trump* (Senate of the United States, 2021).

Six months later, the narrative continued to fray. A Monmouth University poll taken in June found a large gap between how Republicans and Democrats described January 6. While 85 percent of Democrats surveyed insisted it was an "insurrection," only 33 percent of Republicans and 48 percent of independents agreed. Even Republican leaders who initially jumped on the bandwagon appeared to have slowly shied away from using the word.

Regardless, Democrats, the media, and NeverTrump Republicans doubled down on their narrative strategy. On the six-month anniversary of the protest, Joe Biden stated: "Not even during the Civil War did insurrectionists breach our Capitol, the citadel of our democracy. But six months ago today, insurrectionists did." And in a silly Twitter thread, Rep. Andy Kim announced he would donate the blue suit he wore on January 6 to the Smithsonian. "6 months ago today I wore this blue suit as I cleaned the Capitol after the insurrection, now I just donated it to the Smithsonian. It's not hard to not incite or cover up an insurrection."

But despite these somber remembrances of what was frequently called "the worst attack on our democracy since the Civil War," and an event "worse than 9/11," Attorney General Merrick Garland and his prosecutors still hadn't delivered the goods. The overwhelming number of protesters face glorified trespassing and disorderly conduct offenses. One of the most common charges is "parading, picketing, or demonstrating" in Congress, a low level crime frequently committed in US history—and almost never prosecuted—that hardly reinforces the bloodthirsty image of "violent insurrectionists" hunting down terrified lawmakers with guns and zip ties. Moreover, not one American had been charged with the crimes of insurrection or sedition—and Democrats were getting impatient. "Those who hoped he would prosecute January 6 with gusto have been bitterly disappointed," *New York Magazine* writer Andrew Rice confessed in a July piece on AG Merrick Garland. The attorney general's new detractors complained he was being too cautious in not bringing sedition charges against Americans and Republican lawmakers.

The department's head fake "sedition" charge, it appeared, was not satisfying the bloodlust on the Left.

Instead, prosecutors were using a provision in a 2002 law aimed at white-collar criminals to add a felony count to what were largely misdemeanor cases. Joe Biden's Justice Department charged more than 265 protesters with "obstruction of an official proceeding."

Obstruction is a felony punishable by up to twenty years in jail. But the law is not supposed to be used against political activists. It is part of the Sarbanes-Oxley Act, passed in 2002 in response to the Enron and WorldCom scandals.[15] When he signed it into law, President George W. Bush made clear that it was not aimed at Americans involved in political protests but at corporate bad actors attempting to thwart congressional investigations. "To ensure that no infringement on the constitutional right to petition the Government for redress of grievances occurs in the enforcement of section 1512(c) . . . which among other things prohibits corruptly influencing any official proceeding, the executive branch shall construe the term 'corruptly' in section 1512(c)(2) as requiring proof of a criminal state of mind on the part of the defendant,' Bush said in July 2002.

In charging documents, particularly motions seeking pre-trial detention for the accused, prosecutors overhyped the felony obstruction charge as proof that the defendant posed a danger to society and must remain incarcerated before trial. "Taking the Capitol by force to disrupt Electoral College vote count proceedings is the ultimate obstructionist act," the government wrote in a detention motion for protestor Nathan DeGrave.

The attorney representing protestor Brady Knowlton, arrested in April and charged with several offenses including assaulting a po-

---

15   Wilbur A. Glahn, III, *The Sarbanes-Oxley Act: New Criminal Liability for Destruction of Corporate Documents* (McLane Middleton, 2002).

lice officer, told the court that there was no precedent where prosecutors used the obstruction charge in a similar manner. "No court has ever interpreted an 'official proceeding' as that term is used in Section 1512(c) to apply to a legislative function such as the certification of the electoral college vote," Knowlton's lawyer Ronald Sullivan wrote in a June motion to dismiss the obstruction count.

It's highly unlikely the Justice Department will be able to prove the Capitol protest amounted to obstructing an official proceeding as defined by the statute and case law, which is why prosecutors sought plea agreements on the charge during the first several months of the investigation.

By early August, one of the federal judges overseeing Capitol breach cases warned that the government could face a "constitutional vagueness problem" since the statute requires proof of corrupt intent. U.S. District Court Judge Randolph Moss, an Obama appointee, wondered how it differed from other lower-level offenses including "parading" in the Capitol, a misdemeanor faced by hundreds of Capitol defendants. "Unless we can tell the public where that line is, there's a problem," Moss said in an August 3 hearing.

But of course, the legal aspect of the insurrection charge wasn't really that important. To millions of Trump-hating Americans, including the entire national news media, every Democratic politician, and plenty of Republican leaders, January 6 was a deadly, armed insurrection comparable to the worst terror attacks ever perpetrated on American soil. And those involved would be treated accordingly.

CHAPTER THREE:

THE MYTH OF WHITE SUPREMACIST MILITIA GROUPS

YOU CAN'T HAVE AN "INSURRECTION" without some element of planning and organization. Otherwise it is just a spontaneous riot. In the summer of 2020, when BLM activists and Antifa thugs were battling cops in the streets, the Democrats and the liberal media insisted these were "mostly peaceful" demonstrations that had simply gotten out of hand. Antifa itself was portrayed as (at best) a decentralized affinity group and (at worst) a "myth."

After January 6, however, the shoe was on the other foot. Then the Democrats insisted that the Capitol breach was planned and organized for the benefit of Donald Trump, with or without his knowing connivance. This was necessary in order to make their maximalist narrative stick.

It certainly did its work in terms of unifying liberal opinion and shutting down dissent from any source. The trouble would come down the road when the government would be required to prove its case in court. But by then it would be too late. The whole federal apparatus would be weaponized against conservatives in what can only be described as a new domestic war on terror.

*   *   *   *

The notion that white supremacist militia groups loyal to Donald Trump planned and executed an attempted coup of the U.S. government to stop Joe Biden from becoming the next president fed neatly into the left's prevailing anti-Trump narrative. There certainly were people at the Capitol protest who held views that would be considered extreme by mainstream liberals. But none of them represented a palpable threat to the U.S. government.

Nonetheless, the media trotted out self-proclaimed "experts" in the area of domestic terrorism to blame white supremacist militia groups for January 6. "Among the protesters at the Capitol were members of white supremacy groups, including the Proud Boys," Shannon Smith, an associate history professor at St. John's University wrote in a January 7 column. "Their participation in the Jan. 6 events, egged on by Trump, reflects a long history in the U.S. of local, state and national political leaders encouraging white supremacist groups to challenge or overthrow democratic governments."

Insisting that the four-hour disturbance was an act of terror, Jessica Stern, a global studies professor at Boston University, bragged in the university's newspaper on January 15 that she knew some day these dangerous groups would collaborate to wage war against the government. "Authorities are investigating the involvement of a wide variety of hard-right movements, including hard-right militia groups such as the 3 Percenters, neo-Nazis and other white supremacists, Q-Anon conspiracy believers, Proud Boys, and anti-Communist activists," Stern wrote. January 6, Stern concluded, was a domestic terror attack. "Many terrorism researchers have been watching and warning about the growth of various groups on the hard right—white supremacists and anti-government militias—for more than a decade."

Accusations that Trump had a winking affinity for such groups had dogged the president since the start of the 2016 campaign. After the violent "Unite the Right" clash between white supremacists and leftwing protesters in Charlottesville, Virginia in August 2017, where one young woman died, the media repeatedly insisted Trump and militia groups were collaborating to promote a "white supremacist" agenda.

Charlottesville produced one of the biggest media lies of Trump's presidency—the unfounded accusation that he referred to organized rightwing protesters as "very fine people."[1] In addition to two distinct groups of "mutually combative" protesters, some local residents, unaffiliated with any group, also showed up to object to plans to remove a monument of Confederate General Robert E. Lee and rename the park that bore his name.

During a press conference at Trump Tower, the president clearly condemned the violent demonstrators on both sides. "I'm not talking about the neo-Nazis and the white nationalists," he added, "because they should be condemned totally," he said. "They didn't put themselves down as neo-Nazis, and you had some very bad people in that group. But you also had people that were very fine people on both sides. You had people in that group that were there to protest the taking down of, to them, a very, very important statue and the renaming of a park from Robert E. Lee to another name."

Yet, the damage was done. No amount of fact-checking could debunk what had become the accepted truth that Trump's base of support was populated by dangerous white supremacists.

Joe Biden began his run for president with a reference to Charlottesville. "It was there, in August of 2017, that we saw Klansmen, white supremacists, and neo-Nazis come out into the open—their crazed faces illuminated by torches, veins bulging, bearing the fangs of racism. And that's when we heard words from the President of the United States that stunned the world and shocked the conscience of our nation. He said there were some 'very fine people on both sides.'" For effect, he repeated the phrase slowly: "Very fine people on both sides."

---

[1]   Steve Cortes, *Trump Didn't Call Neo-Nazis 'Fine People.' Here's Proof* (RealClear Politics, 2021).

After January 6, reporters solemnly reminded the public that the Charlottesville rally was the precursor to the Capitol protest. "After pro-Trump rioters violently stormed the U.S. Capitol Wednesday, President Donald Trump's message of 'love' to the mob took many Americans back to a dark chapter from the first year of his presidency when he referred to the white supremacists who violently descended upon Charlottesville, Virginia, in 2017 as 'very fine people,'" ABC News reporter Deena Zaru wrote.

News outlets compared the imagery between the two events, including angry white men shouting at police, carrying Confederate flags, and wearing clothes that represented racist or anti-Semitic views. (One Capitol demonstrator was photographed wearing a "Camp Auschwitz" sweatshirt; another wore a t-shirt that read 6MWE, shorthand for "Six Million Wasn't Enough.")

During the House impeachment trial in February 2021, Rep. Jamie Raskin (D-Maryland) played a video clip of Trump's August 2017 press conference in an effort to equate the two events. "He said there were quote, 'very fine people on both sides' when the neo-Nazis, the Klansmen and Proud Boys invaded the great city of Charlottesville and killed Heather Heyer," he intoned. Trump, Raskin claimed, over the years had "conditioned" his supporters to commit "insurrection" on January 6.

Raskin's reference to the Proud Boys also connected the two deadly protests. The Proud Boys and two other groups with a spotty record of stoking violent, race-related battles—the Oath Keepers and Three Percenters—purportedly represented Trump's militant base of support, even though most Americans had never heard of the organizations before he was elected.

Michael Sherwin, the acting assistant U.S. Attorney for D.C. who managed the first few months of the investigation, told CBS's *60 Minutes* in March 2021 that the groups were a high-priority target. "The ten percent of the cases, I'll call the more complex conspiracy cases where we do have evidence, it's in the public record where individual militia groups from different facets. Oath

Keepers, Three Percenters, Proud Boys, did have a plan. We don't know what the full plan is, to come to D.C., organize, and breach the Capitol in some manner."[2]

In his March 2 Senate testimony, FBI Director Wray confirmed that the agency considered January 6 an act of "domestic terror" and specifically named two of the groups as perpetrators. "We're seeing quite a number…what we would call militia violent extremists. We've got a number who self-identify with, you know, the Proud Boys or the Oath Keepers," Wray told Senator Richard Durbin (D-Il.)

When directly asked by Senator Lindsey Graham later in the hearing whether the Oath Keepers are a domestic terror organization, Wray responded somewhat indirectly that "we have individuals who associate themselves with that group who are domestic terrorists."

So, who are these alleged white supremacist "terrorists" who wanted to overtake and seize the Capitol building on January 6?

The Oath Keepers was founded in 2009 in Nevada by a man named Stewart Rhodes, a former Army paratrooper and Yale Law School graduate. Rhodes, fifty-six, seemingly appeared out of nowhere a few months after the inauguration of Barack Obama, promising "to stop a dictatorship from ever happening here," as he told the *Las Vegas Review-Journal* in a March 2009 interview. The group's motto, Rhodes explained, is "Not On Our Watch," a warning that his members would fight the Obama administration's attempts to further encroach on individual freedoms. "My focus is on the guys with the guns, because they can't do it without them. We say if the American people decide it's time for a revolution, we'll fight with you." A one-time libertarian blogger, Rhodes wears an eye-patch from a gun accident and sports a scruffy beard.

His group, according to the Oath Keepers website, "is a non-partisan association of current and formerly serving military, police, and first responders, who pledge to fulfill the oath all military and police take to 'defend the Constitution against all ene-

---

2   Scott Pelley, *Inside the Prosecution of the Capitol Rioters* (CBS News: *60 Minutes*, 2021).

mies, foreign and domestic.'" Rhodes' focus on recruiting active and former military set off warning bells in the minds of liberal journalists who already suspect the US military of being riddled with closeted white supremacists. Membership figures are hard to confirm; estimates ranged at one point from 5,000 to 35,000.

During the Oath Keepers' inaugural meeting in October 2009, Rhodes presented a "Declaration of Orders We Will Not Obey." The list included any attempts by the government to overturn the Second Amendment, expand surveillance of U.S. citizens, or impose any form of martial law.

Rhodes became close with InfoWars host Alex Jones, often appearing on Jones' controversial program. His rhetoric became increasingly caustic; he often talked about a "civil war" and the need to create independent militias.

The Oath Keepers' most notable controversy prior to January 6 was its involvement in the infamous Bundy Ranch standoff, a conflict between the Bundy family and the U.S. government over grazing rights in 2014. Members of the Oath Keepers helped defend Cliven Bundy, a Nevada cattle rancher engaged in a lengthy battle with a federal agency that insisted he was illegally grazing his cattle on government property, during an extended confrontation with law enforcement authorities. Rhodes, however, lost some credibility after he oddly claimed Attorney General Eric Holder was preparing to use a drone to strike the property.

The group's otherwise tame activity over the past several years hardly warrants breathless descriptions of an "armed white supremacist militia." In fact, but for Rhodes' inflammatory rhetoric, the group wouldn't be on anyone's radar screen.

During 2020, Rhodes traveled around the country speaking to gatherings of supporters to warn about the prospect of a stolen presidential election.[3] Oath Keepers reportedly provided security at Trump campaign events and during Black Lives Matter riots.

On November 9, 2020, the day after the news media declared Joe Biden the winner, Rhodes rallied his troops in an online meeting. "We're going to defend the president, the duly elected president, and we call on him to do what needs to be done to save our country. Because if you don't guys, you're going to be in a bloody, bloody civil war, and a bloody—you can call it an insurrection or you can call it a war or fight."

This alarming and potentially incriminating post was included in charging documents against several Oath Keepers for their participation in the Capitol protest. Rhodes is named as "Person One" in every indictment. Yet he himself has not been charged, leading to suspicions that he may have become an informant and that his incendiary rhetoric is part of a manipulative scheme to attract potential "terrorists."

The Oath Keepers conspiracy case is the government's biggest investigation related to January 6. Over the course of several months, the Justice Department arrested at least twenty confirmed or alleged members of the Oath Keepers. Prosecutors painted a dramatic and ominous picture of what the Oath Keepers did before and during the protest. "On the afternoon of January 6, 2021, as a crowd amassed on the central eastern steps of the U.S. Capitol, a troop of camouflaged-clad individuals, many of whom were also wearing combat boots, military grade helmets, and tactical vests emblazoned with Oath Keepers patches, began to assertively and methodically make their way through the crowd and up the steps."

In criminal complaints, the government lifted verbatim a background report prepared by the Anti-Defamation League to define the group as a "large but loosely organized collection of militia who believe that the federal government has been co opted by a shadowy conspiracy that is trying to strip American citizens of their rights."

Some Oath Keepers, the government claimed, attended events to learn "paramilitary combat tactics" before January 6. Court filings detailed extensive communications between Rhodes and other Oath Keepers (or suspected Oath Keepers) in the weeks before the Capitol protest. Some messages were posted on social media, others on encrypted chat applications or on Zello, which is an app that resembles a walkie-talkie. "'Trump said It's gonna be wild!!!!!!!! It's gonna be wild!!!!!!!!," Kelly Meggs, an Oath Keeper from Florida, posted on Facebook on December 22, 2020. "He wants us to make it WILD that's what he's saying. Gentlemen we are heading to DC pack your shit!! Nice, we will have at least 50-100 OK9 there."

Subsequent posts mostly pertained to travel plans. Oath Keepers were traveling from as far away as Texas and Florida to attend Trump's speech and whatever unfolded afterwards. A few days before the protest, Rhodes barked out more orders: "It is CRITICAL that all patriots who can be in DC get to DC to stand tall in support of President Trump's fight to defeat the enemies foreign and domestic who are attempting a coup, through the massive vote fraud and related attacks on our Republic," Rhodes wrote on the group's website on January 4:

> We Oath Keepers are both honor-bound and eager to be there in strength to do our part. As we have done on all recent DC Ops, we will also have well armed and equipped QRF1 teams on standby, outside DC, in the event of a worst case scenario, where the President calls us up as part of the militia to assist him inside DC. We don't expect a need for him to call on us for that at this time, but we stand ready if he does (and we also stand ready to answer the call to serve as militia anytime in the future, and anywhere in our nation, if he does invoke the Insurrection Act).

Rhodes posted another message on the Oath Keepers website the same day:

Oath Keepers has multiple volunteer security teams and PSD teams rolling into DC from all over the nation (from as far away as UT & WY!) and we will be boots on the ground in our nation's capitol on Jan 5-6 to assist in protecting multiple scheduled events, speakers, VIPs, and event attendees. We will also be out on the streets to help keep Trump supporters safe in general as they walk back to and from their hotels, vehicles, or Metro stops (that's when Antifa likes to attack the weak, old, disabled, or families—like the hyenas they are).

On the morning of January 6, a few Oath Keepers were photographed near Roger Stone, a longtime friend of the president's, leading to speculation in the media that Stone was an unofficial liaison between the group and Trump himself. (To date, Stone has not been charged with any such offense.) Roberto Minuta of Newburgh, New York, pictured next to Stone on January 6 in black Oath Keeper regalia, was one of those who apparently volunteered to provide security for Stone, who was seen as a potential target of Antifa violence. Minuta was later arrested and charged with obstruction and unlawful entry. According to charging documents, "Minuta and others affiliated with the Oath Keepers breached the U.S. Capitol grounds, where Minuta aggressively berated and taunted U.S. Capitol police officers responsible for protecting the Capitol and the representatives inside of the Capitol."

Prosecutors characterized him as a flight risk based on a supposed propensity to disobey the law, but a judge released him pending trial as there was no evidence he had actually entered the Capitol, adding, "Mr. Minuta was not engaged in any acts of violence on Jan. 6. I think it is an overstatement of the situation to say that because Mr. Minuta was wearing particular gear he is predisposed to particular acts of violence."

Indeed, it appears that far from acting as a paramilitary force trying to storm and occupy the U.S. Capitol, the Oath Keepers were LARPing, i.e. "live action role playing," enacting a scene designed to look meaningful when, in fact, it accomplished nothing. In short, the government's rhetoric, and big talk by the participants themselves, failed to match reality—or the hope of criminal charges.

It does not appear that the first set of Oath Keepers engaged with police either inside or outside the building. Video showed this first group of about twelve Oath Keepers entering the building around 2:40 p.m. in a "stack" formation, marching single file with their hands on each other's backs. They wore military garb including helmets and reinforced vests. They remained in the building for about twenty minutes and took photos. None had weapons; they didn't vandalize or steal any property.

At about 3:15 p.m., three other Oath Keepers entered on the same (east) side of the building. According to charging documents, they confronted police officers once inside; one defendant, Joshua James, was charged with assaulting or resisting an officer. One allegedly carried, but did not use, a can of bear spray. This is the extent of the heinous violence supposedly committed by the members of this group.

Prosecutors also claimed in their indictment that the group had set up a "quick reaction force" (as referenced by Rhodes, above) and had weapons at the ready in a Virginia hotel. Photos show some Oath Keepers bringing "long boxes," presumably to transport weapons, into one of the nearby hotels. Yet their text communications reveal that the group had decided to leave their weapons in Virginia so as not to run afoul of D.C.'s strict gun control laws.

To date, eight months after the first indictment was handed down—the grand jury added five more between January and August—no Oath Keeper has faced a single charge for possessing illegal firearms or bringing a weapon of any kind into the Capitol.[4]

---

4   Grand Jury, *Indictment* (United States District Court, 2021).

In the *60 Minutes* interview with Scott Pelley, Michael Sherwin confessed that the Oath Keepers' conduct was not as sinister as the public had been led to believe; the "stack" formation was the best evidence the government had against this dangerous "paramilitary group."

> Sherwin: That's what you learn in close, you know, order combat, how you stay with your team to—breach a room where maybe there's a terrorist, to breach a room where maybe there was an Al Qaeda operative.

> Pelley: The infantry calls it a stack.

> Sherwin: Correct. A stack or a Ranger File, a column, a close-quarter combat column going up that staircase.

> Pelley: The Oath Keepers in that stack, what have they been charged with?

> Sherwin: The most significant charge is obstruction. That's a 20-year felony. They breached the Capitol with the intent, the goal to obstruct official proceedings, the counts, the Electoral College count.

Slight problem with Sherwin's analysis that could potentially derail the government's most serious charge against the Oath Keepers and more than 200 other January 6 defendants: by the time the Oath Keepers (and most protesters) entered the Capitol building, both chambers had recessed. How did the Oath Keepers—by walking into the building roughly twenty minutes after the joint session had been suspended—"obstruct" any official proceeding?

In addition to the obstruction count, Oath Keepers faced a variety of nonviolent offenses including conspiracy; aiding and abetting destruction of government property (although they did not damage any property, prosecutors argued that their actions encouraged others to do so); entering restricted grounds; civil disorder; and tampering with documents or proceedings. Prosecutors included as evidence one conversation when the participants debated what type of pants to wear to the Capitol, khakis or jeans.

Some of the initial accusations made by the government were unsubstantiated. In the first set of indictments, the Justice Department tried to portray Thomas Caldwell, a sixty-five-year-old former Naval commander, as a leader of the group. "The detailed and organized nature of Caldwell's planning for the January 6 operation and Capitol assault was uniquely dangerous and continues to impact security in the District and beyond," they alleged. "Everything he did, he did in concert with an anti-government militia. Specifically, Caldwell helped organize a tactical unit of trained fighters that stormed and breached the Capitol on January 6, 2021."

But the prosecutors turned out to be wrong. Caldwell never joined the Oath Keepers, and he never entered the building on January 6. He attended the events in Washington with his wife, Sharon, who had traveled with him the night before from their home in Virginia. The couple told me in September 2021 they wanted to arrive as early as possible to get a seat to hear Trump's speech.

Further, Caldwell's service-related disabilities, including a deteriorating spine, severely limit his physical capabilities. "Moving, sitting for extended periods of time, lifting, carrying, and other physical activities are extremely painful and Caldwell is limited in his ability to engage in them," his attorney wrote in one filing. Caldwell had back surgery in the summer of 2020 and still has shrapnel in his body.

Caldwell's lawyer, David W. Fischer, blasted prosecutors for their rushed and highly prejudiced portrayal of his client, pointing out that the authorities "did virtually no investigation before branding Caldwell a felon, and have provided multiple inaccurate statements to the Court."

> In less than a month, the Government's theory as to Caldwell's role in the claimed conspiracy has morphed from him being the Commander of Oath Keepers . . . who (presumably) led the attack on the east side of the Capitol, to a guy 'associated' with the Oath Keepers. Caldwell's stellar background and military career was, unintentionally, slandered by the Government's sloppy, rushed investigation. As the Court knows, the Government typically takes months and even years to build cases, painstakingly gathering and evaluating evidence and interviewing witnesses. By contrast, in this case the Government charged a 20-year decorated Navy veteran with no prior record based on a few hours of investigation and without giving him the courtesy of an interview.

The wide-ranging conspiracy case against the Oath Keepers has so far revealed no actual conspiracy other than vague plans to show up and "be ready to act" if called on by President Trump. It did produce regular headlines, however. In April, heavy metal singer Jon Schaffer, fifty-three became the first Oath Keeper to take a plea deal. Schaffer pleaded guilty to obstruction of an official proceeding and trespassing with a deadly or dangerous weapon; he reportedly brought bear spray into the Capitol.

Schaffer, described by prosecutors as a founding member of the Oath Keepers, agreed to cooperate with the feds as part of his plea arrangement. "The defendant in this case admits forcing his way into the U.S. Capitol on January 6 for the express purpose of stopping or delaying congressional proceedings essential to our democratic process," FBI Deputy Director Paul Abbate said in an April 16 press release. "These actions are disgraceful and unacceptable."

Oddly, Schaffer was not included in any of the grand jury indictments; in fact, he was never formally indicted at all. Nor is it clear whether he was with the other members at any point that day. There are rumors that he may be in a witness protection program.

New York Times reporter Katie Benner told MSNBCs Rachel Maddow that Schaffer's early cooperation agreement proved the government believes "the Oath Keepers could be a dangerous group. We know that the Oath Keepers, they`re a militia."

So too—according to the media and the Justice Department—are the Proud Boys. Unlike the Oath Keepers, which still maintains a website and accepted membership applications and fees, the Proud Boys doesn't appear to have any formal structure. The group was founded in 2016 by Gavin McInnes, a dual-citizen Canadian/Brit and co-founder of VICE, a digital media and broadcast company that produced documentaries for HBO, among other high-profile endeavors. McInnes left VICE in 2008 and began writing books and hosting his own show online. It's unclear exactly how the group came together.

Proud Boys describe themselves as "Western chauvinists" who oppose political correctness and reject "white guilt." Members have clashed with leftwing protesters over the past few years including at the Charlottesville rally; McInnes was banned from several platforms including Twitter and YouTube before a similar "Unite the Right" protest in Washington, D.C. in October 2018. (Twitter also suspended numerous Proud Boy regional accounts.)

After McInnes gave a speech in New York City in October 2018, Antifa attacked some Proud Boys outside the Metropolitan Republican Club, leading to a violent clash. Ten Proud Boys members were arrested and charged in the brawl.[5]

---

5   Allen Feuer, *Proud Boys Founder: How He Went From Brooklyn Hipster to Far Right Provacateur* (New York *Times*, 2018).

McInnes left the group in November 2018. "I do this reluctantly because I see it as the greatest fraternal organization in the world but rumors and lies and bad journalism has made it's [sic] way to the court system and the [Proud Boys involved in the October brawl]...are facing serious charges," he said in a video announcement.

Enrique Tarrio, the owner of a Florida-based online store called the "1776 Shop," took over the group. During the "social justice" riots and protests in 2020, members of the Proud Boys faced off against BLM and Antifa activists. In August 2020, the groups clashed during a "Back the Blue" rally in Portland. "The two groups sparred for more than two hours, as people exchanged blows, fired paintballs at each other and blasted chemicals indiscriminately into the crowd," the *Washington Post* reported on August 22, 2020. "People lobbed fireworks back and forth. At least one person was hit in the abdomen with a device that flashed and exploded, causing bleeding."

The Proud Boys quickly became the media's counterpunch to the Right on Black Lives Matter. In a September 2020 presidential debate, Fox News host Chris Wallace confronted Trump about his alleged association with militia groups, comparing them to Antifa. "Are you willing, tonight, to condemn white supremacist and militia groups and to say that they need to stand down and not add to the violence in a number of these cities as we saw in Kenosha and as we've seen in Portland? Are you prepared specifically to do it?" Wallace demanded.[6]

Trump correctly noted that almost all of the violence during the George Floyd riots was the work of leftwing groups like Antifa and Black Lives Matter, but Wallace, joined by Biden, pushed for a statement. "Who would you like me to condemn, who?" Trump asked as Biden and Wallace harangued him on national television. Biden spoke up: "The Proud Boys." Trump, who seemed confused by the onslaught, acquiesced. "Proud Boys, stand back and stand by."

6   Audrey Conklin, *Trumps' Proud Boys Comment at Debate Sparks Pushback, Outrage; Tim Scott Asks Him to Clarify* (Fox News, 2020).

Like the Charlottesville comments, Trump's remark was again taken out of context by both the media and some members of the Proud Boys themselves. (He said hours later that he didn't know who the Proud Boys were and reiterated his plea for the group to "stand down [and] let law enforcement do the work.") Tarrio and Joseph Biggs, another Proud Boy leader who would be charged for participating in the January 6 protest, cheered the president's mention. "Standing by sir," Tarrio posted on Telegram. "President Trump told the proud boys (sic) to stand by because someone needs to deal with ANTIFA…well sir! We're ready!!" Biggs replied.

Biggs, thirty-seven, is a retired Army staff sergeant with deployments in Iraq and Afghanistan; he won two Purple Hearts and received a medical discharge from the military for PTSD. At the time of the protest, according to a motion filed by his attorney, Biggs was working for InfoWars and Right Side Broadcasting Network, a pro-Trump online channel.

He reportedly helped plan a large event in Portland in 2019 where Proud Boys and Antifa members violently battled. "Protesters from the competing factions converged near Pioneer Courthouse Square, leading to brief flashes of violence and pointed confrontations," a Portland newspaper reported on June 29, 2020. Antifa threw so-called "milkshakes," which contained wet cement, at Proud Boys, police, and independent journalist Andy Ngo. "Medics treated eight people, including three officers, for injuries, according to police. One officer was punched in the arm, another officer was hit in the head by a projectile and two were pepper-sprayed."

Skirmishes between Proud Boys and leftwing agitators continued after Election Day. In December 2020, Tarrio confronted Black Lives Matter protesters in D.C. after burning a BLM banner that had been taken off an historic black church on December 12.

On January 4, 2021, he was arrested in Washington and charged with vandalism and possessing unloaded magazines after he arrived from Miami to participate in the Capitol protests. Tarrio, like Stewart Rhodes, began rallying his troops before January 6. According to one indictment, Tarrio posted a message on December 29 boasting that the Proud Boys would "turn out in record numbers on Jan 6th but this time with a twist…We will be incognito and we will be spread across downtown DC in smaller teams. And who knows…we might dress in all BLACK for the occasion."

On January 5, Joseph Biggs, a chief organizer of the Proud Boys, sent a text in an encrypted messaging channel confirming that he spoke to Tarrio at around 9:20 p.m. "We have a plan," Biggs tells the group. "I gave [Tarrio] the plan. The one I told the guys and he said he had one." Tarrio, at this point, had been arrested on the banner-burning and ammunitions charge. As a condition of his release, Tarrio could not re-enter Washington.

At 10 a.m. on January 6, Biggs and three other reported leaders of the Proud Boys—Ethan Nordean, Zachary Rehl, and Charles Donahoe—met up near the Washington Monument.

Shortly before 1 p.m., according to charging documents, the four Proud Boys and dozens of other alleged members of the group, charged past barriers that had been breached and eventually entered the Capitol building.[7]

This particular group walked throughout the building. Biggs reportedly entered the Senate chamber at one point, briefly exited the building, then re-entered. None, however, has been charged with a weapons violation or assault. Text messages included in the grand jury indictment show how the members described their action that day.

> NORDEAN posted a message on social media that included a picture of a Capitol Police Officer administering pepper spray on January 6, 2021, with a caption that read, in part…'if you feel bad for the police, you are part of the problem. They care more about federal property (our property) than protecting and serving the people. BACK THE BLACK AND YELLOW.'

---

7   Grand Jury, *Indictment* (United States District Court, 2021).

BIGGS posted a message on social media that read 'what a day.'

REHL posted a message that read, in part, 'I'm proud as fuck what we accomplished yesterday, but we need to start planning and we are starting planning, for a Biden presidency.'

DONOHOE posted a message that read, in part, 'We stormed the capitol unarmed' and then 'And we took it over unarmed.'

All four were arrested within weeks of the protest. In March, they were indicted on numerous counts including obstruction of an official proceeding, abetting destruction of property, trespassing, and disorderly conduct.

They were also, along with at least a dozen other Proud Boys, charged with conspiracy—similar to the Oath Keepers case, but in separate indictments instead of one. The purpose of the conspiracy, prosecutors alleged in both cases, was to "stop, delay, or hinder Congress' certification of the Electoral College vote" on January 6.

Other Proud Boys defendants face more violent charges. Dominic Pezzola, William Pepe, and Matthew Greene are accused of "assaulting, resisting, or impeding" law enforcement officers. At 2:13 p.m. on January 6, Pezzola used a riot shield confiscated by a Capitol police officer to smash in one of the exterior windows. Other Proud Boys assembled on the west side of the complex before entering the building: "Whose house is this?" William Chrestman of Missouri shouted at a crowd of protesters assembled outside. "Do you want your house back?" When the crowd shouted back, "Yes!" Chrestman replied, "Take it!"

Chrestman faces one count of threatening federal officers after telling a Capitol Police officer, "You shoot and I'll take your fucking ass out!"

Another alleged militia group, the Three Percenters, played a much smaller and less coordinated role. Their name is derived from the belief that only three percent of American colonists took up arms against the British during the Revolution. Formed in 2008, it has a much lower profile but became national news when members of the group were accused of participating in a plot to kidnap Michigan Governor Gretchen Whitmer. Membership figures are hard to find; at one point, the group claimed 12,000 members on its Facebook page. But this is unconfirmed and may be greatly exaggerated.

In any case, only a handful of Three Percenters face charges related to January 6. Guy Reffitt was arrested on January 16 at his Texas home; his wife, according to an investigator, told authorities he was a member of the Three Percenters but it's unclear if that statement was accurate. The grand jury indicted Reffitt on January 27 on obstruction of an official proceeding and trespassing charges. (He also faced an additional charge for allegedly threatening his children not to turn him into law enforcement. Reffitt's son told the FBI about the confrontation.)

In June, Reffitt was slapped with a new charge. Prosecutors, five months later, somehow determined that Reffitt had carried a semi-automatic gun to the Capitol grounds that day. (Reffitt did not enter the building.) That same month, the Justice Department announced charges against six alleged Three Percenters. Only one, Russell Taylor of California, was charged with carrying a dangerous or deadly weapon, specifically a knife.

So, to summarize: Roughly fifty confirmed or alleged members of the three "white supremacist militia groups" have been charged with any crime related to January 6. Only a handful are accused of attacking police officers; even fewer face weapons-related offenses. And just one man, Guy Reffitt, is accused of bringing a gun to the Capitol grounds that day, and prosecutors didn't even charge him until five months later.

None of this conduct rises to the level of "domestic terrorism," as FBI Director Wray claimed, or is representative of a menacing, rogue force of crazed militia plotting behind the scenes to overthrow the U.S. government. Militia groups with no firearms? A battle plan comprised of nothing more than braggadocio on social media and in private chat groups? "White supremacists" who, despite volumes of texts and communications between all the participants, never used a racial slur or suggested their actions were fueled by racial issues?

By October 15, 2021, four Oath Keepers had pleaded guilty to various offenses; none was a crime of violence against police or other protesters.

Meanwhile, government and media claims that these groups conspired to "attack" the Capitol on January 6 slowly crumbled. A Reuters report published in August 2021 cited anonymous law enforcement officials admitting the FBI had found "scant evidence" that January 6 was an "organized plot" led by Trump-supporting extremist groups.[8] "FBI investigators did find that cells of protesters, including followers of the far-right Oath Keepers and Proud Boys groups, had aimed to break into the Capitol. But they found no evidence that the groups had serious plans about what to do if they made it inside," officials familiar with the investigation told Reuters. "[S]o far prosecutors have steered clear of more serious, politically-loaded charges that the sources said had been initially discussed by prosecutors, such as seditious conspiracy or racketeering."

Whoever anonymously sourced this story to the press had a clear goal: to downshift public expectations of the January 6 investigations. The conspiracy cases were legally weak; pending trials would further expose the shaky evidence on which they were based.

Nonetheless, Joe Biden's Justice Department treated the accused "militia" men and women like domestic terrorists. The Justice Department sought pre-trial detention for a number of Oath Keepers despite facing no violent charges. Jessica Watkins, a transgender Oath Keeper from Ohio, was arrested in January. Kelly Meggs and Kenneth Harrelson from Florida were arrested in Feb-

---

8   Mark Hosenball, Sarah N. Lynch, *Exclusive: FBI Finds Scant Evidence U.S. Capitol Attack Was Coordinated* (Reuters, 2021).

ruary and March, respectively. All three were sent to the D.C. jail for Capitol defendants; judges repeatedly refused to release them.

As of November 1, 2021, all three remained incarcerated awaiting trial that was delayed from January 2022 until April 2022.

Ditto for Joseph Biggs, Ethan Nordean, Zachary Rehl, and Charles Donohoe, although they are detained in different prison facilities across the country. But the hyperbolic representations both in court and in the media about Nordean's activities on January 6 did not match the charges filed by the government. All four, in fact, face one count of conspiracy; two counts of obstruction; one vague count of "abetting" the destruction of government property; one count of trespassing; and one count of disorderly conduct. Prosecutors still insisted Nordean, facing no violent offenses, should not be released from jail while awaiting trial because it "would leave a man who has the wherewithal to help plan and lead a large group of men in a violent attack to take similar actions in the future in furtherance of his goals."

Seeking Nordean's indefinite incarceration, the Justice Department additionally noted his lack of remorse. "Everything about Defendant's actions on behalf of the Proud Boys since November 4, 2020, all of his actions in Washington, D.C., on January 6, 2021, and all of his actions and statements since then show that Defendant is completely unrepentant. His leadership position in the Proud Boys has not changed, his belief system has not changed, and he is not the least bit sorry for what he has done."

Prosecutors later were forced to admit, under pressure by Nordean's defense attorney, that Nordean did *not* mobilize Proud Boys on January 6 because his cell phone was dead. This was a direct contradiction to the Justice Department's central accusations against him. "[T]he government acknowledged it possessed evidence showing Nordean's phone was without power during the relevant events on January 6," his attorney wrote in a March motion for his release.

Of course, if Nordean is innocent of the charges against him, there is no reason to expect him to show remorse. What is most striking here is the fact that his "belief system" seems to be what is on trial here as opposed to anything he actually did.

Nonetheless, in April, Judge Timothy Kelly, a Trump appointee, revoked Nordean's initial release, granting the Justice Department's demand to keep him behind bars and concurred that his lack of remorse was a factor. "[A]lthough Nordean did not carry or use a weapon that day, he said and did things that day that are highly troubling, as explained in detail on the record," Kelly wrote. "He also celebrated that day, and has expressed no regret or remorse for what he did or what happened."

Judge Kelly made the same argument in ordering pre-trial detention for Biggs, Donohoe, and Rehl. While acknowledging none has a criminal record, Kelly still insisted they posed a danger to society for their supposed "leadership role" in the January 6 "riot." Kelly also continues to delay their trial, repeatedly excluding time from the Speedy Trial Act. (An egregious violation every D.C. District judge has done in January 6 cases.)

All four will remain behind bars until their trial date—currently scheduled for May 2022.

William Chrestman, Guy Reffitt, and Dominic Pezzola also were still being held at the D.C. jail as of October 2021. Christopher Worrell, accused by the government of being a Proud Boy although he was not charged as such, was arrested in Florida in March and indicted on various counts including using pepper spray on a police officer. He was denied bail and remained in the D.C. jail until November 2021. A federal judge authorized his release after reports Worrell was not receiving proper medical care in the jail to treat his non-Hodgkins lymphoma.

By December 2021, however, two men had not been charged: Stewart Rhodes and Enrique Tarrio. It is widely known that both men are "Person One" in the Oath Keepers and Proud Boys indictments, respectively. (Later, I cover legitimate suspicions as to why Rhodes evaded criminal charges and explain that Tarrio once worked as an FBI informant.)

What about other "white supremacists" who were supposedly involved in the protest? The best example the government could muster is the case of Timothy Hale-Cusanelli. An Army reservist working as a security contractor at the Naval Weapons Station in New Jersey, Hale went to the capital on January 6. He was arrested on January 15 after speaking with FBI investigators for five hours. Hale, dressed in a suit on January 6, committed no violent crime and was inside the building for less than twenty minutes.

Naval Criminal Investigative Services wired an informant, a colleague at the military facility, to record a conversation with Hale a few days after he returned from the capital. The informant asked Hale questions about his participation in the Capitol protest and his thoughts about a pending "civil war."

Investigators confiscated Hale's devices and found racially offensive memes and videos including photos of Hale dressed to resemble Adolf Hitler. Some of the material, without question, would lead one to believe Hale is a racist and/or anti-Semite. None of it, however, is against the law.

Naval intelligence investigators even questioned roughly four dozen of Hale's co-workers on his "extremists" views. "The Special Agents asked them a defined set of pre-written questions regarding Defendant's actions on January 6, 2021 [and] Defendant's expression of a white supremacist ideology," government lawyers wrote in a March filing seeking Hale's extended incarceration. "[T]hirty-four (34) of the forty-four (44) interviewees described Defendant 'as having extremist or radical views pertaining to the Jewish people, minorities, and women.'"

Prosecutors used a subhead—"Defendant's White Supremacist Ideology"—in one court filing to detail all of Hale's allegedly racist beliefs, citing answers from the questionnaires given to his co-workers. "White Supremacist and Nazi Sympathizer ideology appears to be the driving force in his life," the government claimed in its request to keep Hale behind bars indefinitely. "Without more, Defendant's White Supremacist, Nazi Sympathizer ideology would not be grounds for pretrial detention. However, Defendant's statements to [the informant] make it clear that his ideology is the driving force behind his stated desire for a Civil War. Given that Defendant's desire for a civil war makes him a danger to the community, this Court can and must consider Defendant's ideology within the context of his dangerousness."[9]

A judge agreed, going so far as to say that "just looking at what [Hale] did on January 6, he would be a free man right now… but his animus" made him a danger to society.

Hale would become the face of "white supremacists" on January 6. But just like the "white supremacist militia" groups, Hale's actions came nowhere close to the media's portrayal of their involvement at the Capitol on January 6.

A court-appointed attorney also is helping advance the "white supremacist" trope, much to the disadvantage of her client.H. Heather Shaner, a D.C.-based lawyer appointed to represent several January 6 defendants who cannot afford the $100,000-plus retainer for a private criminal defense attorney, gives her clients a list of books to read and movies to watch to come to terms with their alleged "white privilege." Shaner, Huffington Post reporter Ryan Reilly explained in a June column[10], "has seized an opportunity to try and educate them on the history their teachers glossed over."

Of course, neither Shaner nor Reilly have any idea what the defendants did or didn't learn in history classes, but no matter. Demeaning January 6 protesters as uneducated, biased "deplorables" from the hinterlands is a common theme in the news media and court documents. Shaner's "remedial social studies program," as Reilly snarkily described it, including urging clients such as Anna Chutk-Lloyd, an Indiana grandmother charged with misdemeanors, to consume a selected list of books and movies. "I tendered a booklist to her," Shaner said[11] about Morgan-Lloyd. "She has

9   Julie Kelly, *The Government's Case Against a 'White Supremacist'* (American Greatness, 2021)
10   Ryan J. Reilly, *A Lawyer For Jan. 6 Defendants Is Giving Her Clients Remedial Lessons In American History,* HuffPost, June 21, 2021
11   Julie Kelly, *Deprogramming of January 6 Defendants Is Underway,* American Greatness, June 23, 2021

read *Bury My Heart at Wounded Knee*, *Just Mercy*, and *Schindler's List* to educate herself about 'government policy' toward Native Americans, African Americans and European Jews. We have discussed the books and also about the responsibility of an individual when confronting 'wrong.'"

Shaner also told the court that Lloyd watched the 'Burning Tulsa' documentary on the History Channel as well as 'Mudbound,' a story of two families, one black and one white, living on the same property after World War II.

During her June sentencing hearing before Judge Lamberth, Morgan-Lloyd offered a mea culpa for her "white privilege," breaking down in tears at one point. "I apologize to the court, to the American people, to my family," she told Lamberth. "I was there to support Trump peacefully and am ashamed that it became a savage display of violence." She said she's never experienced racial negativity but "realizes many people do."

Morgan-Lloyd continued: "I've lived a sheltered life and truly haven't experienced life the way many have. I've learned that even though we live in a wonderful country things still need to improve. People of all colors should feel as safe as I do to walk down the street."

For her five minute jaunt in the Capitol building, a brief excusion that involved no violence and certainly not motivated by any racial malice, Morgan-Lloyd was sentenced to three years probation and a $500 fine.

Like so many accusations about January 6, the notion that it was planned, organized, and executed by "white supremacists" isn't rooted in any evidence. Of the thousands of court filings, which include extensive text messages between co-defendants and social media posts by others, I have seen nothing to support the allegation that the Capitol protest was motivated by race. No racial slurs, no boasts about the superiority of the white race, no crude references to the color of anyone's skin.

Further, the claim makes no sense. White supremacists wanted to overthrow a nearly all-white Congress and hang the white vice president to prevent the inauguration of another white man? Completely illogical, and almost comical.

But facts won't matter. Ingrained in the general narrative of the Capitol protest is the notion that rightwing militias and white supremacists followed Donald Trump's call to overturn the election results that day. And nothing will dislodge that idea from the minds of liberal journalists, judges or voters.

CHAPTER FOUR:

LAUNCHING A NEW DOMESTIC WAR ON TERROR

PAUL HODGKINS TOOK A BUS from Tampa to Washington, D.C. to watch President Trump's speech on January 6. The thirty-eight-year-old press operator traveled alone on the 900-mile journey; he did not bring a weapon or plan to meet up with anyone in the capital.

After listening to the president's speech, he walked toward the Capitol with thousands of Trump supporters. At around 2:50 p.m., Hodgkins entered the building and ended up in the chamber of the U.S. Senate. Hodgkins carried a "Trump 2020" flag and wore a Trump t-shirt. At one point, he raised the flag "in salute," federal prosecutors claimed in a court filing.

He exited the building around 3:15 p.m.

Hodgkins didn't assault a police officer or carry a weapon or damage any property. But he now is a convicted felon who will spend eight months in prison for his nonviolent, twenty-five-minute interlude in a public government building. In June, Hodgkins pleaded guilty to one count of obstruction of an official proceeding, a felony punishable by up to twenty years in jail. (The Justice Department dropped the other four misdemeanors in exchange for his plea.)

Five months after he was arrested, Hodgkins, a working-class American and former Eagle Scout with no criminal record, was branded a "domestic terrorist" by his own government. "The son and grandson of union elevator mechanics, Hodgkins had worked at factories, driven delivery trucks, sold firewood and scrapped metal, and until recent years had a side gig as a wrestler, sometimes making just $25 a match," the *Washington Post* reported[1] in a November 2021 series that featured Hodgkins. "For the past seven years, he had worked late-night shifts at a manufacturing facility, moving large steel coils."

His only political activity prior to January 6 was volunteering to work phone banks for the Trump campaign and waving Trump flags at Tampa intersections, hardly behavior that could be equated with any sort of "terrorist."

Asking for an eighteen-month prison sentence, Mona Sedky, a special assistant U.S. attorney, wanted to make an example of Hodgkins. "The need to deter others is especially strong in cases involving domestic terrorism, which the breach of the Capitol certainly was," Sedky wrote in a July sentencing memo. "Moreover, with respect to specific deterrence, courts have recognized that "terrorists[,] [even those] with no prior criminal behavior, are unique among criminals in the likelihood of recidivism, the difficulty of rehabilitation, and the need for incapacitation."

During Hodgkin's sentencing hearing on July 19, Sedky told U.S. District Court Judge Randolph Moss that the defendant "was part and parcel of an act of domestic terrorism going around him."

So, there it was. After FBI Director Christopher Wray during a March congressional hearing officially designated January 6 as an act of "domestic terrorism," the Justice Department now had permission to refer to U.S. citizens accused of committing no violent crime on January 6 as "terrorists." Prosecutors aren't even required to actually charge any January 6 protester with the crime of domestic terrorism; inflammatory government filings and histrionics in court hearings do the dirty work instead.

---

1   "Before, During, After The Attack," *Washington Post*, October 31, 2021

But Hodgkins' lawyer, an Army reservist about to be deployed for the third time to the Middle East, admonished the prosecutor for her language. "Words have meaning," Patrick Leduc told Moss during the July 19 hearing. "I have been shot at by real terrorists. If we're going to label this as domestic terrorism, where do we draw that line?"

Citing his military oath to fight enemies both foreign and domestic, Leduc choked up defending his client. "Paul Hodgkins is not my enemy." Leduc asked for probation rather than a prison sentence, noting that any jail time would cost Hodgkins his job and apprenticeship to become a mechanic.

Before Moss issued his ruling, Hodgkins begged for mercy. "The felony conviction will cost me several of my civil rights. I will lose the job I love. I will lose the house I rent and have to find a place for my two cats."

Hodgkins said he was "regretful" and apologized for his role in "hurting" the country. He said he went to Washington to "support a president I love." He then uttered a confession-like statement that undoubtedly was music to the ears of the Obama-appointed judge and federal prosecutors: "Joseph R. Biden is rightfully and respectfully the president of the United States."

Leduc, too, asked the judge for leniency. "When you consider that Mr. HODGKINS is not wealthy in any way, shape or form, and rents a home in what is considered the poorest, working class neighborhood in Tampa, and takes his time off on weekends to serve the homeless, is truly noteworthy, and dare I say, incredible," Leduc wrote in a July motion to the court. "Mr. HODGKINS works over 40 hours a week, lives paycheck to paycheck, barely getting by financially, and chooses to serve those EVEN poorer than he. Mr. HODGKINS is a unique Defendant, the likes of which I have not experienced. He is such an honorable, hardworking, gracious and thoughtful citizen, and there is so much to admire in him. If there was ever a person before this court that merit leniency, Mr. HODGKINS possesses every attribute of that very person."

But Moss was unpersuaded. He approved an eight-month prison sentence, effectively rendering Hodgkins unemployed and homeless. Moss scolded Hodgkins from the bench; people were "traumatized and killed" on January 6, the judge claimed. "Democracy requires the cooperation of the governed," he further lectured. "Democracy is in trouble. This is a damage that will persist in this country for decades." He was particularly offended by Hodgkin's Trump flag. "The symbolism of that act is unmistakable. He was staking a claim on the Senate floor, declaring his loyalty to a single individual over a nation."

And there, in a federal courtroom in the nation's capital, was the connection Biden and the Democrats wanted all along: Trump supporter equals domestic terrorist.

The threat of "domestic terrorism" pre-occupied official Washington for the first several months of Joe Biden's presidency. From military brass to Congressional leaders, a day didn't pass without a dire warning about the menace of "domestic terrorists." And as lawmakers confronted any number of crises—the deteriorating situation in Afghanistan, inflation, unprecedented numbers of illegal immigrants flooding the border—the House of Representatives kept its focus on the events of January 6.

*   *   *   *

"We do not believe leaders understood the gravity of the threat. The terrorist danger from Bin Ladin and Al Qaeda was not a major topic for policy debate among the public, the media, or in the Congress. Indeed, it barely came up during the 2000 presidential campaign. Though top officials told us that they understood the danger, we believe there was uncertainty among them."

So concluded the 9/11 commission in its final report issued in July 2004. One of the "top officials" interviewed by the panel was Vice President Richard Cheney. The 585-page document detailed the timeline leading up to the worst terrorist attack on American soil; the war on terror was well underway at the time, with Cheney helping to lead the charge.

Fast forward almost seventeen years to the day when House Speaker Nancy Pelosi convened a press conference on Capitol Hill to announce Cheney's daughter, Representative Liz Cheney, would be one of two Republicans seated on Pelosi's 9/11-style select committee to investigate the events related to January 6.

In a successful attempt to rehabilitate the family name and seek approval from those who just a decade before considered her father a war criminal, Liz Cheney became the GOPs most outspoken critic of her own party during Trump's presidency.

In an interview with Fox News' Bret Baier on the early evening of January 6, Cheney said Donald Trump "lit the flame" of the "assault on the U.S. Capitol." Six days later, Cheney confirmed her intention to vote in favor of impeachment. "On January 6, 2021 a violent mob attacked the United States Capitol to obstruct the process of our democracy and stop the counting of presidential electoral votes," Cheney wrote in a January 12 statement. "The President of the United States summoned this mob, assembled the mob, and lit the flame of this attack. Everything that followed was his doing…There has never been a greater betrayal by a President of the United States of his office and his oath to the Constitution. I will vote to impeach the President."

The Republican daughter of a main architect of the "war on terror" would now be in a position to help Democrats redirect that war against American citizens. It was a fear often expressed by libertarians and progressives when Cheney's father and President George W. Bush galvanized federal resources, including secretive surveillance tools, to root out Islamic terrorists here and abroad. In 2005, Pelosi herself opposed reauthorizing certain provisions of the Patriot Act, insisting it did not "secure the right balance between security and liberty."

Demands for a 9/11-style commission accelerated after White House press secretary Jen Psaki confirmed that her boss had endorsed the idea. "President Biden has made clear his views on the tragic events of January 6th, including where responsibility for them lies. He backs efforts to shed additional light on the facts to ensure something like that never happens again," Psaki assured reporters during a February 16 press briefing, hinting that any commission surely would find Donald Trump ultimately responsible for what happened.

Insisting that "our country has been wounded," Rep. Lee Hamilton and former Governor Tom Kean, co-chairmen of the 9/11 commission, urged the formation of a similar group for January 6. "A full accounting of the events of January 6th and the identification of measures to strengthen the Congress can help our country heal," the pair wrote in a joint letter issued in February.

After the Senate in May rejected the creation of a "bi-partisan" commission comprised of lawmakers from both parties and both chambers, but giving Democrats control of staff selection, Pelosi announced she would move forward with her own inquiry. House Minority Leader Kevin McCarthy appointed five Republican House members, including Rep. Jim Jordan (R-Ohio) and Rep. Jim Banks (R-Ind.), two strong supporters of Donald Trump.

Pelosi quickly scuttled Jordan and Banks; in response, McCarthy pulled all five Republicans. Pelosi then seated Reps. Cheney and Adam Kinzinger (R-IL), two foes of Donald Trump, to work with several Democrats on the inquiry.

The framing of January 6 as an event comparable to 9/11 was not an accident. By equating the two events, Democrats were positioned to advance a new "war on terror," this time against the political Right.

Most Americans who watched the chaos at the Capitol on January 6, 2021 never would compare it to what happened on September 11, 2001. But the ability to put things in their proper context is not exactly a trait shared by politicians or the American news media. In a column for *The Atlantic* published on January 11, Tom Junod recounted his memories of the 9/11 terrorist attack. "The U.S. Capitol did not fall the way the Twin Towers did, but the American idea it embodies was brutalized. We must remember 1/6 the way we remember 9/11," he wrote.

Rebranding the MAGA movement as "Make America Grieve Again," Rep. Steny Hoyer, the third-most powerful Democrat in the House of Representatives, compared the rioters to murderous terrorists. "We grieved on December 7, 1941 and we grieved on 9/11. And yes, we grieved…on January 6th," Hoyer said January 13 on the House floor.

Presidential historian Michael Beschloss insisted that from now on, January 6 should be a "day of national remembrance" to commemorate how the country was "almost fractured" that day. "On both September 11, 2001, and January 6, 2021, terrorist haters of democracy tried to attack our Capitol and Congress," Beschloss wrote. "But on January 6, they actually managed to invade the building and put our leaders and our democracy in danger. We had a close call and must never forget."

January 6 was a "wake up call that we have to confront domestic terrorism," warned former CIA Director Leon Panetta, just like September 11 was a "wake up call to deal with foreign terrorism."

The Department of Homeland Security, created in the aftermath of 9/11, used its National Terrorism Advisory System to issue a heightened threat alert about potential violence committed by their countrymen. "Information suggests that some ideologically-motivated violent extremists with objections to the exercise of governmental authority and the presidential transition, as well as other perceived grievances fueled by false narratives, could continue to mobilize to incite or commit violence," the agency claimed in its January 27 bulletin.[2]

Some unhinged commentators started to insist the Capitol protest was *worse* than the 9/11 terror attacks. In an MSNBC interview in July, Matthew Dowd, a former ABC News contributor and onetime Republican consultant, told Joy Reid that January 6 was worse "because it's continued to rip our country apart and give permission for people to pursue autocratic means."[3] (Dowd was correct, just not in the way he thought.)

---

2   Department of Homeland Security, *National Terrorism Advisory System Bulletin* (DOHS, 2021).
3   Curtis Houck, *This is Absolutely Bonkers* (Twitter, 2021).

The twenty-year anniversary of 9/11 presented more shameful opportunities to connect that horrific day with January 6. One shot was launched by none other than George W. Bush. "[W]e have seen growing evidence that the dangers to our country can come not only across borders but from violence that gathers within," Bush said during a memorial service in Shanksville, Pennsylvania, where Flight 93 crashed after passengers attempted to overtake hijackers. "There's little cultural overlap between violent extremists abroad and violent extremists at home. But in their disdain for pluralism, in their disregard of human life, in their determination to defile national symbols, they are children of the same foul spirit, and it is our continuing duty to confront them."[4]

Pulitzer-prize winning author Spencer Ackerman took to the pages of the *New York Times* to explain how January 6 was the natural progeny of 9/11: "[T]he most durable terrorism in this country is white people's terrorism. A war cannot defeat it. Persistent political struggle can. We need organized grass-roots action to unseat insurrectionist allies from office, to overturn the structural works of white supremacy like voter-suppression laws and to abolish the institutional architecture of the war on terror before it threatens even more American lives and freedoms."[5]

But the hyperbole served a greater cause—to turn powerful government tools against Americans who do not support Joe Biden and the Democratic Party.

*   *   *   *

"When I left the Department as Assistant Attorney General for National Security in October of 2016, the threat from violent extremists, both international and domestic, was rising," Acting Deputy Attorney General John Carlin said in public remarks on February 26, 2021. "But, I never expected that just over four years later, when I returned to the Justice Department to be sworn in on my first day as Acting Deputy Attorney General, that to get

---

4   President George W. Bush, *Speech on 9/11/2021* (ABC News, 2021).
5   Spencer Ackerman, *How Sept. 11 Gave Us Jan. 6* (*New York Times*, 2021).

to the building, I would have to pass through numerous check-points under escort of armed agents in a city under lockdown. I never expected to have to walk through the Department of Justice hallways filled with hundreds of soldiers positioned to protect the Department from terrorists."[6]

Those "terrorists," of course, were anti-Biden protesters and their sympathizers. The hyperbole was not out of character for Carlin, the head of the Justice Department's National Security Division from 2014 until October 2016, to use his platform to portray people aligned with Republicans as a threat. (The National Security Division was created in 2006 to consolidate the federal government's war against terror.)

Carlin's shop, after all, prepared the illicit FISA warrant against Carter Page, which falsely described him as a "foreign agent" of Russia.

Carlin once served as Robert Mueller's chief of staff when he was head of the FBI. In his new role in the Biden administration, he would serve as COS to Lisa Monaco, the deputy attorney general and arguably the person running the day-to-day operation at the Justice Department.

Monaco was part of a tight-knit group of top Obama officials who concocted the Trump-Russian collusion hoax. She too had served as Mueller's chief of staff and preceded Carlin as head of the National Security Division. Like Carlin, she had a hand in promoting the idea Team Trump was in cahoots with the Russians to rig the 2016 election. She often appeared on CNN to push Russian collusion propaganda, including accusations that Michael Flynn violated the Logan Act. She co-authored a 2018 *Washington Post* op-ed demanding the Trump Administration direct more funding to combat "far-right extremism" and "white-supremacist violence."

During her Senate confirmation hearings, Monaco did not face a single question about her involvement in the discredited

---

6   Acting Deputy Attorney General John Carlin, *Remarks on Domestic Terrorism* (United States Department of Justice, 2021).

Russia collusion hoax or her post-election diatribes against Trump and his associates. In April 2021, all but two Republican senators—Rand Paul and Ted Cruz—voted "aye" on her confirmation.

She quickly took the reins at the Justice Department. The agency already had a head start on humiliating those charged in the Capitol breach probe. A database solely dedicated to January 6 defendants is available on the department's homepage and updated on a daily basis. The FBI routinely tweets out the faces of the "most wanted" Capitol protesters, as if they are dangerous criminals on the loose, urging Americans to help identify the suspects.

After Monaco was confirmed, AG Merrick Garland announced that he and Monaco had "reinvigorated the domestic terrorism executive committee," an interagency panel created by Janet Reno after the 1995 Oklahoma City bombing to streamline information sharing. Garland and Monaco quickly asked for $101.2 million in additional funding to combat "unprecedented and troubling levels of domestic violent extremism."[7]

One might think they had in mind the violent extremism displayed in numerous cities all over the country by BLM and Antifa members during the George Floyd riots. But no, their concern is exclusively "white supremacists" aka Trump voters.

On June 15, Garland unveiled his National Strategy for Countering Domestic Terrorism, an assessment Joe Biden ordered on his first day in office.[8] "Our current effort comes on the heels of [a] large and heinous attack…the January 6 assault on our nation's Capitol," Garland said during a speech. "We have now…an enormous task ahead, to move forward as a country, to punish the perpetrators, [and] to do everything possible to prevent similar attacks."

The thirty-two-page document detailed the Biden administration's plan to target alleged domestic terrorists. Prepared by the president's National Security Council, the report presented a list of random attacks, including the 2017 Charlottesville protest and a mass shooting at an El Paso Wal-Mart in 2018, as

---

7   Department of Justice, *Fiscal Year 2022 Funding Request* (United States Department of Justice, 2021)
8   AG Merrick Garland, *Fact Sheet: National Strategy for Countering Domestic Terrorism* (The White House Briefing Room, 2021)

justification for the whole-of-government assault on free speech and political activism on the Right under the guise of a domestic war on terror.[9]

The plan greatly expands the authority and reach of the Justice Department, especially the FBI, and the Department of Homeland Security. Suspected domestic terrorists can be prohibited from government work or joining the military. The government would work with the private sector to prevent "sensitive positions—such as those at airports, seaports, chemical facilities, and other critical infrastructure sites—from being exploited by domestic terrorists."

Those on the government's domestic terror watch list could land on a no-fly list. The regime will find news ways to quash "dangerous conspiracy theories that can provide a gateway to terrorist violence," code for tens of millions of Americans who still believe the 2020 presidential election was stolen.

The report also furthered the falsehood that white supremacists played a key role in the January 6 protest. Systemic racism, Biden's top security advisors warned, is the root cause of domestic terrorism. "Individuals subscribing to violent ideologies such as violent white supremacy, which are grounded in racial, ethnic, and religious hatred and the dehumanizing of portions of the American community, as well as violent anti-government ideologies, are responsible for a substantial portion of today's domestic terrorism. We are, therefore, prioritizing efforts to ensure that every component of the government has a role to play in rooting out racism and advancing equity for under-served communities that have far too often been the targets of discrimination and violence. This approach must apply to our efforts to counter domestic terrorism by addressing underlying racism and bigotry."

Part of the report relied on a threat warning issued in March by Avril Haines, Biden's Director of National Intelligence. Haines, like Monaco, was part of Obama's inner circle. In 2016, as deputy national security advisor, she and Monaco attended secret meet-

---

9   National Security Council, *National Strategy for Countering Domestic Terrorism* (NSC, 2021).

ings to help concoct the Russian collusion hoax. "Haines…and White House homeland-security adviser Lisa Monaco convened meetings in the Situation Room to weigh the mounting evidence of Russian interference and generate options for how to respond," the *Washington Post* reported in June 2017.

Those meetings also included Loretta Lynch, James Comey, James Clapper, and John Brennan, Haines' former boss at the Central Intelligence Agency. Haines learned all the tricks of the trade as Brennan's deputy from 2013 until 2015. Brennan used his last months in office to sabotage Donald Trump's candidacy and incoming presidency then became one of Trump's most virulent foes, routinely accusing the president of any number of crimes including treason.

Despite her ties to both Obama and Brennan, Haines, like Monaco, won the overwhelming support of Republican senators on her confirmation vote; only ten GOP senators voted against her confirmation on the same day Joe Biden was inaugurated. She, like Monaco, picked up where she ended.

Calling January 6 an "assault on our own democracy," Haines quickly produced an unclassified assessment warning domestic terrorism poses "an elevated threat" to the homeland. Her depiction of who presented that threat sounded like someone out of MAGA-world central casting. "Newer sociopolitical developments—such as narratives of fraud in the recent general election, the emboldening impact of the violent breach of the US Capitol, conditions related to the COVID-19 pandemic, and conspiracy theories promoting violence—will almost certainly spur some [domestic violent extremists] to try to engage in violence this year."[10]

Almost a year later, there have been no reported instances of white supremacist violence.

Haines wasn't at all subtle. On top of the category entitled "anti-government/anti-authority violent extremists," Haines included a sketch of the U.S. Capitol building.

---

10   Avril Haines, Director of National Intelligence, *Domestic Violent Extremism Poses Heightened Threat in 2021* (Office of the Director of National Intellience, 2021)

Nebraska Sen. Ben Sasse called Haines a "hero" during an April hearing before the Senate Intelligence Committee. But House Republicans were unimpressed. Haines and other members of Biden's intelligence community were overstepping their bounds by targeting Americans. Rep. Devin Nunes, ranking member of the House Intelligence committee who exposed FISA-gate in his bombshell 2018 memo, condemned Haines for "characterizing wide swaths of American citizens, particularly Republicans and conservatives, as politically suspect, politically violent, and deserving of government surveillance."[11]

He reminded Haines, CIA Director William Burns, and National Security Advisor Paul Nakasone that the "intelligence community exists solely to counteract foreign threats" and reminded the trio what happened in the past when those capabilities have been turned inward, such as the surveillance of Dr. Martin Luther King, Jr. in the 1950s.

Rep. Chris Stewart (R-Utah) asked each official if he or she had statutory authority to spy on Americans "without a foreign nexus." Each replied, "No."

But Biden's intelligence chiefs are marching on, undeterred. After all, as journalist Lee Smith explained in a June column for *Tablet* magazine, "Counterterrorism is a multibillion-dollar Beltway industry, filling a trough that feeds Republican and Democratic constituencies including the State Department, spy services, and Washington-area NGOs and think tanks. As America downsizes its presence in the Middle East, national security bureaucrats and their parasitical private sector partners fear shrinking budgets. Hence the big move from countering violent extremism in Muslim communities to confronting "domestic terrorists." "…All they've done is replace brown teenagers with white middle-age Midwesterners."

---

11   Debra Heine, *Nunes Blasts Democrat Weaponization of Intelligence Community Against Conservatives* (American Greatness, 2021).

*   *   *   *

In February 2019, Couy Griffin received a phone call from President Trump. The leader of Cowboys for Trump had organized an eight-day, 170-mile horseback ride from a farm in Maryland to Washington, D.C. to show support for the president and his agenda, especially Trump's attempt to halt illegal immigration on the southern border. Trump called Griffin to say thank you and invited him to the White House; a few months later, the president hosted Griffin in the Oval Office where the pair were photographed behind the Resolute Desk.

Before the election, Cowboys for Trump—often clad in western gear and carrying American flags—participated in campaign rallies on behalf of the president. The group's now deplatformed website said, "Securing our border, protecting our Second Amendment, and protecting the lives of the unborn are the most vital and key aspects in America's Greatness."

Griffin returned to Washington, D.C. for Trump's speech and rally on January 6. He joined other Trump supporters on the Capitol grounds that afternoon. He did not enter the Capitol building, carry a weapon, or attack anyone including law enforcement officers. He was, to quote a popular phrase used during the 2020 George Floyd riots, a peaceful protester.

But on January 17, Griffin was arrested for his peripheral involvement in the protest. His arrest, and the government's demand to incarcerate him pending trial, were a harbinger of how Trump supporters would be punished merely for being Trump supporters. George Orwell's fictional warning about "thoughtcrimes" became a harsh reality for hundreds of Trump backers, and by extension, the nearly 75 million Americans who had voted to re-elect him.

The criminalization of "resistance" to the new president was a sharp reversal from the nonstop, four-year siege against President Trump. Back then, tens of millions of Americans who refused to accept Donald Trump as the legitimately elected president were not considered "seditionists" but heroes. Celebrities who threatened violence against the president or his family were applauded as patriots, and an endless series of manufactured scandals caused continued speculation in the media that Trump's illegitimate days as president "were numbered."

All that changed on January 6. Meanwhile the same Justice Department that had worked in tandem with Democrats and partisan judges for four years to delegitimize Trump's election now aimed its fire at Trump-supporting Americans for contending that Biden's election was equally suspect. And yet again, innocent lives would be ruined in the pursuit of a political vendetta.

The FBI started arresting people on January 7; a grand jury was empaneled the next day. All cases would be handled by both the U.S. Attorney's Office in the District of Columbia and the Justice Department's National Security Division's Counterterrorism section. A website titled "Capitol Breach Probe," the government's official title for the January 6 investigation, went live and contained all pertinent information about anyone arrested in connection to the protest. It was updated after every new arrest by the FBI, which continued into October.

In a motion filed the day before Joe Biden's inauguration, the Justice Department argued Couy Griffin should remain behind bars pending his trial for two misdemeanors—he was charged with trespassing and disorderly conduct—simply because he rejected the outcome of the 2020 presidential election. "The defendant traveled across country [sic] to participate in an unlawful protest that aimed to overturn a lawful election," acting U.S. Attorney for the District of Columbia Michael Sherwin, the lead prosecutor handling the first few months of the investigation into the Capitol breach, wrote January 19. "The defendant has repeatedly denied the legitimacy of the 2020 Presidential Election, has stated that Biden will never be president, and foresees 'blood running out of the' U.S. Capitol in connection with efforts to prevent a Biden presidency, and has stated that 'nothing is off the table' in preventing a Biden presidency."

"If the defendant denies the authority of the lawfully elected President of the United States, who [sic] election was certified by the Congress of the United States, certainly he would deny the authority of the judicial officers appointed by the President and confirmed by the Senate."

Even though Griffin faced two petty offenses and has a nearly clean criminal record—the New Mexico county commissioner only has one prior conviction for driving under the influence—a magistrate judge agreed he needed to stay behind bars for the safety of the community.

In denying pre-trial release, Judge Zia Faruqui claimed some of Griffin's inflammatory comments before and after the election did not amount to "political speech" protected by the First Amendment. In a post-rally video posted January 7, Griffin had warned of a "revolution" for the stolen election. He also claimed protesters would hold a Second Amendment rally at the Capitol and "if we do, then it's gonna be a sad day because there's gonna be blood running out of that building." He called January 6 a "great day for America."

Faruqui took Griffin's threats seriously. "His statements seem to corroborate that he viewed this as an illegitimate government that he had to take by any means necessary, including violence, to stop, which means to me, I believe, as there continue to be conditions of release that require him to come and show up before me, that he won't listen to those conditions because he may ultimately decide that those conditions are part of a flawed system that he must go by any means to overthrow and disrupt," Faruqui said during Griffin's February 1 detention hearing. (A few days later, the chief judge of the D.C. District Court overruled Faruqui and released Griffin on his own recognizance.)

By immediately hunting down Trump supporters like Griffin, Beltway partisans including federal prosecutors and judges were sending a clear message: Americans who defy the settled narrative that the 2020 election was the freest, fairest, most transparent in U.S. history would be punished. Political dissent will not be tolerated; in fact, it will be criminalized.

Griffin, it turned out, was one of more than one hundred people arrested before January 20 in a show of prosecutorial force aimed at intimidating Americans out of traveling to Washington D.C. to protest on Inauguration Day, a quadrennial American rite of passage.

That isn't speculation. Sherwin, a holdover from the Trump Justice Department tasked with prosecuting every case related to what the Justice Department officially calls the Capitol Breach probe, bragged about it during a March 2021 interview with CBS's *60 Minutes*. Voicing concern about the potential for more violence on Inauguration Day, Sherwin's office used January 6 as a pretext to silence Biden's political detractors. "After the sixth, we had an inauguration on the twentieth so I wanted to ensure and our office wanted to ensure that there was shock and awe, that we could charge as many people as possible before the twentieth," Sherwin told interviewer Scott Pelley. "And it worked."

Sherwin's nationwide manhunt, with the help of every FBI field office in the country, yielded the intended results. "People were afraid to come back to D.C. cuz they were like, if we go there, we're gonna get charged."

So the initial phase of the investigation, Sherwin essentially admitted, had less to do with justice or the rule of law than with the government's desire to keep Americans out of their own capital as the new president was sworn in on January 20.

It was also the start of a legal, personal, and professional nightmare for the first batch of arrestees. Sherwin promised to take these misdemeanor arrests and build sedition cases against American citizens, something that rarely, if ever, is done. "Some of these misdemeanor charges, these are only the beginning, this is not the end. We're looking at significant felony cases tied to sedition and conspiracy," Sherwin said during a January 12 press conference. He announced the formation of a "strike force" to prosecute the most "heinous" offenders.

At the press briefing, Sherwin mentioned two of the most infamous protesters by name: Eric Munchel, the "zip tie guy" as Sherwin called him, and Richard Barnett, the man photographed at a desk inside House Speaker Nancy Pelosi's office. Both were arrested within days of returning home from Washington after turning themselves in to local law enforcement. (Eric Munchel's mom, Lisa Eisenhart, was also arrested.)

The government was already making a public example of Biden protesters, smearing their names before millions of Americans and warning that the worst was yet to come. Barnett's family started receiving death threats immediately after the photo of him went viral on January 6, thanks partly to a tweet by Pelosi's daughter, filmmaker Alexandra Pelosi, who called Barnett a "seditionist."

Just like the case of Couy Griffin, not only was Sherwin's office concocting a flurry of repetitive charges against mostly nonviolent Americans for their participation in the events of January 6, but prosecutors were petitioning federal judges to deny bail to many of the accused, including Barnett and Munchel.

Working with partisan Beltway jurists—several of whom were deeply involved in the four-year legal pursuit of Donald Trump and his associates—the government used detention hearings to conduct one-sided trials based solely on government produced evidence.

Some of the first targets of pre-trial detention were the protesters Sherwin called out in his January 12 press conference.

*   *   *   *

Richard Barnett, a sixty-eight-year-old former fire fighter from Arkansas, turned himself in on January 8 in compliance with the FBI's directive after meeting with FBI agents upon his return home. Known by the nickname "Bigo," Barnett initially faced three counts of trespassing, possession of a dangerous weapon, and theft of government property. Barnett brought to Washington a walking stick that could also be used as a stun gun. (The "Hike and Strike" stun gun and other models can be purchased on Amazon.) He entered Pelosi's office where a photographer, who just happened to be there, instructed Barnett to sit at a desk an act natural. (The desk, it turned out, was not Pelosi's but someone on her staff.) He took a piece of mail.

On January 29, a grand jury—working nonstop since being empaneled on January 8—returned a seven-count indictment against Barnett including obstruction of an official proceeding, a felony punishable by up to twenty years in prison. Prosecutors again sought pre-trial detention for Barnett, insisting he was a threat to the community. After interrogating Barnett's common-law wife Tammy Newburn during a court hearing, the government further concluded that she would not be a suitable custodian if Barnett was allowed to go home because he "actively seeks to hinder and control" her, as Sherwin's office wrote in a memorandum opposing his release.

Beryl Howell, the chief judge of the D.C. District Court overseeing every case involving January 6 defendants, agreed. Condemning Barnett's "brazenly illegal conduct" inside the Capitol, Howell, an Obama appointee and vocal critic of Donald Trump, ruled Barnett was a danger to his community and should remain behind bars.

Barnett obviously should not have been in Pelosi's office. The photographers who, according to Barnett's testimony, invited him to sit at the desk and "act natural" so they could take pictures of him shouldn't have been there either.

Occupying Pelosi's office was not considered a crime when climate change activists, led by Alexandria Ocasio-Cortez in 2018, had swamped Pelosi's office demanding action on the environment.[12] In that instance, the incoming Democratic Speaker quickly capitulated to the rising star's demands. "We welcome the presence of these activists, and we strongly urge the Capitol Police to allow them to continue to organize and participate in our democracy," Pelosi tweeted November 13, 2018.

12   Time, *Alexandria Ocasio-Cortez Joins Climate Change Activists In Protest At Nancy Pelosi's Office* (YouTube, 2018).

Nor was it an act of obstruction or sedition when angry activists crowded into then-Senate Majority Leader Mitch McConnell's office on October 5, 2018 to halt the confirmation of Brett
Kavanaugh.[13] "We have a duty to fight for freedom," the protesters screamed until police officers asked them to leave. They were
not charged with invented felonies and dragged to a secret prison
for months before trial.

Barnett and his fellow protesters, however, were not so lucky.
After nearly four months in jail, Barnett was released from a D.C.
jail in April. Judge Chris Cooper approved home detention for
Barnett; he could only leave his home for work, church, and doc-
tor's visits. (In June, Cooper denied Barnett's request to travel
beyond fifty miles of his home to seek employment.)

Cooper's decision was influenced by a ruling from the D.C.
Court of Appeals in the case of "zip tie guy" Eric Munchel and his
mother that led to their release. The ruling was the first rebuke
of the Justice Department's nonstop pursuit of pretrial detention
orders, particularly for nonviolent offenders, and it had a down-
stream impact on other cases.

*　　*　　*　　*

On January 4, 2021, Eric Munchel and his mother, Lisa Eisenhart, traveled to Washington, D.C. According to court documents,
the pair entered the building through an open door and were not
stopped from doing so by law enforcement inside or outside the
Capitol. Clad in military-style gear—Munchel also carried a taser
with him—they walked through an open door and remained inside for about twelve minutes. Munchel grabbed a stash of zip tie
handcuffs stacked on a cabinet inside one hallway. "Zip ties! I need
to get me some of them motherf---ers," Munchel reportedly said to
his mother.

He was photographed inside the Senate gallery holding the
FlexiCuffs; the picture went viral immediately with the false ex-

13   *Kavanuagh Protestors at Senator McConnell's Office* (C-Span, 2018).

planation that Munchel and others brought them into the Capitol to round-up elected officials. "The photograph spread widely and sparked fears that rioters had planned to take hostages or otherwise detain lawmakers and their staff," Buzzfeed reported on January 10.

Munchel, a thirty-three-year-old bartender from Nashville, turned himself in that same day; he was promptly arrested and charged with four counts including conspiracy and civil disorder. The Justice Department also charged his mother with conspiracy; the U.S. thus argued that a parent and her adult child planning to travel together to the nation's capital to participate in a political protest amounted to conspiracy against the United States government.

As part of their case against Munchel and Eisenhart, prosecutors cited a post-protest interview they had given as proof of their criminal mindset on January 6. "We wanted to show that we're willing to rise up, band together and fight if necessary," Munchel told the Sunday Times. "Same as our forefathers, who established this country in 1776." Prosecutors continued. "The article references EISENHART's talk of violent revolution, as well as her belief that, 'This country was founded on revolution…I'd rather die a 57-year-old woman than live under oppression. I'd rather die and would rather fight."

Just like that, references to the country's founding and admiration for those who fought for independence was evidence of nefarious intent. The language of oppressed dissidents everywhere, the sort of people held up as heroes fighting iron-fisted rule in any number of authoritarian states across the globe, now was considered incriminating speech by the U.S. government.

On January 22, a judge in Tennessee ordered Munchel's release to home confinement. "In our society, liberty is the norm, and detention before trial is an exception," U.S. Magistrate Judge Jeffery S. Frensley said. "I asked the government point blank what [any potential] danger was and they referred to his 'radicalization' and the views that he holds. Mr. Munchel is entitled to his opinions. They are protected by the Constitution. He doesn't have a right to do what he did, but that's an issue for another day."

The Justice Department immediately moved to stay Frensley's order and keep Munchel behind bars awaiting trial. (Prosecutors routinely sought to overrule release orders issued by local judges in the defendant's home state.)

"[I]t is difficult to fathom a more serious danger to the community—to the District of Columbia, to the country, or to the fabric of American Democracy—than the one posed by armed insurrectionists, including the defendant, who joined in the occupation of the United States Capitol," Sherwin's office wrote on January 24.

> Every person who was present without authority in the Capitol on January 6 contributed to the chaos of that day and the danger posed to law enforcement, the Vice President, Members of Congress, and the peaceful transfer of power. The defendant's specific conduct aggravated the chaos and danger. It was designed to intimidate Members of Congress and instigate fear across the country. Make no mistake: the fear the defendant helped spread on January 6 persists—the imprint on this country's history of a militia clad insurrectionist standing over an occupied Senate chamber is indelible. Only detention mitigates such grave danger.

Judge Howell agreed with the government. She ordered Munchel transported to Washington, D.C. In February, Judge Royce Lamberth upheld Munchel's pre-trial detention order; Munchel's public defender appealed the ruling in February as both Munchel and Eisenhart remained behind bars.

The three-person appellate court issued its ruling on March 26: Munchel and Eisenhart, the D.C. Court of Appeals concluded, should be released. Referring to January 6 as "a grave danger to our democracy," the court nonetheless found the Justice Department had not made a convincing case. "That Munchel and Eisenhart assaulted no one on January 6; that they did not enter the Capitol by force; and that they vandalized no property are all factors that weigh against a finding that either pose a threat," wrote Circuit Court Judge Robert Wilkins, appointed to the court by Barack Obama in 2014.

The court issued a split decision, asking the District Court to reconsider instead of overrule the government's detention order. Justice Katsas wanted to "reverse outright" the lower court's opinion. Three days later, prosecutors withdrew the detention motions for Munchel and Eisenhart.

The so-called Munchel ruling acted as a get-out-of-jail card for several January 6 defendants, including Richard Barnett, who were released during subsequent detention hearings. But Eric Munchel's punishment was not over. Since he and his mother were co-defendants in a felonious conspiracy charge, they cannot communicate with each other.

In May, Munchel sought the court's permission to call his mom on Mother's Day. His request was approved. But while Munchel and Eisenhart were released and partially free, others were not.

*   *   *   *

The Justice Department has sought pre-trial detention for at least one hundred protesters, including many first time offenders and some who committed no violent act. The Bail Reform Act, enacted in 1984, sets out specific guidance about who should be held without bail before trial. According to the Justice Department's website, the Act "requires the pretrial detention of a defendant only if a judicial officer determines that no conditions or combination of conditions exist which will 'reasonably assure the appearance of the person...and the safety of any person and the community."

Further, the law lists six factors that must apply before the government can seek pre-trial detention: "An offense with a maximum sentence of life imprisonment or death; an offense for which the maximum term of imprisonment is 10 or more years as prescribed by the Controlled Substances Act; any felony if the person has been convicted of two or more offenses…or comparable state offenses; a serious risk of flight; or a serious risk that the defendant will obstruct justice or threaten a witness."

So in order to meet the "dangerousness" threshold, prosecutors routinely argue that the events of January 6 were so beyond the pale that even if someone did not engage in criminal conduct, his or her mere presence at the Capitol that day made them a threat to society. Prosecutors made the same accusation over and over in detention motions. The Capitol, as Sherwin said, was considered a "crime scene" and each individual, regardless of the severity of their involvement, was part of the crime ring.

Not only was it guilt by association, it was presumed guilty and punished before trial. "Every person who was present without authority in the Capitol on January 6 contributed to the chaos of that day and the danger posed to law enforcement, the United States Vice President, Members of Congress, and the peaceful transfer of power," assistant U.S. Attorney Melissa Jackson wrote in an April memo seeking pre-trial detention for Christopher Quaglin, a New Jersey electrician charged with multiple counts including assaulting police officers—he's accused of shoving officers and using a riot shield as a weapon—and obstruction of an official proceeding.

D.C. Chief Judge Beryl Howell agreed that Quaglin, a new father with only one prior conviction for disorderly conduct, should remain behind bars awaiting trial. Howell also said Quaglin's social media posts "did not display any remorse or regret" and instead celebrated his "role in the riot on January 6."

As of November 1, Quaglin was still in jail.

The Justice Department requested incarceration for nonviolent offenders including a few who are a permanent part of the protest's visual collage. The most notable character to emerge on January 6 is Jacob Chansley, the so-called "QAnon Shaman." He was arrested on January 9 and indicted by the grand jury two days later on various charges including civil disorder, obstruction of an official proceeding, and violent entry into the Capitol building.

Prosecutors did not accuse Chansley of assaulting police or carrying a dangerous weapon. But in typically melodramatic fashion, they asked a judge to keep him in jail without bond. His obstruction of the Congressional proceeding that day, certifying the 2020 Presidential election results, was "nothing short of an attempt to undermine the regular functioning of our Democracy," assistant U.S. Attorney Kimberly Paschall wrote in a February 3 detention memo.

> The offenses committed by the defendant illuminate characteristics inconsistent with a person who could follow orders given by this Court, or indeed, any branch of the federal government. The defendant has espoused disbelief in the outcome of the 2020 Presidential election, and violently acted on that world view. The defendant cannot be trusted to keep from inciting, contacting or coordinating with other radical extremists, intent on continuing to obstruct the normal functioning of our democracy. Given his participation in the obstruction of the normal functioning of the government, and his disbelief in the legitimacy of the current United States government, it is unlikely that the defendant will obey any pretrial release conditions.

Paschall's imputation that denying the legitimacy of the 2020 presidential election means the accused rejects the overall legitimacy of the U.S. government and therefore would not follow court orders can be found over and over in charging documents. It is stunning on its face, considering the fact that millions of Americans have openly and with total impunity denied the legitimacy of the past several presidents for any number of reasons.

Nor is it clear how an attempt to "undermine the regular functioning of our democracy" would constitute a uniquely dangerous criminal offense, given that is what left wing protesters have repeatedly done in the halls of Congress, as for example when they sought to prevent Brett Kavanaugh from being confirmed as a Supreme Court justice. Instead, government prosecutors argued that the attempt to halt the verification of a national election constituted a unique and awful danger to American democracy—as though there were any prospect of it's actually succeeding while surrounded by thousands of police and heavily armed US military in the most secure and defended city in America.

Indeed, such a contention is laughable on its face. Kidnap Mike Pence? Where were they planning to take him? If anyone involved in the Capitol protest actually thought a madcap scheme to change the outcome of a US election armed only with some bear repellant and plastic zip-ties could possibly work out in their favor, they deserved to be charged not with treason but insanity.

Nevertheless, an Arizona magistrate judge agreed with the government in Chansley's case. Judge Deborah Fine not only concurred that he was a danger to the community but that his outlandish costume and national notoriety somehow made him a more likely flight risk. "He was shirtless and carried a bullhorn and a six-foot-long spear with an American flag tied just below the blade," Fine wrote in her order dated January 19. "The Government points out that this costume is how Mr. Chansley is known and that Mr. Chansley's appearance in the costume is has [sic] made him notorious, but that without such face paint and costume, he is not widely known. Without this costume, Mr. Chansley has the benefit of anonymity, which would help him try to flee from prosecution."

All of this was said with a straight face. The question of where Chansley could possibly go to evade federal prosecution was not addressed.

For months, Chansley was bounced to different prisons. (He demanded to be moved from D.C. jail to another facility that offered organic food.) His attorney, Albert Watkins, repeatedly filed motions for his client's release. In May, Watkins detailed how Chansley's mental and physical health were deteriorating under solitary confinement, a situation shared by nearly all of the January 6 detainees.

Solitary confinement is a unique form of punishment generally reserved for the most violent or unruly offenders. Long periods of isolation are well known to be detrimental to a prisoner's mental and physical health and are widely considered inhumane. Yet federal prosecutors and judges routinely insisted on isolating January 6 defendants for months on end, on the pretext of protecting them and other prisoners from infection with Covid-19.

"Since January 9, 2021, Defendant has been subjected to COVID-19 response protocol mandated solitary confinement for 22 plus hours per day," Watkins wrote in May. "Defendant has been compelled to endure cruel and unusual punishment of a nature akin to the gulag of Solzhenitsyn fame."

Watkins has a flair for the dramatic. He often blamed Trump for Chansley's actions and told Judge Royce Lamberth in a May detention hearing that "every one of us in this country have a duty to look in the mirror and ask ourselves what role we played in creating this environment that was so divisive and so alarmingly dysfunctional as to permit, day in and day out, multiple times daily the affirmative representation of untruths by the highest, most powerful leader in the land." In a media interview in May, Watkins called most of the January 6 defendants "fucking short-bus people" and claimed they "are people with brain damage, they're fucking retarded, they're on the goddamn spectrum."

Nonetheless, Watkins fought hard for his client's release. The government again objected, citing his belief in "conspiracy theories," as though that were a federal crime. Prosecutors still insisted Chansley was not authorized to enter the Capitol even though several videos clearly show Chansley and others cooperating with law enforcement outside and inside the building. If they were trespassing, why weren't they arrested on the spot?

Prosecutors also cited Chansley's flag and spear as a potential weapon, even though he was not charged with possessing or using a dangerous weapon.

But Lamberth ultimately had no mercy for Chansley, who already had spent 150 days in jail. In July, despite the fact Chansley is a thirty-three-year-old man who lives with his mother in Arizona and has no criminal record or the financial means to flee the country, Lamberth denied his release from a Colorado jail where he had been sent in June to undergo a court-ordered psychological examination.

Lamberth, appointed to the D.C. District Court in 1987 by Ronald Reagan, clearly was aware of the major hit to the prosecution if he allowed one of the most prolific faces of the "insurrection" out on bond. Longtime Beltway fixtures like Lamberth and others cannot jeopardize the government's case by releasing innocent protesters, particularly a flamboyant one like Chansley.

On September 3, Chansley pleaded guilty to the obstruction of an official proceeding charge. The government asked for a forty-one to fifty-one month sentence. During his sentencing hearing in November, Chansley explained to Lamberth how his extended incarceration, including 317 days in solitary confinement, had impacted him. "I am not a violent man," Chansley told Lamberth. "I am not an insurrectionist. I am certainly not a domestic terrorist. I am a good man who broke the law. And I'm doing everything I can to take responsibility for that."

While Lamberth acknowledged that Chansley's words of repentance were "the most remarkable I've ever heard" in his tenure on the bench, he nonetheless sentenced Chansley to 41 months in prison. "What you did was horrific," Lamberth lectured.

Watkins gave an impromptu press conference after the hearing; he said he wanted to have a beer with President Trump and tell him "you've got a few fucking things to do…including clearing this fucking mess up and taking care of a lot of the jackasses that you fucked up because of January 6."

Another legal clown show with an innocent man used as human fodder, all to bolster the disintegrating narrative about January 6.

*   *   *   *

One of the more egregious examples of how the Justice Department would use pre-trial detention to punish Trump supporters is the case of Bruno Cua.[14] The high school senior from central Georgia traveled to Washington to hear the president's speech. His parents, Joseph and Alise, went with him. The Cua family lives on a three-acre farm; Dr. Alise Cua had quit her career as a veterinarian to home-school Bruno and his two younger siblings.

After Trump's speech, the Cuas walked to Capitol Hill. Bruno climbed on the scaffolding erected outside, then entered the building—his parents did not. He carried a small collapsible baton with him as he wandered through the hallways. Bruno is seen on surveillance video walking around the inside of the Senate chamber. At one point, Cua reportedly is heard saying, "they can steal an election, but we can't sit in their chairs?"

The Cua family drove home late on January 6.

Bruno was arrested by the FBI on February 5. Three law enforcement officials in his hometown of Milton, Georgia reported him to the FBI after seeing Cua's photo on a "persons of interest" list produced by the D.C. Metropolitan Police department after January 6.

Atlanta's FBI field office tweeted the news of Cua's arrest on February 6. The grand jury returned a crushing twelve-count indictment against the eighteen-year-old, including assaulting a plain-clothed Capitol police officer and carrying a "deadly or dangerous weapon" into the Capitol.

---

14   Julie Kelly, *A Family on Trial for January 6* (American Greatness, 2021).

Although Bruno had no criminal record—he had run-ins with local police over his driving, which included a report he menaced another driver on the road with his Trump-flag adorned truck—a judge ordered him kept behind bars. And it wasn't only because of Bruno's actions on January 6; it was because his parents, who were not accused of any crime related to the Capitol protest, were somehow complicit. Magistrate Judge Baverman said Bruno should not be released to his parents because they "were maybe not instigators but aiders and abettors [in Cua's alleged crime] and didn't take steps to stop their child from going off the rails."

Federal prosecutors also sought to keep Bruno in jail. The government cited Bruno's social media posts as proof he posed a threat. (Like many teenagers, Bruno was a social media loudmouth and braggart.) But the Justice Department condemned his parents as well.

Federal prosecutors interrogated Joseph Bruno about his private conversations with his son after the riot. The government demanded to know if they punished Bruno once they returned home, and condemned the parents for not doing a better job monitoring his social media accounts.

Here was one exchange from a February 12 detention hearing between Joseph Cua and an assistant U.S. attorney about a post-election rally he and his son attended.

> Cua: It was a rally around . . . the election results, we should see the real results and that type of thing.

> U.S. government: Do you recognize that that is not true?

> Cua: Yes, I do.

> U.S. government: But you recognize also
> that you participated in that activity with your
> son? Do you share in the responsibility in your
> son's belief and his actions?

In other words, believing an election was stolen is a crime, attending a rally to protest it is a crime, and taking your son to a rally is akin to child abuse.

One prosecutor told the court his parents should not be custodians if their son was released because the boy was "home-schooled" and had "ingested" his parents' political beliefs as though they were some kind of toxin. The government even threatened to charge Bruno's parents.

Bruno was sent to a prison in Oklahoma City that became a transfer station of sorts for most January 6 defendants denied bond. He first was sent into a fourteen-day isolation quarantine then into the general population while his family's lawyer prepared motions for his release. From jail, Bruno wrote to Judge Randolph Moss, begging to go home. "I miss my family more than anything in the world, I have never been away from them like this. I just want to go home to my Mom and Dad, I am truly sorry."

Then, Bruno caught COVID-19. His lawyer notified the court and again asked for his release. Bruno also had been assaulted by another inmate, according to the attorney. But the government again objected. In addition to his alleged actions at the Capitol, the prosecutor cited Bruno's failure to wear a face mask on January 6 as proof he would not protect his community. "The government has grave concerns about the defendant's willingness to take precautions against the spread of the COVID-19 pandemic."

Moss signed Bruno's release order on March 10, but not before giving his parents another scolding:

> [I]t is true that Cua's parents bear some
> responsibility for Cua's actions—they were
> the ones that drove him to Washington D.C.,

permitted him to bring and carry a baton to the Capitol, and allowed him to scale the scaffolding, leading to Cua's breach of the Capitol building. The Court is convinced, moreover, that Dr. and Mr. Cua deeply regret permitting their son to act as he did and that—for his sake—they will do all that they can to ensure that he does not take any action that might risk revocation of his pretrial release or other criminal exposure.

Moss further cited comments made by Alise Cua in her son's detention hearing. "I ask for your forgiveness for just my failures as a mom, and I am very well aware of them, and I just—I'm really just hoping that we get a chance to prove that this is behind us. We just want our family together.... [W]e are completely broken and completely just, honestly and truthfully, remorseful to the core of our beings, and we're asking for a chance."

No doubt, music to the ears of federal prosecutors. A family of Trump supporters is broken and humiliated, reduced to abject groveling. Mission accomplished!

By mid-2021, Joe Biden's Justice department was still pursuing pre-trial detention for Trump supporters. In June, Robert Morss was arrested and charged with several offenses including attacking a police officer. Morss is a former Army Ranger with three tours of duty in Afghanistan, and a graduate of Penn State University. At the time of his arrest, he was working as a long-term substitute high school history teacher. For six months after his involvement in the Capitol uprising, he volunteered for his community and taught children without incident. Now the government considered him such a menace that they wanted him put behind bars indefinitely.

According to the government's criminal complaint, Morss and others breached a police barrier, then attempted to enter the lower west terrace tunnel to gain access to the building. He is accused of entering a broken window and attempting to take riot shields from police in order to create a "shield wall" against police amassed inside the tunnel. Morss also was in the same area where Rosanne Boyland died.

During the raid of his home in June, the FBI seized a box of Legos. At first, investigators said they had found a "fully constructed U.S. Capitol Lego set," but later had to admit the set was still in the box, unassembled.

In the government's July filing asking the court to keep Morss behind bars in a D.C. jail for months awaiting his trial, assistant U.S. Attorney Melissa Jackson wrote, "It is difficult to fathom a more serious danger to the community—to the District of Columbia, to the country, or to the fabric of American Democracy—than the one posed by someone who knowingly and eagerly engaged in a violent insurrection to occupy the United States Capitol and abort the certification of a lawful and fair election."

On July 20, Magistrate Judge Michael Harvey denied Morss' petition for release. Repeatedly referring to defendants as "rioters," Harvey outrageously suggested that Morss' military service, a factor that usually weighs in favor of release, should be held against him. "His status as an Army ranger is undermined since he's willing to use his training to organize…political violence." There is no evidence, however, that Morss used his military experience to "organize" anything that day. This is pure projection on the judge's part, seemingly reflecting his own bias.

In short, the detention hearings, rather than cogently and objectively presenting reasons why a defendant should be kept behind bars, instead became a venue for theatrical, partisan rants from both judges and prosecutors. Due process, the presumption of innocence, the right to a speedy trial, and the exercise of "blind justice" were all cast aside in service to the Democrats' political agenda: to punish and criminalize dissent from their partisan narrative.

CHAPTER FIVE:

WHAT KILLED BRIAN SICKNICK?

BY THE END OF THE DAY on January 6, 2021, four people would be dead. All four were supporters of Donald Trump.

Ashli Babbitt, an unarmed veteran, was shot and killed by a United States Capitol Police officer inside the building. When news of her death spread through the crowd that day, protesters became enraged at police, which led to many of the altercations captured on video and in photographs.

Four dead Trump supporters ran counter to the Democrats' narrative that January 6 was an armed insurrection by lethal white supremacists aimed at overthrowing the seat of government power. Lawmakers, not protesters, were supposed to be the victims; headlines announcing the deaths of four Americans protesting the incoming president threatened to seize the spin.

Questions undoubtedly would arise about the cause of death for the four protesters; even water-carrying news organizations would be forced to examine the details of Babbitt's shooting. Concealing for months the identity of her shooter would have been impossible.

Enter Officer Brian Sicknick.

The Democrats and news media stooped to many new lows during the Trump era. Blatant lies about Trump-Russia election collusion based on a phony "dossier" topped the list. So, too, did claims about Brett Kavanaugh's unsubstantiated sexual behavior in the 1980s or the notion that a pro-life teenager from Kentucky smugly "disrespected" a native elder and Vietnam veteran at the March for Life in 2019.

But exploiting the death of Sicknick, a bike patrol officer, would take Democrats and the media to a new political cellar. For months, they openly and knowingly lied about what happened to the thirteen-year veteran of the US Capitol Force to smear Trump supporters as violently enraged cop killers.

Just as the tear gas clouds cleared and the public began to process the chaotic imagery the following day, rumors circulated that a police officer had been killed in the melee. In the late hours of January 7, USCP issued the following statement.

> At approximately 9:30 p.m. this evening, United States Capitol Police Officer Brian D. Sicknick passed away due to injuries sustained while on-duty. Officer Sicknick was responding to the riots on Wednesday, January 6, 2021, at the U.S. Capitol and was injured while physically engaging with protesters. He returned to his division office and collapsed. He was taken to a local hospital where he succumbed to his injuries. The death of Officer Sicknick will be investigated by the Metropolitan Police Department's Homicide Branch, the USCP, and our federal partners. Officer Sicknick joined the USCP in July 2008, and most recently served in the Department's First Responder's Unit. The entire USCP Department expresses its deepest sympathies to Officer Sicknick's family and friends on their loss, and mourns the loss of a friend and colleague. We ask that Officer Sicknick's family, and other USCP officers' and their families' privacy be respected.

Sicknick, his older brother, Ken, told ProPublica on January 8, texted him the night of January 6. Brian told Ken he had been sprayed twice with pepper spray but was fine. At some point, the officer collapsed and was taken to George Washington University hospital. His family received a text on January 7 that said Brian had a blood clot and suffered a stroke; his family rushed from their home in New Jersey when they learned Brian was on a ventilator, but they didn't make it in time.

Immediately, coverage of Babbitt's shooting and interest in how the three other Trump supporters died, to the extent it was even reported, vanished. The political world quickly devolved into a state of rage and revenge; Trump supporters were not just insurrectionists but cop killers. Further, they had murdered one of their own. Sicknick, the public was told, a single man who had served in the U.S. military, also backed Donald Trump.

Nancy Pelosi ordered Capitol flags to be flown at half-staff. "The perpetrators of Officer Sicknick's death must be brought to justice," she said in a statement released January 8. "The violent and deadly act of insurrection targeting the Capitol, our temple of American Democracy, and its workers was a profound tragedy and stain on our nation's history. But because of the heroism of our first responders and the determination of the Congress, we were not, and we will never be, diverted from our duty to the Constitution and the American people."

Jeffrey Rosen, the acting attorney general, pledged to promptly investigate Sicknick's alleged murder. "Our thoughts and prayers are with the family and fellow officers of U.S. Capitol Police Officer Brian D. Sicknick, who succumbed last night to the injuries he suffered defending the U.S. Capitol, against the violent mob who stormed it on January 6th," the nation's top law enforcement official wrote. "The FBI and Metropolitan Police Department will jointly investigate the case and the Department of Justice will spare no resources in investigating and holding accountable those responsible."

NeverTrump Republicans also got in on the act. Senator Mitt Romney quickly issued a statement. "I am heartbroken by the death of Officer Brian Sicknick in the line of duty as he was protecting the U.S. Capitol and all of us inside the building. I hope the perpetrator who claimed Officer Sicknick's life is brought to justice."

Conservative radio host Hugh Hewitt opened his January 8 show by asking Ben Sasse, the anti-Trump Republican senator from Nebraska, about the president's "culpability for the insurrectionists and the rioters breaking into the Capitol and murdering a Capitol Policeman?" Sasse responded that "blood was actually being shed" in the Capitol by "a mob that was incited by the president of the United States."

Details about how Sicknick died were initially vague. Then the *New York Times* published a bombshell.[1] "A United States Capitol Police officer died Thursday night from injuries sustained when he engaged with a pro-Trump mob that descended on the U.S. Capitol the day before," Marc Santora, Mike Baker, and Megan Specia reported January 8. "[P]ro-Trump rioters attacked that citadel of democracy, overpowered Mr. Sicknick, 42, and struck him in the head with a fire extinguisher, according to two law enforcement officials. With a bloody gash in his head, Mr. Sicknick was rushed to the hospital and placed on life support. He died on Thursday evening."

Even though the *Times* account was sourced to anonymous officials, no one questioned its veracity. No journalist bothered to track down a hospital report or ask for any other verification.

Yet despite wall-to-wall coverage by every network and newspaper, in addition to independent journalists and bloggers on the scene that day, no proof of the fire extinguisher attack was found. Sicknick's brother, in fact, told ProPublica on January 8 that his brother had texted him on January 6 to say that he "got pepper-sprayed twice" but was "in good shape." The family was told Sicknick later collapsed, was rushed to the hospital, put on a ventilator, and later died from a stroke caused by a blood clot.

---

1   Mike Baker, *A Capitol Police Officer Dies from Injuries Sustained During the Pro-Trump Rampage* (New York Times, 2021).

Nonetheless, the *Times'* gruesome account was immediately accepted as fact. Every major news organization, from the *Wall Street Journal* to CNN, repeated their description of what happened to Sicknick. "A Capitol Police officer died Thursday night of injuries he suffered while responding to the mob of President Trump's supporters who attacked the Capitol," *Wall Street Journal* reporter Andrew Duehren wrote on January 8. (As of September 1, the article remains online in its original form with no correction or retraction.) "The officer, Brian D. Sicknick, was struck in the head with a fire extinguisher during Wednesday's unrest, according to a law-enforcement official."

"The flags at the U.S. Capitol are at half-staff this morning for the police officer, Brian Sicknick, who was murdered this week," CNN's Jake Tapper solemnly reported on January 10. Noting flags were not at half staff at the White House, Tapper claimed the reason was "because Officer Sicknick was the enemy of the terrorist mob."

"Officer Sicknick was pummeled by a rioter wielding a fire extinguisher, according to witnesses," the *Washington Post* editorial board alleged in a January 11 opinion piece.

Raheem Kassam, writing for the National Pulse in February, catalogued numerous segments at CNN where hosts repeated the fire extinguisher tale.[2] "The network has repeatedly claimed, without evidence, that Officer Brian Sicknick was definitely killed by Trump supporters with a fire extinguisher. Poppy Harlow claimed: "We turn now to a tribute happening soon for fallen Capitol Hill police officer Brian Sicknick who died—was killed. He was killed when one of the rioters hit him with a fire extinguisher." Anderson Cooper asserted: "[A] Capitol police officer was beaten reportedly with a fire extinguisher." Ana Cabrera stated: "Officer Brian Sicknick died after being hit in the head with a fire extinguisher during the hours long attack." Erin Burnett asked: "Why is Trump trying so hard to make those claims the focal point of the Senate trial? Charging him with inciting insurrection? Does he think that

---

2   Raheem J. Kassam, *CNN Repeatedly Claimed Capitol Officer Sicknick Died Due to a Fire Extinguisher Hit…
Now They've Quietly Admitted That May Not be True* (The National Pulse, 2021).

the lie would justify a mob of his supporters trampling a woman? Does he think that the lie justifies police officers being beaten by a hockey stick and a crutch like we saw in the video on January 6th? Or does he think that the lie justifies the death of Officer Brian Sicknick who was working at the Capitol on the day of the riot and died after being hit in the head with a fire extinguisher?"

Wolf Blitzer allowed Rep. Ted Lieu to assert, unchallenged: "This was an insurrection and attempted coup where multiple people died including a law enforcement officer that reportedly was bludgeon [with a] fire extinguisher."

MSNBCs Joe Scarborough ranted for weeks on his morning program about Sicknick's murder at the hands of deranged Trump voters. In one segment, he warned Republican senators who wanted to "move on" from the events of January 6, including Utah Senator Mike Lee. "You don't get a mulligan when you kill a cop, Mike," Scarborough raged. "When you abuse police officers, jam police officers' heads inside a door, and bash police officers' brains with fire extinguishers, you don't get a mulligan. Especially if you're the one responsible for bringing those cop killers up to Capitol Hill." Republican senators, Scarborough claimed, are "not only cop killers, but these people are traitors to the United States of America." Scarborough, like the rest of the media, never acknowledged his role in promoting the lie.

Some conservative media outlets also ran with the falsehood. In a column arguing for Trump's conviction in the Democrats' second impeachment trial, *National Review*'s Andrew McCarthy, a former federal prosecutor, insisted Sicknick had been "murdered" and his killing should be part of the Democrats' impeachment strategy. "When Officer Sicknick needed a president, Donald Trump was missing in action," McCarthy wrote on January 17. "When America needed a commander-in-chief to protect the seat of its democracy, Donald Trump wouldn't be disturbed—he was busy watching television."

Tiana Lowe at the *Washington Examiner* took aim at Senator Josh Hawley, blaming the first-term Republican senator for Sicknick's death. "When he told followers to 'STAND UP,' they listened and murdered a cop while storming the Capitol," Lowe tweeted on January 8. "He lost. Make him pay."

Even U.S. military leadership, at a time when Afghanistan was on the verge of a Taliban takeover, commented on his death. "We mourn the deaths of the two Capitol policemen," the joint chiefs of staff wrote in a January 13 statement. (Democrats tried to tie the alleged suicide of another Capitol Police officer to January 6.)

Federal prosecutors included Sicknick's death in charging documents against the first set of Capitol defendants, claiming that "approximately 81 members of the Capitol Police and 58 members of the Metropolitan Police Department were assaulted, and one Capitol Police officer died."

Sicknick's death created all sorts of beneficial optics for the Democrats just as impeachment efforts were underway. Police officers and mourners lined the streets of Washington, D.C. on January 10 for a formal procession that included dozens of police vehicles and a hearse carrying Sicknick. People made posters featuring Sicknick's official photo with the words "hero" and "RIP."

House impeachment managers included the *Times* story in their official memo detailing the evidence against Trump: "The insurrectionists killed a Capitol Police officer by striking him in the head with a fire extinguisher."

On February 1, the House of Representatives passed a resolution stating, "The remains of the late United States Capitol Police Officer Brian D. Sicknick shall be permitted to lie in honor in the rotunda of the Capitol from February 2, 2021, through February 3, 2021." The rare honor usually is reserved for presidents and other dignitaries; only four individuals—two Capitol Police officers killed during the 1998 Capitol shooting, Reverend Billy Graham, and civil rights icon Rosa Parks—who were not either a government or military official have lain in honor in the Rotunda.

Lawmakers of both political parties attended the solemn ceremonies one week before the Senate impeachment trial began. A motorcade carrying Sicknick's family and remains arrived at the Capitol the night of February 2. An honor guard carried Sicknick's urn and a folded American flag up the Capitol steps. House members and USCP officers filled the darkened Rotunda as Sicknick's urn and flag were placed on a podium covered in black.

Rep. Steny Hoyer saluted the display, as did dozens of Sicknick's USCP colleagues. Joe and Jill Biden arrived around 10:30 p.m. Holding hands, they walked slowly to the display as the room was silent. Biden placed his hand near the red box inscribed with Sicknick's full name that contained his ashes. Both placed their hands over their hearts for several seconds and Joe Biden gave the sign of the cross.

They walked over to a row of floral displays. Joe Biden shook his head as Jill Biden comfortingly rubbed his back.

The next day, Congressional leaders, D.C. Mayor Muriel Bowser, and Sicknick's family attended a socially distanced memorial service. Senate Majority Leader Charles Schumer opened the service. "Brian was a peace keeper,' Schumer said while wearing a face mask. "He was caught in the wrong place at the wrong time on a day when peace was shattered." Holding up a photo of Sicknick, Schumer called his death "a senseless tragedy" and wondered aloud why his family had to "pay such a high price for his devoted service."

The Air Force band played "America the Beautiful." House Speaker Nancy Pelosi commended Sicknick's "heroism" and promised to "remember his sacrifice." Following the two-hour service, attendees including Senate Minority Leader Mitch McConnell and House Minority Leader Kevin McCarthy stood outside as bagpipes played "Amazing Grace." Sicknick's remains were again placed in a hearse. Another motorcade transported the urn to Arlington National Cemetery, where it was buried.

The proceedings rivaled that of a state funeral for a president or Supreme Court Justice. In hindsight, these over-the-top theatrics should have raised red flags.

In fact, just as officials were preparing for Sicknick's memorial, CNN published a report questioning the official narrative of the officer's death. It was a preemptive strike, of course, intended to soften the blow of still-pending autopsy results. (Even though Sicknick had been cremated, the D.C. Medical Examiner's Office had refused to release his cause of death.)

"Investigators are struggling to build a federal murder case regarding fallen U.S. Capitol Police officer Brian Sicknick, vexed by a lack of evidence that could prove someone caused his death as he defended the Capitol during last month's insurrection," CNN's Evan Perez and Daniel Shortell reported on February 2.[3] "According to one law enforcement official, medical examiners did not find signs that the officer sustained any blunt force trauma, so investigators believe that early reports that he was fatally struck by a fire extinguisher are not true."

CNN then proffered the new storyline: Sicknick died after suffering a reaction to a chemical spray. "One possibility being considered by investigators is that Sicknick became ill after interacting with a chemical irritant like pepper spray or bear spray that was deployed in the crowd."

The *New York Times*, which had already slowly backed away from the fire extinguisher story by using more vague descriptions of his death in follow-up coverage, quietly retracted its January 8 article. At the top of the original article, the paper printed this: "UPDATE: New information has emerged regarding the death of the Capitol Police officer Brian Sicknick that questions the initial cause of his death provided by officials close to the Capitol Police."

Of course, it wasn't an update; it was a retraction. Not only did the paper abandon its initial account, one that infected January 6 coverage for weeks and ended up in an official impeachment document, the *Times* also subtly changed the portrayal of its sources. At first, the fire extinguisher account was attributed to law enforcement officials; the "update" was attributed to officials "close" to law enforcement—whatever that means.

---

3   Evan Perez, David Shortell, Whitney Wild, *Investigators Struggle to Build Murder Case in Death of US Capitol Police Officer Brian Sicknick* (CNN, 2021).

With few exceptions, the *Times'* retraction was ignored. No one in Congress rushed to remove the article from the impeachment memo; in fact, lawmakers continued to promote the lie. "Twenty-nine days ago, officer Sicknick…was murdered on the steps just outside this hallowed floor," Rep. Alexandria Ocasio-Cortez said during an overwrought floor speech on February 5.

The whole thing started to reek of a cover-up. In late February, Sicknick's mother Gladys told the *Daily Mail* she thought her son died of a stroke. When Senator Charles Grassley asked FBI Director Chris Wray in March how Sicknick died, Wray uncomfortably said the agency could not "disclose or confirm the cause of death." Wray then told Senator Ted Cruz that he believed it was appropriate that Capitol Police categorized Sicknick's passing as a "line of duty death."

Wray then smugly commended Congress' interest in Sicknick's death: "I think it speaks well of Congress that they're so interested in somebody who's lost his life protecting all of you.," he told the Senate Judiciary Committee on March 2.

So, after all the publicized theatrics, from the president to the FBI Director down to rank-and-file Capitol police, there was no way official Washington and the news media would let the Sicknick "murder" storyline fade away. It was time to concoct a new narrative, one that would sustain the biggest falsehood about January 6—and that would cost two men their reputations, their livelihoods, and their freedom.

*   *   *   *

On March 15, the Justice Department announced charges in connection with an "attack" on Officer Brian Sicknick.[4] Pennsylvania resident Julian Khater, thirty-two, was arrested after he got off a plane at Newark Airport; restaurant owner George Tanios, thirty-nine, was arrested at his home in West Virginia. Each was charged with three counts of assault on a federal officer with a dan-

---

4   United States Department of Justice, *Two Men Charged with Assaulting Federal Officers with Dangerous Weapon on January 6* (DOJ News, 2021),

gerous or deadly weapon and one count of conspiracy to injure an officer along with several other offenses.

Tanios told me in October that his fiancé, Amanda, encouraged him to take a break from working one hundred hours a week at the popular sandwich shop he owned in a West Virginia college town to go see Trump's speech. "You'll regret it if you don't go," she told him. His parents, immigrants from Lebanon, spent a lot of time in Trump's casinos in New Jersey, Tanios told me. He supported Trump as an "outsider fighting for us." But Trump was only part of the reason he decided to go to the nation's capital that week. "They didn't cheat him, they cheated us," he said of the 2020 presidential election.

Tanios and Khater traveled to Washington on January 5. They went to D.C. on the morning of January 6 to watch Trump's speech, then walked to the Capitol. Tanios had a backpack with a few cans of chemical spray in case they needed to defend themselves against leftwing protesters, they later testified. Tanios, a gun owner, left his firearm at home since D.C. imposes strict gun control laws.

Both arrived at the Capitol complex shortly after 2 p.m. and stood on the west side of the building where most of the clashes between police and protesters were taking place. Officers from the D.C. Metro Police force and USCP started attacking the crowd after 1 p.m. with flashbangs, sting balls with rubber bullets, and tear gas.

That's when Khater allegedly took bear spray out of Tanios' backpack and sprayed the chemical toward the officers. "The video shows Khater with his right arm up high in the air, appearing to be holding a canister in his right hand and aiming it at the officers' direction while moving his right arm from side to side," the Justice Department said in a press release. "The complaint affidavit states that Officers Sicknick, Edwards, and Chapman, who were all standing within a few feet of Khater, each reacted to being sprayed in the face. The officers retreated, bringing their hands to their faces and rushing to find water to wash out their eyes."

Tanios was about to take a shower at around 9:00 p.m. on Sunday, March 14 when he heard banging on his front door. Wearing a robe, Tanios ran to see what was happening. "Then I heard, 'put your fucking hands up!'"

About fifteen agents raided his home, interrogated Amanda, and took Tanios to jail. "I had no idea what I was being arrested for," he told me. "No one would answer me. Some of the agents seemed to feel bad about it. One [agent] said they had been arresting people all over but they had never arrested anyone without a criminal record like this."

Four days later, Tanios' attorney visited him in jail and read the charges including conspiracy to injure an officer and three counts of assault on a federal officer with a dangerous weapon— chemical spray. "I thought I was going to have a heart attack, I begged them to take my handcuffs off because my heart dropped," he said. "I told them, 'I am not a cop killer.'"

Despite having no criminal record, both men were denied bond. A federal judge berated Tanios for supporting Donald Trump. "Everyone in our country knows what happened on January 6," U.S. Magistrate Judge Michael Aloi lectured during a March 22 bond hearing. "We also generally know . . . that they were supporting the president who would not accept that he was defeated in an election. And so we have created this culture, radicalized by hate, and just refusal to really accept the result of a democratic process."

January 6, Aloi claimed, was "an assault on our nation's home." Even though Tanios was not accused of spraying Sicknick or anyone on January 6, Aloi ordered Tanios to remain behind bars because of his involvement in the Capitol protest. "I don't think I have ever seen anything play out in a way that was more dangerous to our community."

Tanios and Khater were transported to the D.C. jail for January 6 defendants.

But the case looked sketchy from the start. Video evidence amounted to what Tanios' lawyer called "tiny limited seconds of evidence" that failed to show that any liquid from Khater's spray container came in contact with police.

Further, the original accusation, that Sicknick had been hit with potent bear spray, was disputed by an FBI investigator on the case.

A court filing included this exchange:

> Attorney: Did Khater use the bear spray that day?
>
> Agent: Not that I know of, but that's for further investigation—the investigation is still going on regarding the bear sprays.
>
> Attorney: OK. So it's your understanding that Khater used the smaller canister of OC spray with the black handle that was sort of like on a keychain or could be a keychain?
>
> Agent: That's according to my investigation, which is still going on.
>
> Attorney: You don't have any reason to believe that the bear spray was deployed that day at all, do you?
>
> Agent: I have the bear spray cans myself and I haven't submitted them for analysis, so that's what I would need to do. That's a very serious thing that I have to be sure on in a scientific way the best I can.

Julian Khater's lawyer argued the officer could have been hit with tear gas used by their own colleagues on the scene. At one point in the government's video evidence, Khater is heard saying, "I've been hit."

In a save-face effort, the *New York Times* produced an unconvincing video purporting to show the attack on Sicknick. "New videos obtained by The New York Times show publicly for the first time how the U.S. Capitol Police officer who died after facing off with rioters on Jan. 6 was attacked with chemical spray," the *Times* reported on March 24. "A thin stream of liquid is visible shooting from a canister in Mr. Khater's hand. It is unclear in the video what Mr. Khater is firing, and prosecutors have alleged that Mr. Tanios brought two smaller canisters of pepper spray to the Capitol in addition to two cans of Frontiersman bear spray. Officer Sicknick reacts immediately to the spray, turning and raising his hand."[5]

For that alleged action, George Tanios and Julian Khater would spend months in jail, denied any chance for their families to make bond. "[W]ithout the violent efforts of these specific individuals to injure and/or incapacitate law enforcement officers who were executing their duties and protecting our democracy, the barrier lines would never have been breached, and rioters would likely not have gained entry into the Capitol Building," prosecutors wrote to the D.C. District court in April seeking their continued detention. "The defendants were spokes in the wheel that caused the historic events of January 6, 2021, and they are thus a danger to our society and a threat to the peaceful functioning of our community."

The men filed numerous character letters describing their work ethic and family support; Tanios and his fiancée have three small children and he worked six days a week a week running his restaurant.

Tanios and Khater, as is the case for nearly all January 6 protesters, would face much harsher treatment by the justice system

5   Evan Hill, David Botti, Dmitriy Khavin, Drew Jordan and Malachy Browne, *Officer Brian Sicknick Died After the Capitol Riot. New Videos Show How He Was Attacked* (New York Times, 2021).

than dozens of violent Antifa and BLM protesters who had attacked police with chemical spray and other weapons in nationally televised riots the summer before.

For example, Kevin Phomma was arrested in Portland in August 2020 and charged with assaulting federal officers with bear spray during that city's months-long occupation by Antifa. "As Portland officers began dispersing the crowd, Phomma was witnessed pepper spraying officers," a Justice Department press release read. "Phomma doused several officers with pepper spray while they attempted to arrest him. Once in custody, officers discovered the pepper spray was in fact a powerful bear deterrent pepper spray. While searching Phomma, officers also found a sheathed, three-inch dagger attached to his hip."[6]

Unlike Khater and Tanios, who belonged to no organized group, the active Antifa member was not charged with three counts of assaulting an officer with a dangerous or deadly weapon. Instead, he was charged with civil disorder and several other offenses.

"Phomma was later released," the Justice Department confirmed in the same statement.

But a funny thing happened while Khater and Tanios languished in solitary confinement conditions in the D.C. jail awaiting a new hearing seeking their release: The D.C. Medical Examiner's Office finally issued its overdue autopsy report on Officer Sicknick.

"On Wednesday, January 6, 2021, an unprecedented incident of civil insurrection at the United States Capitol resulted in the deaths of five individuals. The District of Columbia Office of the Chief Medical Examiner, Dr. Francisco J. Diaz, issued determinations on April 7 as to the cause and manner of death for four of those individuals and today issues the cause and manner of death of the remaining individual."

The office confirmed what his family said on January 8: Brian Sicknick died of natural causes, a stroke caused by blood clots—confirming what his family had been told on January 7.

6   United States Attorney's Office, District of Oregon, *Portland Man Charged with Civil Disorder After Assaulting Police Officers with Bear Spray* (United States Department of Justice, 2020).

In other words, Brian Sicknick was not murdered. By anyone.

The *Washington Post* got ahead of the story before the report went public so the medical examiner's office could put the preferred Beltway spin on the results. Acknowledging the autopsy "will make it difficult for prosecutors to pursue homicide charges in the officer's death," the paper included comments from Diaz to support the initial narrative that Trump supporters were responsible for Sicknick's death. "Diaz's ruling does not mean Sicknick was not assaulted or that the violent events at the Capitol did not contribute to his death," *Post* reporters Peter Hermann and Spencer Hsu wrote April 19. "The medical examiner noted Sicknick was among the officers who engaged the mob and said 'all that transpired played a role in his condition.'"[7]

There is no way to know if that is true. Even the snippets of video made public don't show Sicknick involved in any of the more heated physical confrontations between police and protesters. He was wearing a face covering and at one point appears to wash something out of his eyes. The more likely scenario is, given the copious amount of tear gas cops deployed against the crowd that day, Sicknick was hit with friendly fire.

That report should have been enough to justify the release of Khater and Tanios. But the next month, a federal judge denied their motion for bond. Judge Thomas Hogan, eighty-two, an appointee of Ronald Reagan, refused to let them out of jail even to home confinement. Julian Khater's family offered a $15 million bond package, an amount, as one scribe noted, three times higher than the bond for serial sexual harasser and accused rapist Harvey Weinstein.[8]

"They attacked uniformed police officers and I can't get around that," Hogan said during the May 11 hearing. While acknowledging their "excellent backgrounds," Hogan ruled the pair should remain behind bars because they, in Hogan's view, attempted to "halt democratic processes in their attack on Congress."

---

7   Peter Hermann, Spencer Hsu, *Capitol Police Officer Brian Sicknick, Who Engaged Rioters Suffered Two Strokes and Died of Natural Causes, Officials Say* (Washington Post, 2021).

8   Jordan Fischer, Eric Flack, Stephanie Wilson, *Capitol Rioter Accused of Bear Spraying Police Willing to Pay $15M Bond to Get Out of Jail* (WUSA9, 2021).

(Again, neither man went inside the building and the alleged altercation happened after Congress took a temporary recess.)

Both men appealed the judge's ruling; the D.C. Circuit Court denied Julian Khater's appeal in July.

But a month later, the appellate court issued a well-deserved smackdown of Hogan's ruling to keep Tanios behind bars. "ORDERED and ADJUDGED that the district court's May 12, 2021 order be reversed and the case remanded for the district court to order appellant's pretrial release subject to appropriate conditions, including home detention and electronic monitoring," the appellate court announced on August 9. "On this record, we conclude that the district court clearly erred in determining that no condition or combination of conditions of release would reasonably assure the safety of the community."

Ten days later, Hogan allowed Tanios to be released to home incarceration. He offered no apology for his errant judgement that robbed Tanios of five months of freedom. As of October 2021, no trial date had been set for either man.

But the damage had been done. Tanios told me he cannot sell his shop—"Who will buy a business with this name attached to it?" he said—and has been wrongly and unfairly branded a cop killer by the media. "In the court of public opinion," he lamented, "we've all been destroyed." Tanios showed me an email sent to him by Airbnb the day after his arrest, notifying him that his account was cancelled. DoorDash, an online food delivery service, cancelled Tanios' account in April.

To this day, one can search for articles or news segments about Brian Sicknick and nearly all still report that he was killed in the line of duty on January 6. "Five people died including a police officer," is the standard line.

Sicknick's employer also continues to perpetuate this lie. After the medical examiner released its report confirming he died of a stroke, the agency issued a statement: "The USCP accepts the findings from the District of Columbia's Office of the Chief Medical Examiner that Officer Brian Sicknick died of natural causes.

This does not change the fact Officer Sicknick died in the line of duty, courageously defending Congress and the Capitol. The United States Capitol Police will never forget Officer Sicknick's bravery, nor the bravery of any officer on January 6, who risked their lives to defend our democracy."

A report prepared by two Senate committees examining the security failures at the Capitol twice mentioned Sicknick's death. "USCP Officer Brian Sicknick, a 13-year veteran and member of the First Responder Unit, was stationed on the West Front of the Capitol, where rioters attacked him with bear spray. Officer Sicknick passed away at 9:30 p.m. on January 7."

Joe Biden repeatedly deceives the American people about Sicknick's death. After Russian President Vladimir Putin in June accused the U.S. of holding political prisoners related to Biden's January 6 investigation, Biden responded that Capitol protesters went "into the Capitol [to] kill a police officer."

This statement from the president of the United States grotesquely misrepresents not only what occurred on January 6, but the intentions of those involved in the protest. Yet no one in the press seems interested in issuing the kind of fact checks that were routine when Donald Trump was president.

During a White House ceremony in August to sign legislation honoring law enforcement agencies who responded to the January 6 protest, Biden issued another gross distortion when he claimed numerous officers were injured and hospitalized "and others were lost forever. May their souls rest in peace and rise in glory."[9] Biden recalled how he and Jill attended the Sicknick memorial "after he lost his life" in the line of duty.

But truth will not wash the imaginary blood from the hands of Trump supporters. Democrats, the media, and Trump-hating Republicans shamefully repeat the lie without fear of contradiction to this day.

And seeding the falsehood about Brian Sicknick would be just the start of the United States Capitol Police's bad behavior related to January 6.

---

9   President Joe Biden, *Remarks by President Biden at Signing of H.R. 3325, Awarding Congressional Gold Medals to Those Who Protected the U.S. Capitol on January 6* (The White House Briefing Room, 2021).

CHAPTER SIX

WHOSE SIDE ARE THEY ON?
THE ROLE OF THE CAPITOL POLICE

AFTER JANUARY 6, Democrats finally found a police force they could praise and did not want to defund: The United States Capitol Police.

As part of the legislative branch, the USCP is protected from Freedom of Information Act requests. Oversight of the 2,000-member force is administered by four congressional committees and a small Capitol Police Board composed of the sergeants-at-arms for the House and Senate, the Architect of the Capitol, and the agency's chief-of-police. USCPs annual budget jumped from $464 million in 2020 to $515 million in 2021, a budget that rivals that of police forces in many mid-sized cities.[1]

Initially, Capitol police were heralded as heroes on January 6; but for their bravery that afternoon, who knows how many lawmakers would have been killed, the media pondered aloud. Some officers undoubtedly acted courageously, moving elected officials and staff to safer quarters, protecting cherished property inside the building, and calming a few heated flashpoints.

---

1   First Branch Forecast, *Capitol Police Release 2019 Complaints Data With Significant Omissions That Reduce Clarity* (First Branch Forecast, 2020).

Overall, however, the role of the Capitol police force is not as clear-cut as the media or Congressmen on both sides of the aisle want the public to believe. Contradictory images showed Capitol Police at one point fighting with demonstrators, firing teargas and rubber bullets, while in other videos they appear to be admitting demonstrators to the Capitol and posing with them for selfies. When it was revealed that the USCP had declined additional support from the National Guard, many on the right found it suspicious. Meanwhile some on the left accused them of complicity in the insurrection and of being riddled with white supremacists.

The USCP is not exactly free of controversy. Prior to January 6, USCP faced serious scrutiny for its lack of transparency and the conduct of some USCP officers. Internal complaints at the agency skyrocketed between 2016 and 2020; several pending lawsuits described allegations of racial discrimination and sexual harassment. An investigative report by Roll Call published just a few months before the Capitol protest detailed accusations contained in a wrongful dismissal suit filed by a former officer.

"A male Capitol Police officer allegedly used the department's computer to solicit sex on Craigslist, send sexually explicit emails and attempt to buy an illicit drug from Qatar, according to filings in one officer's gender discrimination lawsuit that summarizes internal department documents," reporter Chris Marquette wrote on September 24, 2020. "Another male officer allegedly stored sex toys in his Capitol Police vehicle, photographed himself masturbating, and took photos of a handcuffed, partially nude woman in the back of the car, the lawsuit states. A male commander allegedly asked a female subordinate to have sex with him in his hotel room. The officers all received some form of punishment, described by an expert on police conduct as light. None of them were demoted or fired."[2]

Demands for accountability and greater access to USCP materials prompted Rep. Rodney Davis in 2020 to introduce a re-

---

2   Chris Marquette, *Exclusive: Capitol Police Disciplinary Reports Show Pattern of Misconduct* (Roll Call, 2020).

form bill that required USCP to produce a semi-annual report on the "functions and activities of the United States Capitol Police" and make the information available to the public.

Such calls for transparency and accountability ended on January 6. From the start, USCP leadership acted as propagandists for the "insurrection" narrative. Officers were immediately trotted out to the media to recount their harrowing stories of survival. Lawmakers bestowed Congressional medals and proposed massive increases to USCPs annual budget.

The agency's chief, Steven Sund, set the tone with a lengthy statement the day after the Capitol protest: "United States Capitol Police (USCP) officers and our law enforcement partners responded valiantly when faced with thousands of individuals involved in violent riotous actions as they stormed the United States Capitol Building," Sund wrote in the January 7 press release. "These individuals actively attacked United States Capitol Police Officers and other uniformed law enforcement officers with metal pipes, discharged chemical irritants, and took up other weapons against our officers. They were determined to enter into the Capitol Building by causing great damage. The violent attack on the U.S. Capitol was unlike any I have ever experienced in my 30 years in law enforcement here in Washington, D.C."[3]

Sund resigned the next day amid threats he would be fired by House Speaker Nancy Pelosi. A Senate report issued in June outlined several missteps by Capitol Police under Sund's leadership, faulting the agency for failed intelligence that did not properly assess the potential threat on January 6.[4] The security review, conducted by the Senate Rules Committee and the Senate Homeland Security Committee, concluded USCP did not prepare officers and failed to provide enough equipment to deal with the protesters. Communication systems were inadequate. (The report also inaccurately claimed that three officers "ultimately lost their lives" as a result of the protest.)

---

3   Steven Sund, Chief of Police, *Statement Regarding the Events of January 6, 2021* (United States Capitol Police, 2021).

4   United States Senate, *Staff Report—Examining the U.S. Capitol Attack: A Review of the Security, Planning, and Response Failures on January 6* (Committee on Homeland Security and Governmental Affairs, Committee on Rules and Administration, 2021).

"[S]everal USCP officers have stated that they received no warning about the possibility of violent protests on January 6 from USCP officials," the Senate report said. "Line officers raised concerns about USCP leadership's lack of communication about the potential threats on January 6, with some saying they did not receive the January 3 Special Assessment and others were made to feel that 'it was business as usual.' One USCP Inspector told the Committees that they expected January 6 to be just like the previous two Million MAGA Marches in terms of crowd size and the potential for violence. Multiple officers also reported that no meetings were held prior to January 6 to brief officers and provide emergency plans, which typically occurs for major events. The Capitol Police Labor Committee stated, USCP leadership 'failed to share key intelligence with officers in advance, they failed to prepare adequately, they failed to equip our officers with a plan and on that very day, they failed to lead.'"

Sund was replaced by Yogananda Pittman, who wasted no time using her new post to help politicize the events of January 6. In her first official statement, she stressed the agency's grief about the "loss" of Brian Sicknick—the USCP stuck with the story that he was killed in the line of duty even after an autopsy revealed the true cause of death—and suggested that another officer, Howard Liebengood, who reportedly committed suicide on January 9, did so because of the trauma he suffered during the protest.

Pittman immediately ordered a military-style lockdown of the Capitol grounds. Helping to fuel dire warnings that Joe Biden's inauguration would create an opportunity for "violent insurrectionists" to strike again, Pittman closed down streets several days before the event and erected non scalable fencing around the perimeter of the building.

Though their presence had not been requested by the mayor or Democratic leaders before the protest, thousands of National Guard troops were now ordered to D.C. to help secure the complex. After the inauguration, Pittman recommended the fencing remain in place. "In light of recent events, I can unequivocally say that vast improvements to the physical security infrastructure must be made to include permanent fencing, and the availability of ready, back-up forces in close proximity to the Capitol," Pittman said on January 28.

It didn't take long for the department to receive its reward. The House Appropriations Committee proposed a $1.9 billion emergency spending bill "to respond to the tragic events" of January 6; most of the new funds were allocated for Capitol Police and the Architect of the Capitol.[5] The slush fund included:

- $31 million in overtime and hazard pay, retention bonuses, and tuition reimbursements as a reward for USCP response to January 6.

- $4.4 million for a Wellness and Trauma Support program named after Harvey Liebengood, the officer who allegedly committed suicide after January 6. (In June, the agency hired an emotional support dog, Lila, to help officers cope.)

- $250 million for physical security measures at the Capitol including "pop-up" fencing.

- $200 million to create a dedicated Quick Reaction Force within the Capitol Police that would be a "ground force equivalent of the 113th Wing within the District of Columbia Air National Guard at Joint Base Andrews, which defends National Capital Region airspace."

- $100 million to the Architect of the Capitol and the Capitol Police for COVID mitigation.

- Joe Biden signed the bill into law in July 2021.

5   Chair Rosa Delauro, *Emergency Security Supplemental to Respond to January 6th, Bill Summary* (House Committee on Appropriations, 2021).

As the Biden White House and Congressional Democrats continued to ramp up their rhetoric, USCP officers contributed to the theatrics. Rank-and-file officers became instant media darlings; their unchallenged and, in many cases, unsubstantiated accounts were told to sympathetic journalists who expressed their alarm about the cruelty, racism, and bloodlust of Trump supporters.

Officer Harry Dunn, a thirteen-year veteran of the force, gave a rage-filled interview to ABC's *Good Morning America* in February in which he described what he endured that day.[6] Dunn, armed and dressed in riot gear for his TV appearance, called the protesters "terrorists" who tried to "disrupt this country's democracy." In the interview, he told ABC News correspondent Pierre Thomas on February 22 that as he looked out at the sea of supporters holding Trump flags on the east side of the building, he assumed that they were armed. "I'm gonna get shot, they gonna take me out." This was of course mistaken—more a reflection of his own ingrained assumptions than of actual reality.

During one exchange with protesters, Dunn supposedly told the group that he had voted for Joe Biden. Dunn claimed a woman wearing a pink MAGA shirt yelled to the crowd, "Hey, this nigger voted for Joe Biden, guys." Others started to repeat the slur. "Everybody, everybody joined in with them. A large number in that crowd were racists," Dunn said. After the chaos ended, Dunn said he told a fellow officer he had been called the n-word "a couple dozen times today."

No video of protesters using this word has so far been made public. If it existed, we can be fairly sure it would have been released. Perhaps it will be proven in due course. Until then, we are entitled to be skeptical of this inflammatory claim.

But Dunn did offer some truth in the interview, confirming that police used "smoke grenades, gas grenades, pepper balls... flashbangs." Dunn claimed the weaponry was used by "everybody," suggesting that protestors had come prepared with these

---

6   Pierre Thomas, Victor Ordonez, Eliana Larramendia, *Capitol Police Officer Recounts Jan. 6 Attack: Exclusive* (ABC News, 2021)

munitions. But a trove of open-source videos only show police, not protesters, using explosive devices and sting balls against the crowd assembled outside.

Dunn appeared on CNN a few months later with a USCP colleague, Sergeant Aquilino Gonell, who complained that Republican House members did not support a January 6 commission. "We gave them time to get to safety and they [sic] not appreciating that," Gonell told CNN anchor Pamela Brown on June 5. "We put our lives, while they were running, we held the line and that to me, we sacrificed so much for them."

Gonell, a military veteran and immigrant from the Dominican Republic, accused lawmakers of violating their oath of office to "put their country before their party." On January 20, 2021, Gonell took a medical leave from the department.

The pair, according to their Twitter accounts, hold deep contempt for Donald Trump and strong political views. In a now-deleted tweet, Dunn took a selfie while wearing a t-shirt with an image of Colin Kaepernick holding his knee and foot on the face of Donald Trump. "I hate @TuckerCarlson what an out of touch asshole that has no clue about anything that doesn't look like him or agree with him," Dunn tweeted in 2019. After Steve Bannon defied a subpoena to testify before the January 6 committee, Dunn tweeted the hashtag, #FuckSteveBannon."

Gonell's Twitter feed includes numerous profane posts about the former president and Republicans. One tweet featured a cartoon of Trump that Gonell labeled "Traitor Trump." Another tweet showed an image of Trump's charred head. Gonell mocked the disabled governor of Texas after Greg Abbott announced an executive order banning vaccine mandates. "Wheelchairs and ramps should be ban (sic) in Texas…" One post included a horsehead on the body of Rep. Marjorie Taylor Greene.

It is thus a fair presumption that both officers are highly partisan and, as such, not unbiased or fully reliable.

Dunn and Gonell also participated in the first public hearing of Nancy Pelosi's January 6 select committee.[7] Before his opening

---

7   Julie Kelly, *Another Partisan Stunt by the U.S. Capitol Police* (American Greatness, 2021).

remarks, Dunn asked for a moment of silence in honor of Brian Sicknick, his "fallen colleague [who] died from injuries he sustained in the line of duty defending the Capitol of our beloved democracy." This was already known to be false. Dunn repeated the same accounts he gave in the ABC News interview, including the claim—impossible to verify—that a woman in a pink MAGA shirt called him a "nigger" and that others joined in.

"In the days following the attempted insurrection, other black officers shared with me their own stories of racial abuse on January 6," Dunn read from his prepared opening statement. "One officer told me he had never, in his entire forty years of life, been called a 'nigger' to his face, and that that streak ended on January 6. Yet another black officer later told he had been confronted by insurrectionists inside the Capitol, who told him to "Put your gun down and we'll show you what kind of nigger you really are!"

Gonell described the fighting at the Capitol on January 6 as "medieval"-no one brought a sword or mace or arrived on horseback-and insisted it was worse than what he saw while serving in Iraq.

He called lawmakers who had visited the D.C. jail holding January 6 defendants under pre-trial detention orders "pathetic." The House members, including Marjorie Taylor Greene, Louie Gohmert, and Matt Gaetz, "shouldn't be elected officials any more," Gonell told the committee.

Two D.C. Metro Police officers joined Dunn and Gonell for the hearing on July 27; the agencies had worked together on January 6 to secure the Capitol and attack protesters outside the building with explosive devices, rubber bullets, and chemical spray.

A ProPublica investigative report published on January 17 embedded dozens of videos posted on Parler that showed the attacks. (Some January 6 protesters speculate the reason Parler, and not Facebook, was deplatformed was to cut off access to videos and photos showing what police actually did during the protest.)

A video recorded at 12:59 p.m. and posted in the ProPublica piece showed Capitol police in full riot gear walking on the lower terrace on the west side of the building. Dressed in black, officers' uniforms don't display a name or badge number. At 1:19 p.m., a group of officers stationed on the upper west terrace aim long guns at the crowd. "The gas is coming over," one man said.

At 1:45 p.m., after nearly a half hour of nonstop attacks on the crowd, a man approached a line of D.C. police standing behind metal racks. "You know what you're doing is wrong," he said.

"The cops were shooting at us for a while, then they stopped," one user said. "They're firing their tear gas at us, the flash-bang grenades, but there's nothing they can do." Another woman shouts at officers, "We're done with the police. You're going to have Antifa, Black Lives Matter and the Republicans all hating you guys!" After word of Ashli Babbitt's shooting reached the crowd, one man scolded a cop: "Don't kill no more of our patriots. You guys won't kill Black Lives Matter, but you'll shoot us."

But police officers instead argue *they* are the victims of MAGA cultists. Officers Michael Fanone and Daniel Hodges, like Dunn and Gonell, gave angry, emotional testimony while recounting their near-death experiences.[8] Hodges at least a dozen times referred to the protesters as "terrorists" and said they called police "stormtroopers" and "traitors" for the way they were handling the crowd. Video shows Hodges trapped in a doorway, crying out in pain. "I led the charge through the midst of crowd control munitions, explosions and smoke engulfing the area, terrorists were breaking apart the metal fencing and bike racks into individual pieces presumably to use as weapons," Hodges said. (Only two men were charged with using a bike rack as a weapon.)

Rep. Adam Kinzinger (R-Il), appointed by Pelosi to serve on the committee, famously sobbed after hearing the group's testimony. (Kinzinger announced in October he would not seek re-election after Illinois Democrats eliminated his congressional district in the decadal remap process.)

---

8   *Capitol and D.C. Police Testify on January 6 Attack* (C-Span, 2021).

Officer Fanone, who became the face of law enforcement after January 6, giving nonstop interviews on CNN and appearing on the front cover of *Time* magazine in August, pounded the table and raged that it was "disgraceful" that his colleagues weren't getting more respect from Republicans in Congress.

After the hearing ended, the four officers smiled for photos and embraced committee members.

*   *   *   *

Seated behind the officers during the hearing was David Laufman, a D.C. attorney working with Dunn and Gonell on a pro bono basis. Laufman and his co-counsel, Mark Zaid, prepped the officers before their testimony. "We find ourselves in the middle of 2021 astonishingly and painfully in a circumstance where American democracy feels like it's hanging by a thread," Laufman told the *National Law Journal* in July. "The ability as a lawyer to help clients who are law enforcement officers tell their story to Congress and the American people about what happened that day will hopefully raise consciousness throughout the country about the dangers of this menace to our democracy and help mitigate the threat that remains before us."

After Tucker Carlson called Dunn an "angry, leftwing activist" on his show, Laufman and Zaid issued a statement condemning his remarks. "Our client has served 13 years in law enforcement and on January 6, 2021, fought against an insurrectionist violent crowd—no doubt many of them Carlson's supporters—to protect the lives of our elected officials, including Vice President Pence," they wrote in a July 22 statement.[9]

Laufman and Zaid are no strangers to political theater in the nation's capital, particularly when it comes to vilifying Donald Trump. Laufman was a top deputy in the National Security Division at Barack Obama's Justice Department, the same agency that handled the illicit FISA warrant on Trump campaign adviser

---

9   Graig Graziosi, *Harry Dunn's Lawyers Hit Out at Tucker Carlson After He Brands Capitol Police Officer 'Angry' Activist* (Yahoo News, 2021).

Carter Page. Laufman also was involved in the investigation of Hillary Clinton's email server; he and disgraced FBI agent Peter Strzok interviewed Clinton in 2016.

In 2018, Laufman represented a friend of Christine Blasey Ford, the woman who accused Supreme Court Justice nominee Brett Kavanaugh of sexually assaulting her in 1982. Monica McLean, a former FBI agent and Ford's "beach friend," reportedly pressured a friend of Ford's to change her story. Laufman called the allegations "absolutely false" but the Senate Judiciary Committee investigated McLean for tampering with a "critical witness" during Kavanaugh's confirmation process.[10]

Mark Zaid, an expert in Beltway lawfare, actually called for a "coup" against Donald Trump on January 30, 2017, just days after his inauguration as president. He represented the so-called "whistleblower" who leaked details of Trump's July 2019 call with the Ukrainian president, which prompted the president's first impeachment trial. In an August 2021 profile piece in the Washingtonian, Zaid said he "is hopeful we don't have another person like Trump" in the White House again.

Pelosi's January 6 select committee was an extension of what people like David Laufman started in 2016 under the Obama Justice Department and people like Mark Zaid continued in 2019: the wholesale destruction of Donald Trump and everyone around him. Officers Harry Dunn and Aquilino Gonell were just the latest actors to animate another Trump-centered crisis.

In fact, the USCP pushed hard for a January 6 commission. When Republicans refused to pass legislation authorizing the inquiry, anonymous officers sent a letter to members of Congress threatening to withhold security. Reiterating the false claim that USCP officers died because of the Capitol protest—"some officers served their last day in a US Capitol police officer uniform, and not by choice"—the unnamed officers warned Republicans in the House and Senate that they are "privileged" because

---

10   Office of the Chairman, Senator Chuck Grassley, *Memorandum Re: Senate Judiciary Committee Investigation of Numerous Allegations Against Justice Brett Kavanaugh During the Senate Confirmation Proceedings* (United States Senate, 2018).

they are kept safe by Capitol Police. "That privilege exists because the brave men and women of the USCP protected you, the members."

*   *   *   *

Officers Dunn and Gonell had something else in common: Both were in the west terrace tunnel under the Capitol where Rosanne Boyland, a Trump supporter from Georgia, died. It was the scene of fierce fighting between protesters and police in the late afternoon of January 6. Law enforcement used heavy amounts of chemical spray inside the tunnel and outside the premises to subdue protesters.

A motion filed by Joe McBride, a lawyer representing Ryan Nichols, detailed the horrific activities inside the tunnel, which is underneath the traditional inauguration platform used every four years to swear in the new president. McBride watched three hours of official surveillance video related to his client's case: "Screams and cries for help keep pouring out of the tunnel. The place has literally turned into the Gates of Hell. Ryan is about eight feet from the entrance, and is keeping an eye on the middle-aged White woman with the red shirt and red MAGA hat. As Ryan watches the woman, he sees Officer Badge # L359, wearing a long-sleeve White-shirt, begin to beat a man for no apparent reason. This same officer in the White-shirt started beating the man at 2:06:15 in the video, which equates to approximately 4:06 pm. This officer beats the man so badly that the man crawls over to the woman with the MAGA hat. White-shirt swings for the man one last time but misses and knocks the woman's MAGA hat off instead. Then for reasons that no fair minded or decent human being will ever understand—White-shirt turns his attention to the woman and begins to pulverize her. The weapon this officer appears to be using is a collapsible stick, designed to break windows in emergency situations. This stick is neither designed nor to be used against another human being."

In their congressional testimony, Dunn and Gonell vaguely described how they gave medical aid to a woman who needed help. "In the Crypt, I encountered Sergeant Gonell, who was giving assistance to an unconscious woman who had been in the crowd of rioters on the west side of the Capitol," Dunn said in his prepared remarks on July 27. "I helped to carry her to the House Majority Leader's office, where she was administered CPR."

That's all he said. Gonell added a little more detail in his opening statement, but not much. "But it was not until around 4:26 pm, after giving CPR to one of the rioters who breached the Capitol in an effort to save her life, that I finally had a chance to let my own family know that I was alive."

Neither officer explained what actually happened to the woman and the committee members didn't bother to ask. But the timeline offered by Dunn and Gonell, substantiated by video clips and a lengthy report in the *New York Times*, seems to confirm they are the officers who handled Boyland, one of four people who died on January 6.[11]

Here is what transpired: At around 4:20 p.m., police pushed a mob of protesters out of the tunnel causing many to tumble down the steps. The tunnel leads to the inside of the Capitol building; it's unclear right now why dozens of protesters were inside that tunnel. It is likely, since cell phone service had been shut off, that they didn't realize the joint session had been suspended. Some later told me the mob was so dense they had nowhere to go and were looking for an exit through the tunnel.

Boyland at this point was already unconscious, according to witnesses. Edward Lang, who would be arrested a week later and detained for months, tried to help Boyland and others being physically crushed by the crowd. They repeatedly asked police to stop pushing so they could administer aid.

"In the chaos, two men spotted Ms. Boyland on the ground and dragged her away from the door," the *Times* reported on Jan-

---

11   Evan Hill, Arielle Ray, Dahlia Kozlowskey, *Videos Show How Rioter Was Trampled in Stampede at Capitol* (*New York Times*, 2021).

uary 15. "The men laid Ms. Boyland out on the steps and attempted to resuscitate her. At least two individuals can be seen
on video providing CPR. At the top of the steps, another man,
wearing a purple jacket, can be seen apparently negotiating with
the police so that the rioters can get Ms. Boyland assistance."

Police, presumably Gonell, then move her into the Capitol
Rotunda. Several minutes later, D.C. Metro paramedics responded to a call for emergency medical help and found "two Capitol
Police officers in the Rotunda performing CPR on Ms. Boyland,
who the officers said had collapsed in the protest." She was transported to a hospital and died at 6:09 p.m.

A time stamp on body cam footage shows Boyland on the
ground at 4:26 p.m. Her friend, Jason Winchell, is heard on the
video screaming, "She's gonna die! She's dead!" As protesters battle with police, Winchell keeps yelling her name and asking for
help. "[R]ioters dragged Ms. Boyland from the door and attempted but failed to resuscitate her," the *Times* reported in a follow-up
article on January 28. "They then carried her back to the police
battling rioters at the doorway, who moved her into the Capitol
Rotunda, where paramedics eventually reached her."

An August court filing on behalf of Jacob Lang included a
sworn affidavit by Phillip Anderson detailing what happened before Gonell and Dunn handled Boyland's body. Anderson said
police were using a spray that was not tear gas that made it "impossible" to breathe and caused people to collapse.[12]

"There were many others who collapsed because of these
toxins, as I did. The police continued to use excessive force, by
hitting me and others. One of the people that fell in the crowd
was a woman by the name [of] Rosanne Boyland. Several people
gathered to give her CPR; all while the police officers hit them
over the head repeatedly," Anderson testified.

Police continued their assault on the crowd. "Not only were the
people that were trying to help being hit physically, but police were
also spraying mace (or some other type of gas) on everyone who was

---

12   Julie Kelly, *What Did the Capitol Celebrity Cops Do to Roseanne Boyland?* (American Greatness, 2021).

down. After Rosanne Boyland fell, the weight that continued to gather on top of her left [her] unconscious. At first, she reached out and held my hand firmly, and shortly thereafter her grip loosened

On April 7, the D.C. Medical Examiner's Office ruled her death an accident and claimed she died of "acute amphetamine intoxication." A regular user of Adderall, a common drug to treat attention deficit disorders that contains amphetamines, Boyland probably had some detectable level in her system at the time of her death. Overdoses by Adderall, however, are extremely rare; Boyland would have had to ingest roughly 25 times her normal daily dose to die of it.

But what exactly happened to Boyland—and how much of a role law enforcement played in her death—may never be known. Video clips released in August and September show disturbing scenes of police and protesters assaulting each other as Boyland lay motionless on the ground, her midsection exposed. A brief clip, likely edited by the government to prevent the public from seeing precisely what happened, shows an officer begin to drag her body back into the tunnel. The video stops seconds afterwards.

Her family said the D.C. coroner repeatedly refused to release the full autopsy report. The D.C. police department also denied her family's request for footage recorded on body-worn cameras by D.C. police near Boyland when she died.

Exactly what Dunn and Gonell did with her body, and whether D.C. officers physically assaulted her prior to her death, is yet to be known.

Dunn and Gonell weren't the only cops in on the action. USCP rank-and-file acted as useful political props to keep January 6 in the news. In February, Nancy Pelosi announced she would introduce legislation to award the department a Congressional Gold Medal. Pittman thanked Pelosi for acknowledging the officers "at a time when they're experiencing tremendous emotions and exhaustion."

In March, two USCP officers filed a lawsuit in the D.C. District Court against Donald Trump. James Blassingame and Sidney

Hemby directly blamed the president for injuries, both physical and emotional, that they sustained that day. "The insurrectionist mob, which Trump had inflamed, encouraged, incited, directed, and aided and abetted, forced its way over and past the plaintiffs and their fellow officers, pursuing and attacking them inside and outside the United States Capitol, and causing the injuries complained of herein," the pair wrote in a March 20 filing.

Hemby said he was crushed against a door, sprayed with a chemical irritant, and suffered cuts and abrasions. Blassingame also claimed he was crushed against a door and repeatedly called "nigger" by Trump supporters. "The insurrectionists struck Officer Blassingame in his face, head, chest, arms, and what felt like every part of his body. Insurrectionists used their fists and had weapons that ranged from flagpoles to stanchions and building directional signs, water bottles and other objects he could not identify. The threats and attacks on Officer Blassingame seemed endless. Officer Blassingame's sole focus was to do what he could to survive."

Both officers have since suffered severe emotional distress, according to the lawsuit. And Trump isn't the only one to blame. "Trump's followers engaged in conduct that was extreme and outrageous, and so beyond the bounds of decency that it is regarded as atrocious and utterly intolerable in a civilized society. This extreme and outrageous conduct was intended to cause James Blassingame's emotional distress or was carried out with reckless disregard of whether the conduct would cause James Blassingame to suffer emotional distress."

The pair asked for $75,000 in compensatory damages and an unspecified amount in punitive damages. Their injuries cannot be verified and it is also unclear who, if anyone, has been charged with attacking either officer. No evidence has so far been provided either on video or in charging documents of Hodges either being squeezed in the door or abused with racist slurs.

Some police were indeed injured to various degrees in the fighting. But it is also worth noting that nothing that occurred at the Capitol protest in terms of either physical or verbal abuse was not also done to cops all over the country during the BLM/ Antifa riots the previous summer. Needless to say, no indictments were brought against these rioters for "extreme and outrageous" behavior "beyond the bounds of decency."

Blassingame is represented by lawyers working for the Protect Democracy Project, part of an expansive NeverTrump operation funded by leftwing billionaire and eBay founder Pierre Omidyar. Advisors to the group include NeverTrump "conservatives" such as Mona Charen, Linda Chavez, and Matthew Dowd. Protect Democracy, in addition to several Omidyar-funded nonprofits, was formed in 2017 to resist Trump's presidency. [13]

Seven more USCP officers filed a separate civil lawsuit in August, but this time, Trump wasn't the only target. The officers also sued members of the Proud Boys, Oath Keepers, and Three Percenters; Ali Alexander and the "Stop the Steal" organization; Trump confidante Roger Stone; "Walk Away" founder Brandon Straka and several others accused of organizing the assault.[14] Claiming allegations of election fraud were racist because of questions about ballot-counting in major cities such as Detroit, Philadelphia and Milwaukee that have large black populations, the officers—Conrad Smith, Danny McElroy, Byron Evans, Governor Latson, Melissa Marshall, Michael Fortune, and Jason DeRoche—accused Trump and his co-defendants of violating the Ku Klux Klan Act and the D.C. Bias-Related Crime Act.

Officers claimed injuries related to chemical sprays and tear gas; Officer Latson said he was pushed and allegedly called a "nigger" by protesters, as was Officer Fortune. All accused the defendants of causing emotional injuries.

"Racism and white supremacy pervaded Defendants efforts from the outset," the plaintiffs' lawyers wrote as though this were a self-evident truth. "Defendants targeted false claims of election fraud at cities and states with significant Black populations…and

13   https://protectdemocracy.org/our-staff/
14   *Smith v. Trump,* Complaint, Case No.: Case 1:21-cv-02265

sought to intimidate and threaten officials from those and other jurisdictions into overturning the will of the voters. They relied on white supremacist groups and sympathizers to organize and hold rallies and to help plan and carry out the Capitol Attack. Participants in the Attack directed racial epithets at Black officers protecting the Capitol. And after breaching the Capitol, the attackers paraded the Confederate flag and other symbols of white supremacy through the Capitol's halls."

Trump and the other defendants supposedly "aided and abetted" assaults on the seven officers, the lawsuit claimed. Describing the events of January 6 as "terrorism," the officers accused Trump and his supporters of attempting "to strong-arm the American public to accept the unlawful and undemocratic subversion of the 2020 Presidential election in violation of law and in contravention of the demonstrated will of the electorate."

Meanwhile USCP continued to fuel the notion that Washington could come under attack at any moment, animating more "insurrection" theater for the Democrats. Fencing and National Guardsmen remained in place at the complex for months. Amid absurd rumors allegedly promoted by QAnon that Trump would be "reinstated" as president during a secret inauguration on March 4, Pittman issued a bulletin warning of another threat to the Capitol and promising to step up security measures. "We have obtained intelligence that shows a possible plot to breach the Capitol by an identified militia group on Thursday, March 4," Pittman claimed. "We have already made significant security upgrades to include establishing a physical structure and increasing manpower to ensure the protection of Congress, the public and our police officers."[15]

March 4 came and went. Nothing happened.

Three months later, with no threat in sight, they were still stoking the atmosphere of crisis. On June 5, the agency conducted what it called a "routine" training exercise at the Capitol. "Please

15   United States Capitol Police, *Press Release: Capitol Police Increase Security Following Threat* (United States Capitol Police, 2021).

do not be alarmed if you see emergency vehicles and low flying helicopters," USCP notified residents in a tweet.

*   *   *   *

But Capitol Police still could not explain why so many officers allowed protesters into the building. Open source video taken by Trump supporters and journalists on the scene showed several instances when USCP employees opened doors or, at the very least, did not resist entry into the Capitol.

Senator Ron Johnson, one of the few Republicans with access to USCP surveillance footage, sent a letter to Pittman in June asking for clarification on one recording which showed a USCP officer directing several people toward open doors from the inside around 2:30 on January 6.

"Over the span of a 14-minute period, approximately 309 unauthorized individuals entered the Capitol on January 6 through the upper west terrace doors," Johnson wrote to Pittman. "At approximately 2:26 p.m. on January 6, a security camera showed a male inside the Capitol attempting to open one of the upper west terrace doors to exit the building. This unauthorized individual, who was by himself at the time, walked through a narrow hallway to the double doors and attempted to exit through the left door by pushing the door's crash bar. The door did not open and the individual turned around and walked back through the hallway and away from the doors. Approximately seven minutes later, at 2:33 p.m., security footage showed five unauthorized individuals walking down the same hallway, past a police officer. The security footage, which did not include audio, appeared to show the police officer gesturing toward the doors as these individuals walked past him. Once at the double doors, one of the five individuals pushed the left door's crash bar and this time, it opened. All five individuals exited the building at approximately 2:33 p.m."[16]

16   Senator Ron Johnson, *Letter Dated June 10, 2021* (United States Senate, 2021).

Johnson noted that several officers formed a line but did not stop protesters from entering. After Ashli Babbitt was shot around 2:45 p.m., those officers retreated, again allowing more people to "surge" into the building, Johnson said. He asked whether Pittman had interviewed the officers and for copies of the transcribed interviews. "If not, I respectfully ask for the opportunity to interview these officers."

It started to look like USCP couldn't tell the truth about anything related to January 6. The Architect of the Capitol, technically a member of the USCP department, floated the idea that protesters caused $30 million in damages including "broken glass, broken doors, and graffiti," J. Brett Blanton told a congressional committee in February. "Statues, murals, historic benches and original shutters all suffered varying degrees of damage, primarily from pepper spray accretions and residue from chemical irritants and fire extinguishers. This damage to our precious artwork and statues will require expert cleaning and conservation."[17]

Blanton's estimate made big headlines. "Capitol Riot Costs Will Exceed $30 Million, Official Tells Congress," the *New York Times* reported on February 24. An NPR headline screamed, "Architect Of The Capitol Outlines $30 Million In Damages From Pro-Trump Riot," on the same day.

That wasn't true, either. In seeking restitution from January 6 defendants, the Justice Department admitted the building only sustained about $1.5 million in damages. It is unknown how much of that was actually caused by police officers using chemical sprays inside the building.

After reinforcing the Democrats' narrative that January 6 was a deadly, dangerous terror attack, the USCP announced plans to take its show on the road. On the six-month anniversary of the Capitol protest, Pittman introduced a long list of initiatives the agency would pursue including the purchase of new equipment and "state-of-the-art campus surveillance technology, which will enhance the ability to detect and monitor threat activity." The wellness program would be expanded and new officers would be hired.

---

17   Julie Kelly, *Another January 6 Falsehood: $30 Million in Damages to the Capitol* (American Greatness, 2021).

Citing an enhanced threat against lawmakers, Pittman said the unaccountable agency would expand beyond the borders of Washington, D.C.: "The Department is also in the process of opening Regional Field Offices in California and Florida with additional regions in the near future to investigate threats to Members of Congress." Pittman had claimed in congressional testimony that the number of threats against members of Congress had doubled since 2017 with the "overwhelming majority of suspects residing outside" Washington, D.C.

"Tim Barber, a USCP spokesman, said the plan was to open several additional regional offices as the department charged with protecting Congress transforms itself in the aftermath of the attack, which exposed serious deficiencies in the Capitol Police's gathering and dissemination of intelligence, preparedness and training," the *New York Times* reported on July 6. "Much like the Secret Service, which has field offices in multiple states and countries, the Capitol Police need to be able to monitor and quickly investigate threats against lawmakers wherever they occur, Mr. Barber said."

So a secret police force shielded from complying with public accountability laws and clearly beholden to Democrat politicians will operate offices across the country, face no scrutiny, and harass citizens and lawmakers they deem to be "threats."

What could possibly go wrong?

In the months following the Capitol protest, the U.S. Capitol Police did nothing to earn the public's trust. The agency's lawyers, in coordination with the Justice Department, fought attempts to access 14,000 hours of footage that could give the public a broader picture as to what happened on January 6 as major parts of the original narrative—the death of Officer Sicknick, the idea it was an "armed insurrection," the accusation it was "incited" by President Trump's speech earlier in the day, which contradicted simultaneous claims the event had been pre-planned by militia groups—crumbled under scrutiny. USCP and the Justice Department also denied requests seeking access to email correspondence between USCP officials, the

Capitol Police board and other entities including the FBI and Department of Homeland Security.

The security system footage and the emails, USCP argued, are not public records. "For the USCP to function and properly execute its mission, its leadership must be able to communicate, including by email, without fear or apprehension that those messages will be made public merely upon request," the Justice Department wrote in response to a lawsuit filed by Judicial Watch seeking the documents. "This is especially so during rapidly unfolding, dangerous events such as the January 6 attack on the Capitol. Court-ordered disclosure of these emails would undoubtedly chill those important communications. Releasing the requested email correspondence to the public could frustrate the investigation of the House Select Committee or other congressional committees, and could also be expected to compromise ongoing criminal proceedings against those who attacked the Capitol."

A lawyer for USCP stated that he searched for emails between the acting chief and the FBI, DOJ, and DHS between January 1 and January 10, 2021. "I reviewed approximately 214 emails located by that search, the majority of which were duplicates of one another," James W. Joyce, general counsel for the agency, said in an affidavit. "These emails primarily concern Inauguration preparations, concerns and condolences regarding officer injuries and fatalities, personal correspondence about Chief Steven Sund's resignation and Acting Chief Pittman's elevation, and fencing."

In September, the agency announced the results of thirty-eight internal investigations related to complaints about officer conduct on January 6.[18] The USCP's Office of Professional Responsibility identified twenty-six officers; twenty were cleared of any wrongdoing. Of the remaining six officers, three were cited for "conduct unbecoming," one was cited for failure to comply with commands, one was cited for "improper remarks" and one was cited for improperly disseminating information. All six were referred for disciplinary action.

---

18   United States Capitol Police, *Press Release—UPDATE: USCP's January 6 Internal Investigations* (United States Capitol Police, 2021).

Once again claiming confidentiality privileges, the agency did not disclose the names of the officers involved—except for one Capitol Police officer who was indicted on two charges of obstruction for advising an acquaintance to delete possibly incriminating social media posts. The officer, Michael Riley, responded to the pipe bomb alert in the early afternoon of January 6. No suspect was charged and the alleged perpetrator who set the pipe bombs still has not been identified.

Just like everything else related to the Capitol Police, there appeared to be more to the story as to why Riley, of the hundreds of USCP officers on the scene, including several who either attacked protesters or let them into the building, has been charged. In a message to his unnamed acquaintance, Riley said he "agrees with your political stance," presumably meaning that Riley is himself a Trump supporter. He then warned the man that the Justice Department would start charging everyone inside the building; after he learned the man had turned himself into the FBI on January 20, Riley deleted the Facebook messages between the two.

Why did USCP wait to charge Riley nearly nine months later? Was he singled out because he was a Trump supporter? We may never know.

But nothing damaged the agency's credibility more than the killing of Ashli Babbitt. The agency's handling of her shooting should give all Americans pause—and prompt Republicans in Congress to raise hell—about USCP plans to expand its reach across the country.

CHAPTER SEVEN:

DID ASHLI BABBITT HAVE TO DIE?

ASHLI BABBITT WAS ON VACATION in Mexico with her husband, Aaron, in late 2020 when she decided to go to Washington on January 6. "She was an avid Trump supporter, she knew that's where she had to be," Micki Witthoeft, Ashli's mom, told me in an interview in July. "She went to all the [Trump] rallies if there was one nearby. She was the political one at our house."[1]

Ashli traveled from her home in California, where she and Aaron operated a pool cleaning business, to the nation's capital. After watching the president's speech, she, like tens of thousands of Trump supporters, headed toward Capitol Hill. A clip of Ashli walking to the Capitol, Witthoeft said, is the only video she has seen of her daughter that day. In the video, Ashli boasted (implausibly) that three million "patriots" were in Washington to support Donald Trump. "That brings me peace. She was in her zone, so happy, having a great day. Until that son-of-a-bitch shot her," Witthoeft told me.

At 2:43 p.m. on January 6, a U.S. Capitol Police officer shot Ashli as she attempted to climb through a broken window in front of the Speaker's Lobby, a long hallway adorned with paintings of past speakers. (In 2020, Pelosi ordered the removal of four portraits of former speakers who had served in the Confederate Army.)

---

1   Julie Kelly, *Ashli Babbitt's Mom Speaks* (American Greatness, 2021).

Draped in a Trump flag, the unarmed Air Force veteran is seen shouting at three police officers guarding the doorway. At one point, she jumps up and down, clearly agitated. The officers talk calmly among themselves then inexplicably walk away, at which point three men smash the doors' windows with a flagpole and a helmet. "Break it down! Let's fucking go!" one man screams.

Off to the left, an officer with a gloved hand aims his gun diagonally toward a broken window through which Ashli is climbing. "There's a gun! Gun!," a man screams.

The officer takes a step forward and fires one shot; Ashli falls backwards, hit in the neck. People scream. Several police officers attempt to treat her wound while protesters who witnessed the shooting begin yelling at the officers. They attempt to clear people out of the jammed hallway.

The appalling video released months later on Tucker Carlson's three-part documentary shows three Capitol officers carrying her body, face up and head-first, down a set of stairs before attempting to administer any medical assistance–and transported her to Washington Hospital Center where she was pronounced dead.

Witthoeft, fifty-seven, told me her oldest child was a "tomboy" who was "determined and strong willed." Ashli decided in high school she wanted to join the military, so her mom had to sign a document that allowed Ashli to enroll in the Air Force at age seventeen. The terror attacks of September 11, 2001, which occurred while Ashli was in high school, "strengthened her conviction to serve."

Ashli graduated from high school in 2013. On her twenty-first birthday, Witthoeft told me, Ashli suffered life-threatening injuries following an explosion at Camp Bucca detention facility in Iraq; she was airlifted to a hospital in Germany.

She served in the U.S. Air Force for fourteen years with eight tours overseas. After her death, the *Air Force Times* reported that "Babbitt…was on active duty from April 2004 to April 2008, and was a reservist from October 2008 to July 2010. The Air National

Guard said she was a guardsman from July 2010 to July 2016." Her deployments included Afghanistan, Iraq and the United Arab Emirates. She was awarded the Iraq Campaign Medal and the Global War on Terrorism Expeditionary Medal. Ashli was a security forces airman, providing security at Air Force bases, and achieved the rank of senior airman. Contrary to deceptive media portrayals, Ashli was not a "trained military killer."

Witthoeft's daughter-in-law called her on January 6 with the news that Ashli had been shot. "We knew from the news reports that someone had been shot and killed at the Capitol. So when she called to say Ashli was shot, I just knew. I could tell in her voice. We hoped there was time to pack a bag and get to D.C., but there wasn't."

During an interview for "Capitol Punishment," a documentary on January 6 produced by filmmaker Nick Searcy, Ashli's husband Aaron described how he learned his wife was dead. "I got that phone call saying they saw Ashli on TV and my heart sank," he told Searcy. "You just go numb at that point." Aaron said he saw her laying on the ground; news channels aired the scene over and over. "I recognized the clothes she was wearing, her face. The side profile of her hair."

Aaron, physically fit with a long beard, gravely voice and tatoos on one arm, said he "went into a panic" and knew at that moment "she was looking for me." He started calling hospitals, trying to get information about her whereabouts. When his brother called the D.C. Metro police department, the dispatcher said, "Somebody's already called here, we didn't effin shoot her."

Then, Aaron said, the officer hung up on his brother.

Ashli was cremated and her ashes scattered in the Pacific Ocean near her favorite dog beach in February. An animal lover, Ashli's German Shepherd died of grief when she did not return home.

But like everything else related to January 6, the normal rules did not apply to the death of Ashli Babbitt.

Usually, when a police officer shoots and kills an unarmed suspect in plain sight, the name of the officer is quickly released.

Cyberspace is filled with demands for justice; the victim is glorified no matter the circumstances.

The nation submits to collective soul-searching about how such a thing could happen in America. Lawmakers and celebrities console the family; the officer's social media account, work history, and personal life are fully vetted by the news media and given wall-to-wall coverage. If the shooter is white and the victim is black, the officer is vilified as a racist even if race had nothing to do with it.

None of that happened after Ashli Babbitt was shot and killed. The media had no interest in reporting the name of the federal officer who killed her, only interest in Babbitt's history and political views. Ashli, in the days after her death, got what she deserved as both a Trump supporter and alleged adherent to QAnon, according to the news media.

Ashli's political views, such as believing the election was stolen, automatically made her a QAnon conspiracist in the eyes of the liberal media. But even if she had been a hardcore follower of QAnon—so what? Believing in weird or farfetched theories isn't a crime. Do those who still believe the 2016 election was stolen by Vladimir Putin deserve to die for their wrongheaded views? Of course not. In Ashli's case, however, allegations she followed QAnon seemed to make her shooting a justified homicide.

"Woman Killed in Capitol Embraced Trump and QAnon," blared the headline of a January 7 *New York Times* article: "Her social media accounts suggest that she also, increasingly, embraced the conspiratorial thinking of QAnon, which has asserted that the 2020 presidential election was stolen by an elite Satan-worshiping cabal, and that it was up to ordinary people to reinstate Mr. Trump. Her social media feed was a torrent of messages celebrating President Trump; QAnon conspiracy theories; and tirades against immigration, drugs and Democratic leaders in California." In other words, she got what she deserved.

The first paragraph of an NBC News article on her death said nothing about her status as a veteran or questioned what led to her shooting. "Ashli Babbitt, the woman who was shot and killed Wednesday in the riot in the halls of the U.S. Capitol, apparently by Capitol Police, was an ardent supporter of President Donald Trump and a follower and promoter of many well-known radical conservative activists as well as leaders of the QAnon conspiracy theory movement, according to her social media profiles," reporters Brandy Zadronzy and Mosheh Gains wrote on January 7. "Babbitt's Twitter account was almost singularly focused on radical conservative topics and conspiracy theories. Babbitt was a loyal Fox News watcher, according to thousands of tweets to Fox News hosts, but she also engaged on social media with the conspiracy news internet site InfoWars. In 2020, Babbitt began to tweet with QAnon accounts and use QAnon hashtags. QAnon conspiracy theorists subscribe to a false belief that high-profile Democrats and Hollywood celebrities are ritually sacrificing children and that Trump is fighting to stop it."

Claiming QAnon supporters were "central to the storming of the Capitol," Vice reporter David Gilbert on January 7 documented several of Babbitt's Q-related tweets including a photo of her wearing a Q t-shirt in September 2020. The *Los Angeles Times* traced Babbitt's "radical path [that] led to Trump, Qanon, and a deadly insurrection" in a January 7 article.

There is zero evidence for Gilbert's claim that QAnon supporters were "central" to storming the Capitol. How would he even know such a thing? But of course, he was not required to provide any because his readers (and his editors) already believed it was true. It was a logical extension of the narrative they had spent four years constructing about Trump and his supporters.

Time magazine claimed Babbitt's death would be used to recruit domestic terrorists. "Babbitt's emergence as a martyr for many of the different groups that made up the pro-Trump mob is no surprise," Vera Bergengruen wrote on January 10 in a lengthy article that unconvincingly attempted to tie the Capitol riot to the history of white supremacy. "White women's deaths have long been leveraged for propaganda, from the 19th century Ku Klux Klan to the militia movements of the 1990s to Donald Trump's 2016 presidential campaign, which often invoked their killing at the hands of undocumented immigrants." A security expert told Bergengruen that "this woman will be used as a martyr figure to inspire others to radicalize towards violence."

The *Washington Post* immediately tasked four reporters to scrub Ashli's social media accounts, review court and military records, and interview family and friends. Her journey to MAGA world, the reporters wrote on January 10, "was one of paranoid devotion and enthusiasm that only increased as Trump's fortunes waned. She avidly followed the QAnon conspiracy theory, convinced that Trump was destined to vanquish a cabal of child abusers and Satan-worshiping Democrats. She believed Wednesday would be 'the storm,' when QAnon mythology holds that Trump would capture and execute his opponents.

The paper noted her "undistinguished military career" and "personal travails." Backing Donald Trump, the *Post* concluded, "gave her life purpose." Her name was certain to "become synonymous with the feverish movement that had propelled thousands of Americans to desecrate a pillar of their government."

Some online bloggers were even less kind. Writing for Medium on January 8, writer Manny Otiko called Babbitt a traitor who fought against her own country and died because she bought into "ridiculous conspiracy theories." Babbitt, Otiko warned, didn't merit any sympathy or memorial tributes. "She should be remembered as a terrorist, like Timothy McVeigh, who died because she couldn't tell B.S. from the truth."

Otiko's comparison is absurd and overheated. Timothy McVeigh famously blew up a Federal office building in Oklahoma City with a truckload of fertilizer that killed 168 people including fifteen children under the age of five. Ashli Babbitt was an unarmed civilian seeking access to the chambers of government. She probably shouldn't have been there, but the only person she put at risk by doing so was herself.

Rep. Markwayne Mullin, a Republican House member from Oklahoma, likewise claimed that the unnamed officer had no choice but to shoot Babbitt. "They were trying to come through the front door, which is where I was at in the chamber, and in the back they were trying to come through the speaker's lobby, and that's problematic when you're trying to defend two fronts," he told ABC's *Good Morning America* on January 7. "When they broke the glass in the back, the [police] lieutenant that was there—him and I already had multiple conversations prior to this—and he didn't have a choice at that time. The mob was going to come through the door, there was a lot of members and staff that were in danger at the time. And when he [drew] his weapon, that's a decision that's very hard for anyone to make and, once you draw your weapon like that, you have to defend yourself with deadly force."

Mullin praised law enforcement's "restraint" and insisted they "did the best they could" on January 6. (Photos later showed the officer holding his gun inside the chamber prior to the fatal confrontation with Babbitt.)

Only one House Republican, Rep. Darrell Issa of California, called Babbitt's family after the shooting. "I was confused as to why he was calling me because I don't live in his district but I figured out later it was because my business is in his district," Aaron Babbitt told Newsmax's Greg Kelly in April.

During the House impeachment trial, Rep. Eric Swalwell from Ashli's home state of California explained that "Ashli Babbitt attempted to climb through a shattered window into the House lobby. To protect the members in the lobby, an officer discharged his weapon." Swalwell later pushed back on her supposed "martyr" status. "This must be made clear & cemented as the ground truth: The officer who defended hundreds of people from Ashli Babbit (sic) & the armed mob behind her is an American hero. Don't take my word for it, DOJ investigated & justified his actions. My family is grateful for his bravery," Swalwell tweeted in July.

Small problem, though: there was no "armed mob" behind Ashli Babbitt. To the contrary, police officers were standing right behind her. At the time he made these comments, Swalwell must have known this very well.

Nor were there "hundreds of people" at risk: the chamber was relatively empty with the exception of a few lingering representatives and a number of police. One video showed people walking through the hallway unaware that a lethal threat in the form of a 5'2" unarmed woman lurked just yards away. Documents released months later indicated Byrd gave no warning to Ashli or anyone around her; Ashli would have easily been overpowered by the officers outside the door and arrested.

The video of Ashli's shooting went viral immediately—and the recording itself wasn't without controversy.

The moment was captured on film by John Sullivan, an independent journalist from Utah, also known as "Jayden X." Sullivan's background and role are ambiguous. In 2020, Sullivan was involved in the George Floyd protests; he founded a group called Insurgence USA to fight police brutality. During a June 2020 protest in Utah, Sullivan told the crowd that "racism is still real in America and that needs to change. It's not enough to voice your words, put those words into action... make change happen."

Sullivan was arrested in July for violence related to an altercation with pro-police protesters in Provo, Utah. He traveled to Portland several times during the summer of 2020 as a journalist-activist. The *Washington Examiner* reported Sullivan also ran "an antifa Discord server that featured other left-wing activists discussing tactics and strategy at protests."

In August 2020, according to a report by Fox News, Sullivan participated in a protest near the White House. "We...about to burn this s— down," Sullivan said. "We gotta...rip Trump right out of that office right there. We ain't about...waiting until the next election."

In sum, Sullivan has a proven pedigree as a left-wing activist. Yet on January 6, he showed up at the Capitol and recorded about ninety minutes of the protest. After he followed a crowd into the building, Sullivan is heard yelling, "There are so many people. Let's go. This shit is ours! Fuck yeah. We are all a part of this history." At another point in his video, Sullivan says, "We gotta get this shit burned," sounding every bit the pro-Trump firebrand.[2]

Trump supporters, after seeing Sullivan's video, smelled a rat. Why was a known BLM activist infiltrating a huge crowd of Trump supporters? Sullivan's presence and attempt to provoke the crowd, to many, seemed to prove that leftwing agitators played a more significant role in the riot than the media wanted to admit.

Sullivan continued to film the chaos inside until he reached the area outside the Speaker's lobby after 2:30 p.m. He described his experience shortly afterwards in a January 14 *Rolling Stone* profile:

> I remember just seeing, like, five or six guns just poke out of these doorways And I just remember screaming, 'Gun, there's a gun! There's a gun! Guys, there's a gun!' I see her start trying to climb through the window, and I'm like, 'Don't go in there, don't go in there,' but I know she could not hear me. So my thought was to get that moment on camera. I wanted to show the gun firing, and the bullet hitting her, and how she dropped to the ground. The guy who was pointing a gun at her was leaning with an intent to shoot; he was not playing. There's a difference between holding a gun up and warning somebody versus, like, really leaning into it. I was like, all right, I'm going to show the world why she died. And I'm not going to let her death go in vain. Because I didn't think that she deserved to die.

2   Jayden X, *The Insurrection Of The United States Capitol And Shooting Of Ashli Babbitt* (YouTube, 2021).

Sullivan continued: "I remember she dropped to the ground, and I don't think that's the part I was ready for. That was emotional for me. I remember just like looking into her eyes, like she was staring at me. She's just staring straight at me, and I just see her soul leave her body, just the light just leave her eyes. I felt a lot of anger, I felt a lot of sadness and sorrow, frustration. I don't think I could ever have prepared myself for it. This was the first time I saw somebody die. I'm still trying to deal with it." [need citation]

Sullivan reportedly sold his footage to CNN, NBC and other news outlets for $90,000. In February, he was indicted on several counts including civil disorder and trespassing. A superseding indictment handed down in May added more charges and sought the forfeiture of the money he collected for selling his footage.[3]

As the months wore on, however, one thing became clear: No one was supposed to film that shooting let alone capture any image of the federal officer responsible for her death.

*   *   *   *

The cover-up started less than twenty-four hours after Ashli died. USCP Chief Steven Sund confirmed her identity and that she died as a result of the shooting. "As per the USCP's policy, the USCP employee has been placed on administrative leave and their police powers have been suspended pending the outcome of a joint Metropolitan Police Department (MPD) and USCP investigation."

The media took Sund's cue. Every article and news segment for months omitted the name of the officer. And when some online sleuths incorrectly speculated about it, USCP quickly issued a statement. "As the investigation continues into the events of January 6, 2021, it's important to correct misinformation some in the media have reported, and that's been shared on social media," a February 23 press release read. "Reports identifying Special Agent David Bailey as the officer involved in the shooting in the Speak-

---

3   Grand Jury: *USA v. Sullivan, Indictment* (United States District Court, 2021).

er's Lobby are inaccurate. The Department will share additional information once the investigation is complete."[4]

Chalk it up as another lie by U.S. Capitol Police. The agency never disclosed the name of the officer—nor did the U.S. Department of Justice when it announced in April that the investigation into Ashli's shooting was closed and the officer involved would not face charges. The U.S. Attorney's Office for the District of Columbia, the same office handling the sprawling investigation into the Capitol breach, and the D.C. Metropolitan Police department allegedly conducted an investigation and "found insufficient evidence to support a criminal prosecution." The D.C. police department notified Ashli's family.

Investigators only considered whether the unidentified officer violated Ashli's civil rights under 18 U.S.C. § 242. "The investigation revealed no evidence to establish beyond a reasonable doubt that the officer willfully committed a violation of 18 U.S.C. § 242. Specifically, the investigation revealed no evidence to establish that, at the time the officer fired a single shot at Ms. Babbitt, the officer did not reasonably believe that it was necessary to do so in self-defense or in defense of the Members of Congress and others evacuating the House Chamber," the Justice Department concluded.[5]

The department apparently did not consider whether the officer used excessive force or possibly committed second-degree murder or manslaughter—charges typically filed against law enforcement officials who kill an individual while on duty. No—Ashli's death, unlike the case of George Floyd, was a civil rights matter, not a criminal one.

Once again, the media refused to demand the name of the now-exonerated officer. Journalists were uninterested in any aspect of the investigation; not one major news organization sought the details.

---

4   United States Capitol Police, *Press Release: U.S. Capitol Police Statement regarding Media Misidentification of Officer* (United States Capital Police, 2021).

5   United States Department of Justice, *Four Former Minneapolis Police Officers Indicted on Federal Civil Rights Charges for Death of George Floyd; Derek Chauvin Also Charged in Separate Indictment for Violating Civil Rights of a Juvenile* (DOJ News, 2021).

Tucker Carlson, one of the few media personalities willing to cover the increasingly egregious conduct of the Justice Department and Ashli's shooting, said the decision not to pursue charges was "the new standard for murder in our country." Carlson read a statement issued by Terry Roberts, the lawyer representing her family, that said they disagreed with the Justice Department's decision but would continue to pursue a civil lawsuit.

"The shooting death of US Veteran Ashli Babbit was murder, plain and simple," Carlson said on his April 15 show. "Babbitt did not represent a threat. The officer did not warn Babbit and disappeared after he shot her in cold blood. This case is far from over."

Republicans also started to take notice. Rep. Paul Gosar (R-Ariz.) confronted FBI Director Chris Wray during a June 15 congressional hearing:

> Gosar: Director Wray, do you know who executed Ashli Babbitt?

> Wray: No, I don't know the name of the person.

> Gosar: Do you agree that Ashli Babbitt was unarmed?

> Wray: No, I can't weigh in on the facts and circumstances of that case.

> Gosar: It's disturbing. A Capitol Police officer that did the shooting...appeared to be hiding, lying in wait and appeared to give no warning. When police officers around the

country are routinely identified after a shooting, why hasn't that officer been named?

Wray: I don't want to comment on that case. I haven't been directly involved in that and so I can't agree or disagree with your characterization.

Gosar: Do you believe in lethal force against unarmed citizens including a 100-pound woman?

Wray: I won't answer a hypothetical.

Gosar: That wasn't a hypothetical. That's actually what happened.

On July 6, Gosar issued a statement. "Six months ago today, Ashli Babbitt, a 110-pound woman with nothing in her hands, not a rock, not a stick or a bat, was shot dead by a still unknown Capitol Hill police officer. Her death has been ruled a homicide. Yet, we have very little information about her death." Gosar said he and Trump wanted answers about the officer who killed Ashli and an update on the investigations, noting that common practice after a police shooting involves releasing the name of the officer and circumstances before and after the deadly shooting. "It is unjust to sweep Ashli's death under the rug by merely saying she was in the wrong place at the wrong time, as so many have. Her life mattered. We do not allow the execution of citizens by street 'justice' in our country," Gosar said.

Donald Trump finally started raising the issue, too. In an email to supporters on July 1, Trump asked a simple question: "Who shot Ashli Babbitt?"

Voters wanted accountability from their representatives. A listener called into a North Dakota radio show on July 27 to press Senator Kevin Cramer, a Republican, to disclose the officer's name. Cramer's constituent told the first-term senator that the public had a right to know who killed Ashli. "Why do you have a right to know?" Cramer retorted. He then referred to Ashli as a "criminal" who did not comply with the officer's commands. When the caller pushed back, Cramer explained the officer wasn't a suspect in any crime and admitted he was "grateful" for his actions on January 6.[6]

*   *   *   *

Speculation swirled for months about the officer's identity. In July, Paul Sperry, an investigative reporter for Real Clear Investigations, confirmed his name: Lt. Michael L. Byrd. Sperry pointed to overlooked testimony by the acting House sergeant-at-arms who revealed Byrd as the officer who shot Ashli Babbitt. (Byrd's name was removed from C-SPAN and CNN transcripts of the congressional hearing.)

Sperry reported that the January 6 shooting wasn't the only time Byrd was careless with a firearm. "In February 2019, Lt. Byrd was investigated for leaving his department-issued Glock-22 firearm unattended in a restroom on the House side of the Capitol, even though the potent weapon, which fires .40-caliber rounds, has no manual safety to prevent unintended firing. Fortunately, the abandoned gun was discovered by another officer during a routine security sweep. A Glock-22 was used in the Babbitt shooting."[7]

Byrd finally came forward in August after USCP cleared him of any wrongdoing and concluded that his actions were "consistent" with agency policy. But more than seven months later, the agency still refused to publish his name. "The officer in this case, who is not being identified for the officer's safety, will not be fac-

6   Andrew Kaczynski, *Full Exchange With the Radio Caller, from the Jay Thomas Show Yesterday* (Twitter, 2021).
7   Paul Sperry, *Naming the Capitol Cop Who Killed Unarmed Jan. 6 Rioter Ashli Babbitt* (RealClearInvestigations, 2021).

ing internal discipline," USCP announced on August 23. "This officer and the officer's family have been the subject of numerous credible and specific threats for actions that were taken as part of the job of all our officers: defending the Congress, Members, staff and the democratic process."

A few days later, Byrd talked to NBC News' Lester Holt.[8] Holt started by claiming that Byrd, a black Capitol Police officer, had been "in hiding for months" after video of the shooting went viral. "They talked about killing me, cuttin' off my head, you know, very vicious and cruel things," Byrd said. Holt interrupted. "Racist things?" he prompted. Byrd said he was subjected to "racist things" as well.

Byrd, a twenty-eight-year veteran of the force, immodestly told Holt that he had showed the "utmost courage" on January 6. Indeed, he made several sketchy comments in the interview. He said he heard reports of "shots fired through the House main door onto the floor of the chamber," but Holt acknowledged those alleged reports were "false." Byrd also insisted he yelled commands at protesters, including Babbitt, to "get back, stop." But that account is not verified by any video or witnesses on the scene, including John Sullivan. There's also no indication Byrd gave Ashli any warning before firing his gun or that she could see him brandishing his weapon from her angle.

"I know that day I saved countless lives," Byrd told Holt. "I know members of Congress, as well as my fellow officers and staff, were in jeopardy and in serious danger. And that's my job." Incredibly, Byrd said that if he had to do it over again, even knowing she was unarmed, he would have still shot her.

Byrd's job also involved helping create optics related to January 6. Not only did he instruct lawmakers to put on gas masks because of a "disbursement" of tear gas in the building but also warned them to remove the pins that signified they were members of Congress. That move made headlines in the days after the Capitol protest.

---

8   Lester Holt, *Capitol Police Officer Who Killed Ashli Babbitt While Defending House Chamber Speaks Out* (YouTube, 2021).

Byrd teared up in the interview after Holt read part of the USCP statement commending him for "potentially sav[ing] Members and staff from serious injury and possible death" at the unarmed hands of Ashli Babbitt. "Those words meant a lot because that's exactly what I did," Byrd said.

He expressed no remorse or second thoughts; he didn't have to. Democrats and the news media had protected him for months, demonizing Ashli as a Trump fanatic and conspiracy nut, and explaining why her fate was deserved. Why would Byrd show any sympathy for her? His sense of accomplishment in the killing of an unarmed Trump supporter was endorsed by the most powerful interests in the country.

After the interview aired, Aaron Babbitt, Ashli's widower, had harsh words for Officer Byrd. "I don't even want to hear him talk about how he's getting death threats and he's scared," Aaron Babbitt told Tucker Carlson on August 26. "I've been getting death threats since January 7, two, three, five, 10 a day and all I did on January 6 was become a widower. So, you're going to have to suck it up, bud, and take it."[9]

Carlson himself, noting that armed officers were both in front of and behind Babbitt at the time, described her killing as an "execution." He mocked the idea that Babbitt posed a threat. "Michael Byrd executed an enemy of the Biden administration so they're praising him. In fact, he's the victim here." Carlson asked Terry Roberts, the family attorney, if he could recall a time when the name of an officer involved in a fatal had been concealed. "Not to my knowledge, I've never seen it," Roberts replied.

Correct. Because it never happened—until January 6. After that, the normal practices of law, journalism, and politics were discarded and replaced with secrecy, vengeance, and heartlessness.

Byrd's account gave the media another opportunity to misrepresent the events of January 6 while defending his actions. In his syndicated column, the *Washington Post's* Clarence Page

---

claimed "five officers" died—four from suicide plus Officer Sicknick's murder—because of the Capitol protest. "I, too, was saddened by Babbitt's death, not because I think she was a martyr but because she was so sadly misled," Page wrote. "She wasn't shot because of her beliefs as much as for her actions in service of Trump's big lie that Democrats were stealing the White House from its rightful Republican owners, regardless of dozens of court decisions that have decided otherwise."

George Washington University law professor Jonathan Turley, however, explained that Byrd's exoneration set a dangerous precedent, not to mention being an egregious double standard of justice. "Under this standard, hundreds of rioters could have been gunned down on Jan. 6—and officers in cities such as Seattle or Portland, Ore., could have killed hundreds of violent protesters who tried to burn courthouses, took over city halls or occupied police stations during last summer's widespread rioting." Given Byrd's accepted explanation for what he did, and the Justice Department's refusal to prosecute him, Byrd would have been justified in shooting "ten or more" people that day, Turley wrote.[10]

But the vitriol against Ashli Babbitt continued. The blogosphere was filled with more vilification of her as a QAnon fanatic who had it coming. Chauncey DeVaga, a writer for Salon, warned that Byrd would endure the "full weight of white supremacy" for killing a white woman.[11] Others cheered the death of a "traitor."

Given what we know about the actual events of that day Byrd's account of his own actions and experience seems highly overwrought. But it is also revealing insofar as it goes to the mindset of those inside the Capitol. Clearly they thought their lives were in danger. On the other hand, his comments also reflect a prejudicial view of Trump and his supporters, one that is widely shared among liberal elites, that these people are simply not rational and cannot be treated like normal citizens. They have no rights that anyone needs to recognize. Indeed, they are

---

10   Jonathan Turley, *Justified Shooting or Fair Game? Shooter of Ashli Babbitt Makes Shocking Admission* (JonathanTurley.org, 2021).

11   Chauncey Devega, *Black Cop Shoots White Woman: The Saga of Michael Byrd and Ashli Babbitt* (Salon, 2021).

not even human. They are mad dogs who need to be put down without remorse.

Internal documents obtained by Judicial Watch in October seemed to show that, contrary to the confident and bravado displayed in the Holt interview, Byrd was a mess after the shooting. One officer told investigators that Byrd was "shaking…he was nervous, teary-eyed, and appeared very upset. His voice also shaky when he called for medical assistance over the radio." His immediate emotional state belied the calm narrative he attempted to spin to the media.

"These previously secret records show there was no good reason to shoot and kill Ashli Babbitt," Judicial Watch President Tom Fitton stated after a review of the documents. "The Biden-Garland Justice Department and the Pelosi Congress have much to answer for over the mishandling and cover-up of this scandalous killing of an American citizen by the U.S. Capitol Police."

Meanwhile Ashli's mother has a message for those who continue to vilify her. "You only have awful things to say? Well, my daughter fought for your right to say them," she told me. "You're welcome."

CHAPTER EIGHT:

WHAT WAS THE ROLE OF THE FBI?

J UST AS THE INVESTIGATION into the "terror attack" of January 6 was in full swing, court proceedings in the alleged 2020 kidnapping of Governor Gretchen Whitmer began in Michigan. News of the shocking plot—several men alleged tied to militia groups planned to abduct Whitmer and leave her stranded on a boat or hold a "trial" over her lockdown policies—made headlines as early voting was underway in the critical swing state.

Trump and Whitmer sparred throughout 2020 over her refusal to reopen her state. On April 17, Trump tweeted demands to 'liberate" three states—Michigan, Virginia, and Minnesota. Washington Governor Jay Inslee quickly came to the defense of his three Democratic colleagues. Trump, Inslee tweeted, "is fomenting domestic rebellion and spreading lies" by insisting it was time to open back up after initial COVID-justified lockdowns.

When thirteen men allegedly tied to militia groups were arrested on October 7 on federal and state charges for planning to kidnap Whitmer from her Michigan vacation cottage, Team Biden and Whitmer herself made the most of the timely political gift. "There is a through line from President Trump's dog whistles and tolerance of hate, vengeance, and lawlessness to plots such as this one," Biden said in an October 9 statement. "He is giving oxygen to the bigotry and hate we see on the march in our country."

Whitmer, a first-term governor once rumored as a possible Biden running mate but now facing political headwinds over the state's protracted lockdown, embraced the role of victim. "When I put my hand on the Bible and took the oath of office 22 months ago, I knew this job would be hard. But I'll be honest, I never could have imagined anything like this," Whitmer said in a press conference the day the charges were announced. She claimed rightwing militias interpreted his "stand back and stand by" comment about the Proud Boys—even though the group was not involved in the kidnapping scheme—as a "rallying cry, as a call to action." (Trump's remark was made a week before the arrests; the plot had been hatched months before.)

It's impossible to know how or if the shocking news impacted voting at that time. But as defense lawyers prepared for the high-profile trial to begin in mid-2021, explosive revelations about the FBI's central involvement in the kidnapping plot threatened to undermine the government's case—and raised legitimate questions whether the agency conducted the same type of operation on January 6.

In a press release announcing the arrest of six of the plotters on federal charges, the Justice Department detailed the elaborate plan. "This group used operational security measures, including communicating by encrypted messaging platforms. On two occasions, members of the alleged conspiracy conducted coordinated surveillance on the Governor's vacation home…and discussed detonating explosive devices to divert police." The wanna-be kidnappers planned to use a taser gun on Whitmer then either abandon her in a boat on a nearby lake or transport her to Wisconsin to stand trial. "These alleged extremists undertook a plot to kidnap a sitting governor," the assistant FBI special agent in charge said in the statement. "Whenever extremists move into the realm of actually planning violent acts, the FBI Joint Terrorism Task Force stands ready to identify, disrupt, and dismantle their operations, preventing them from following through on those plans."

But the Justice Department's description failed to match reality as court documents and testimony would show. Far from the FBI thwarting the operation, the FBI itself enlisted participants, organized and funded training and surveillance trips, and used paid informants working with FBI agents to lure unsuspecting "militia" members into attempting to execute the plot.

The scheme centered around a group called the Wolverine Watchmen, an unknown "militia" group formed online in late 2019 by another man who faced state, not federal, charges related to the plot. (The man, Joseph Morrison, created a Facebook page for the new group four days after he was arrested on a weapons charge, which was pleaded down to a misdemeanor with time served—one day in jail.) It was essentially a small online group of malcontents, more smoke than fire.

An extensive expose published in July 2021 by BuzzFeed News detailed how the plot went down and the close involvement of at least twelve FBI agents and informants. Contradicting the government's early claims, the site's investigative reporters concluded the following: "An examination of the case by BuzzFeed News also reveals that some of those informants, acting under the direction of the FBI, played a far larger role than has previously been reported," Ken Bensinger and Jessica Garrison wrote on July 22. "Working in secret, they did more than just passively observe and report on the actions of the suspects. Instead, they had a hand in nearly every aspect of the alleged plot, starting with its inception. The extent of their involvement raises questions as to whether there would have even been a conspiracy without them."[1]

In April 2020, at an anti-lockdown rally in Michigan, alleged "militias" including the Three Percenters and the Wolverine Watchmen surrounded the Capitol building in Lansing. Protesters were clad in military garb, some carried weapons including firearms. An FBI informant who was present secretly

---

1   Ken Bensinger, Jessica Garrison, *Watching the Watchmen* (BuzzFeed News, 2021).

told his handlers via a recording device that one of the so-called militia groups was preparing to "breach" the building. "Then something surprising happened," Bensinger and Garrison explained. "The Michigan State Police stood down and let the protesters—including those in full tactical gear—enter the building unopposed. They could even bring their guns, so long as they submitted to a temperature check for COVID-19."

Photographers were inside snapping pictures of protesters clashing with law enforcement. Some banged on office doors, calling out for Whitmer; it's unknown if she was in the building at the time. A blow-by-blow account of the chaos was posted on social media including "menacing" photos of militiamen lined up in hallways and confronting police. News outlets from local stations to *Forbes* and CNN covered the protest.

A sentencing memo for the first defendant to plead guilty in the Whitmer case confirmed the group's original plan was another "attack" on the Michigan state house before the election. The plotters wanted "to recruit 200 people to storm the Capitol, try any politician they caught for 'treason,' and execute them by hanging them on live television."

As it turned out, however, the insurrectionary plot had the government's fingerprints all over it. Every man involved in the kidnapping scheme had an FBI handler. According to a filing by one defense lawyer, "the government has shared ID numbers linked to 12 confidential informants but, with one exception, has not provided background on how they were recruited, what payments they may have received from the FBI, where they are based, or what their names are." The lead informant, known as "Big Dan," was paid at least $54,000 by the FBI for seven months of work, a sum that included reimbursing him for a loss when he sold his home out of fear his identity would be revealed.

Further, BuzzFeed warned, defense lawyers could potentially "add weight to the theory that the administration is conducting a witch hunt against militant groups—and, by extension, that the

Jan. 6 insurrection was a black op engineered by the FBI." Such a suggestion sounds outlandish at first. But the parallels seemed to increase as more court filings in the Whitmer case coincided with other reporting on January 6.

Lawyers defending the men facing federal charges accused the government of entrapment. In September, defense counsel asked a federal judge in Michigan to delay the October trial date for ninety days, partially so investigators could probe the conduct of key FBI assets.

The FBI special agent in charge, Richard Trask, had been arrested in July for assaulting and attempting to choke his wife after the couple attended a swingers' party. Trask was fired a few months later and removed as a witness.

But that wasn't the full extent of the sketchy behavior by lead FBI agents. Special agent Jayson Chambers, while working the Whitmer case, also coaxed "Big Dan" to enlist another man in Virginia to concoct a plot to kill Virginia Governor Ralph Northam. Chambers made clear to "Big Dan" what he was supposed to convince "Frank," his target, a disabled Vietnam veteran, to do. "The mission is to kill the governor specifically," Chambers texted. He further instructed "Big Dan" to tell "Frank" how to build an explosive device, an approach similar to the one used in the Whitmer scheme.

Trask's partner, Special Agent Henrik Impola, encouraged "Big Dan" to delete texts after others in the group suspected he was working with the feds. Impola advised "Big Dan" to finger someone else as the informant. "Impola is telling his F.B.I. paid informant to lie and implicate someone else as a federal agent," one defense attorney wrote in a motion asking the government for all cell phone data between the men. "This behavior . . . casts a dark shadow over the credibility of this investigation." But the Whitmer caper was only part of a much larger undertaking by the FBI in 2020. Operation Cold Snap, BuzzFeed reported, was a "far-reaching, multi-state domestic terrorism investigation." A separate press release issued by the Justice Department announcing arrests in the Whitmer case confirmed that "the FBI began an investigation earlier this year after becoming aware through social media that a group of individuals was discussing the violent overthrow of certain government and law enforcement components." Special Agent Impola also testified that "he was aware of other FBI investigations in Baltimore and Milwaukee and Cincinnati and Indiana involving other militia members . . . who were attending the national conference in Dublin."

That conference was organized by one of the plot's leaders, a man named Stephen Robeson, a convicted felon—and a longtime FBI informant, according to one defense attorney. In June 2020, Robeson organized a "National Militia Conference" in Dublin, Ohio and urged his contacts from across the country to attend. (Robeson, in addition to being an FBI informant, also founded the Wisconsin chapter of the Three Percenters, again raising questions whether these groups are organic or constructs of the federal government.)

And there was another tie between the Whitmer plot and January 6 that may be more than mere coincidence: the head of the Detroit FBI field office, the agency that managed the informants and agents involved in the Whitmer caper, was promoted as head of the D.C. Field Office. He would play a central role in directing the bureau's national dragnet to find and arrest "insurrectionists" after January 6.

[NB I have trimmed the D'Antuono material so that it is limited to factual statements, without the heavy innuendo, and cut the reference to Wray's whereabouts because no actual point is being made and the subject is not raised again.] Now, why would Steven D'Antuono, who just pulled of what the public at the time believed was a massive sting operation to catch militia men who wanted to abduct the governor of one of the largest states in the country, quickly be moved to Washington, D.C.?

The Whitmer drama provided a compelling backdrop to what was happening in the government's biggest January 6 conspiracy case. Distrust of the FBI was sky-high among Republicans for the agency's corrupt investigation into Donald Trump's 2016 presidential campaign, which included illicit FISA warrants and the use of confidential human sources. Suspicions that the FBI participated in the chaotic events of January 6 would not be hard to bolster among most rank-and-file Republicans.

During the Trump era, Democrats and Republicans abandoned their traditional positions on federal law enforcement. The Republican Party that embraced the Patriot Act and generally trusted the agency to work within legal and Constitutional constraints now viewed the FBI as a crucial part of the "Deep State," a hostile agent loyal to the Democratic Party. Democrats and progressives who historically viewed the FBI as a rights-crushing, racists Gestapo of sorts suddenly canonized people like former FBI deputy director Andrew McCabe.

One fact was not up for dispute, however; the agency has a long history of meddling in domestic political affairs starting with J. Edgar Hoover, the FBI director whose name is emblazoned on FBI headquarters in Washington. Hoover authored a memo in 1956 that called for the agency to track Americans he perceived as enemies of the state. The new program, COINTELPRO, launched that year to surveil suspected members of the Communist Party in the United States. Gradually, other groups–the Ku Klux Klan, the Black Panther Party, Puerto Rican nationalists, and the Socialist Worker's Party–were added to COINTELPROs target list.

Some of the abuses ended after the Church Commission, a Senate select committee tasked with investigating COINTELPRO, accused the FBI of acting unlawfully. "What happened to turn a law enforcement agency into a law violator? Why do those involved still believe their actions were not only defensible, but right?" the committee's final report asked.

In the early 1990s, the FBI accelerated its focus on the white Christian Right after the events at Waco, Texas and Ruby Ridge; the FBI launched PATCON, short for Patriot Conspiracy, an alleged movement of Christian extremists. In one case, the FBI created a fictional rightwing militia group to use it as an organ to collect information about other suspected militia members. "The tactics of FBI agents infiltrating militias, as well as paid informants being coerced into spying on these groups, and, in some instances, even providing the means and encouragement to carry out violent plots before being arrested, have been criticized as constituting entrapment by using agent provocateurs—agents posing as criminals to justify the financial and social expenses of counter-terrorism," a 2011 study published by Rutger's University concluded.

Was this the case with January 6?

A small handful of journalists not buying in to the groupthink of January 6 started raising more red flags. In June, Revolver News, a new website founded by Darren Beattie, a former aide to Donald Trump, published a lengthy report raising questions about the number of unindicted co-conspirators in the Oath Keepers case, including Stewart Rhodes.[2] Rhodes is widely accepted as "Person One" in the multi-defendant case. Communications between Rhodes and other Oath Keepers conspirators were cited as evidence in every case; it was obvious he was calling the shots.

But nine months after the first arrests, he was still a free man.

"Given…Stewart Rhodes's actions and words leading up to and on 1/6, and given that Rhodes is the leader of the major militia group associated with 1/6—why no indictment for Rhodes?" Beattie asked. Citing similarities to the Whitmer case, Beattie continued, "If it turns out that an extraordinary percentage of the members of these groups involved in planning and executing the Capitol Siege were federal informants or undercover operatives, the implications would be nothing short of staggering. This would be far worse than the already bad situation of the government knowing about the possibility of violence and doing nothing. Instead, this would imply that elements of the federal government were active instigators in the most egregious and spectacular

---

2   Darren Beattie, *Unindicted Co-Conspirators in 1/6 Cases Raise Disturbing Questions of Federal Foreknowledge* (Revolver, 2021).

aspects of 1/6, amounting to a monumental entrapment scheme used as a pretext to imprison otherwise harmless protestors at the Capitol—and in a much larger sense used to frame the entire MAGA movement as potential domestic terrorists."

Given the FBI's long history of using false-front groups as flypaper to attract dangerous radicals, and then moving them to commit actionable crimes, this kind of speculation seems far from unreasonable.

Beattie's reporting went viral, earning hits on "Tucker Carlson Tonight" and scorn by the media and those invested in the January 6 "insurrection" narrative. Rhodes then gave an interview, which seemed more like damage control, to the *New York Times* that revealed he had been interviewed by the FBI in May. "Against the advice of a lawyer, Mr. Rhodes spoke freely with the agents about the Capitol assault for nearly three hours," reporter Alan Feuer wrote in a July 9 article. Rhodes told Feuer that his underlings had "gone off mission" and that he was "frustrated" so many entered the building. "Prosecutors overseeing the investigation of Mr. Rhodes have long admitted that they have struggled to make a case against him. His activities seemed to stay within the boundaries of the First Amendment, one official with knowledge of the matter said."

But Rhodes' posts and texts before January 6 were highly inflammatory, and contradicted his portrayal in the *Times*. Further, the argument that his online activity and his conduct that day—he did not enter the building, but neither did dozens of other protesters nonetheless charged for various crimes—were protected by the First Amendment also contradicted the government's stance that the events of January 6 rose to the crime of insurrection, not a legitimate political protest. That certainly wasn't the case for Thomas Caldwell, one of the first Oath Keepers arrested and indicted, who also did not enter the building.

Beattie followed up his initial reports with an updated piece in October that summarized the Justice Department's nine-month prosecution of the Oath Keepers.[3] Rhodes, Beattie explained, established the conspiracy, recruited the people involved, gave instructions including the use of illegal weapons, and activated the conspiracy, including the entrance into the building in a stack formation, that afternoon. Still, Rhodes remained uncharged.

So did a man named Ray Epps. In another bombshell at Revolver, Beattie noted that despite egging on protesters on both January 5 and 6, the government had not charged Epps with any offense. He is clearly seen on at least three occasions encouraging people to storm the Capitol. During a confrontation between Trump supporters and BLM/Antifa activists at Black Lives Matter Plaza across from the White House late on January 5, Epps told Trump supporters what they need to do the next day. "We need to go *in* to the Capitol," Epps, wearing a Trump hat, yelled, pointing east toward the building. "Peacefully!"

Some people smell a rat. They loudly shout "no" in response and a few start chanting "Fed! Fed! Fed!"

For ninety minutes, Epps, who looks and sounds every bit the aging Marine sergeant that he is, tried to convince people to head to the Capitol on January 6. The next day, Epps is at it again. Shortly after Trump began his speech around noon, Epps is seen hollering at passersby, "After the speech, we are going to the Capitol. Where our problems are!" A half hour later, Epps whispered into the ear of Ryan Samsel just seconds before Samsel charged up the steps and became the first to breach the police line on the west side of the Capitol.

As it turns out, Epps is more than a retired Marine who loves his country. He also is the former head of the Arizona chapter of the Oath Keepers, the group still run by Stewart Rhodes. They are photographed together at various events in 2011.

Beattie also noted that after landing on the FBI's most wanted Capitol protesters roster as early as January 8, Epps' photo was quietly scrubbed from the list in July.

3   Darren Beattie, *Federal Protection of "Oath Keepers" Kingpin Stewart Rhodes Breaks The Entire Capitol "Insurrection" Lie Wide Open* (Revolver, 2021).

But despite overwhelming evidence that Epps repeatedly attempted to incite the crowd over an eighteen-hour period, by November 1, he had still not been arrested. How could a man on the FBI's most wanted list for six months, then suspiciously removed, remain scot-free while others accused of mere trespassing were hunted down by the FBI?

A few days after Beattie's piece was posted, Attorney General Merrick Garland testified before the House Judiciary Committee. Rep. Tom Massie played a video montage of Epps' clips from January 5 and 6 and challenged Garland to explain them.

> Massie: You said this is one of the most sweeping [investigations] in history. Have you seen that video, or those frames from that video?

> Garland: So as I said at the outset, one of the norms of the Justice Department is to not comment on pending investigations, and particularly not to comment on particular scenes or particular individuals.

> Massie: I was hoping today to give you an opportunity to put to rest the concerns that people have that there were federal agents or assets of the federal government present on January 5 and January 6. Can you tell us, without talking about particular incidents or particular videos, how many agents or assets of the federal government were present on January 6, whether they agitated to go into the Capitol, and if any of them did?

> Garland: So I'm not going to violate this norm of, of, of, the rule of law.

Inconsistencies are also appearing in the prosecution of the Proud Boys. Enrique Tarrio, the head of the group, was arrested on January 4 in Washington on an outstanding warrant for burning a Black Lives Matter flag during a counterprotest in December 2020. Tarrio also had two high-capacity firearm magazines in his car at the time of his arrest.

As part of his release, Tarrio was ordered to leave the city; he could not attend the protest on January 6. (The release was temporary. In August, Tarrio was sentenced to five months in prison for the offenses.) Yet Tarrio, up until that point, had led most of the pre-planning discussions about what the Proud Boys would do on January 6. The fact he wasn't actually in the city that day doesn't override the fact he was intimately involved beforehand. As with Rhodes, any "conspiracy" to "attack" the Capitol came at the direction of Tarrio.

The timing of his arrest, which prevented him from joining a large group of Proud Boys on January 6, and the fact he had not been named in any Proud Boy indictment led to speculation he might be working with the feds.

After all, he had done so before. A January 2021 report by Reuters revealed that Tarrio had a history as a government informant. "A Federal Bureau of Investigation agent and Tarrio's own lawyer described his undercover work and said he had helped authorities prosecute more than a dozen people in various cases involving drugs, gambling and human smuggling,' Aram Roston disclosed in the January 27 article. "The records uncovered by Reuters are startling because they show that a leader of a far-right group now under intense scrutiny by law enforcement was previously an active collaborator with criminal investigators." Tarrio's cooperation with the government came after he was charged in 2012 for fraud.

When asked for comment, Tarrio told Roston he didn't "recall any of this."

Then came a bombshell from the *New York Times*: the group of Proud Boys in the capital on January 6 included at least two federal informants who were in constant communication with their FBI handlers. "The informant, who started working with the F.B.I. in July 2020, appears to have been close to several other members of his Proud Boys chapter, including some who have been charged in the attack," Alan Feuer wrote on September 25. The *Times* had received access to confidential records documenting the informants' activities. "The F.B.I. also had an additional informant with ties to another Proud Boys chapter that took part in the sacking of the Capitol."[4]

In passing, let it be noted that the term "sacking" connotes burning, pillage and looting such as last occurred in Washington during the War of 1812. This kind of loose terminology is constantly applied to the events of January 6, fostering public confusion and a misleading view of what transpired.

Aside from the revelation about FBI informants within the Proud Boys during the Capitol protest, Feuer also suggested that the information did not prove the Proud Boys conspired to "stop, delay, or hinder Congress' certification of the Electoral College vote," as the government alleged in indictments. The informant, according to the documents Feuer viewed, repeatedly said the Proud Boys' plan was to maintain a defensive posture and prepare to fight leftist agitators such as Antifa.

A few weeks later, Feuer followed up with an article over a dispute between Joe Biggs, the Proud Boys leader on the ground that day, and Ryan Samsel, one of the first protesters to knock down barriers around 1:00 p.m. on January 6. Video shows the two briefly speaking before Samsel confronted Capitol police stationed in front of a slim row of metal racks. Samsel told investigators, according to Feuer, that Biggs urged him to breach the line. "[W]hen he hesitated, the Proud Boys leader flashed a gun, questioned his manhood and repeated his demand to move upfront and challenge the police."

---

4   Alan Feuer, *Among Those Who Marched Into the Capitol on Jan. 6: An F.B.I. Informant* (New York Times, 2021).

Biggs' attorney denied Samsel's account, telling Feuer that Biggs was not armed on January 6. But the account added a new wrinkle to what may have transpired in the moments before the group of Proud Boys first overran barriers and law enforcement.

Biggs also had a relationship with the FBI. He turned himself in to two agents, including "one he'd known for a long time," according to his lawyer, on January 20. In a court filing, Biggs' lawyers described how his client routinely met and spoke with the FBI, including agents at the Portland FBI field office, about his plans to organize Proud Boys rallies in that city as a counterdemonstration to Antifa protests. In 2018, FBI agents in Florida, where Biggs lives, started questioning "what Biggs meant by something politically or culturally provocative he had said on the air or on social media concerning a national issue, political parties, the Proud Boys, Antifa or other groups," his lawyer wrote.

In July 2020, Biggs met for two hours with two FBI agents in Daytona Beach to seek any information Biggs might have about Antifa networks in Florida. Biggs and the agents continued to communicate regularly; on January 16, Biggs contacted one of the Daytona Beach agents to discuss his involvement in the January 6 protest. The Proud Boy leader turned himself in a few days later. He has remained behind bars, denied bail, ever since.

Obviously, the FBI knew what Biggs was up to for months before the January 6 protest. He was in close contact with agents; it's hard to imagine Biggs did not inform them what the group's plans were for January 6.

Unanswered questions about what the FBI did—or didn't do—before and after January 6 persisted throughout 2021. With trials delayed until mid-2022, embarrassing disclosures confirming the presence at the Capitol of FBI informants or undercover agents would remain secret for months—unless regime-friendly outlets like the *Times* were allowed to get in front of the disclosures first.

But one fact not in dispute was the FBI's nationwide manhunt to round up January 6 protesters in a show of force usually reserved for the country's most dangerous criminals. Agents were let loose to capture hundreds of Capitol protesters in their own homes or their place of work. Families were awakened at dawn by armed officers screaming commands, children were terrified, neighbors were horrified. The over-the-top displays were intended to inflict maximum fear and humiliation. The stories were something straight out of a totalitarian nightmare.

*   *   *   *

"Mommy, why are they locking Daddy's hands?"

The little girl heard asking the question on a home security video is the daughter of Casey Cusick, the vice president of Global Outreach Ministries in Melbourne, Florida. Cusick and his father, James, the founder of the church, were arrested on the same day for entering the Capitol on January 6.

FBI agents went to Casey Cusick's home on June 24 with an arrest and search warrant; the officers, with guns drawn, asked the family to exit the home so they could "clear this residence." Casey's wife, carrying a toddler on her hip and holding the hand of her three-year-old daughter, asks repeatedly to see the warrant but officers ignore her.

About fifteen minutes away, Casey's father, a seventy-three-year-old pastor, Vietnam War veteran, and Purple Heart recipient, was handcuffed in front of his adult daughter, Staci, and their neighbors. "[T]here's just no reason for it. He did nothing to deserve what we saw this morning," Staci later told a reporter for the Gateway Pundit. "I don't understand why they would feel okay doing this to someone like him. I think they felt bad about it, but they kept saying it's their job." Agents confiscated the clothes he wore to the protest on January 6.

So what crime did the Cusicks commit that required such a show of force, a display that traumatized their family including young children? The same four misdemeanors charged in the overwhelming majority of Capitol breach cases: Entering and Remaining in a Restricted Building, Disorderly and Disruptive Conduct in a Restricted Building, Violent Entry and Disorderly Conduct in a Capitol Building, and Parading, Demonstrating, or Picketing in a Capitol Building.

And what, exactly, did the agents think they would find in their homes nearly six months after the protest? Firearms they never used? Detailed plans to lead the "insurrection?" Incriminating MAGA hats?

What happened to the Cusicks happened all over the country for months as the FBI executed raids of people's homes, even those charged with low level offenses. The purpose is clear; to humiliate the accused in front of their neighbors and give fodder to local news reporters who can breathlessly tell their viewers that an "insurrectionist" lives among them.

FBI Director Chris Wray boasts during congressional hearings that every one of the FBI's fifty-six field offices is involved in the Capitol breach probe. From Alaska to New York, homes have been ransacked and reputations crushed. The accused were often interrogated for hours without a lawyer present and before a warrant was shown.

Since mid-January, the FBI's Joint Terrorism Task Force has conducted excessive raids related to the Capitol breach probe, creating their own campaign of terror in the process. Coincidentally—or perhaps not—D'Antuono, the FBI brass whom Wray moved from the Detroit field office to Washington, D.C. just a few weeks before the election, promised a scorched earth approach. "Just because you've left the D.C. region, you can still expect a knock on the door if we find out that you were part of criminal activity inside the Capitol. Bottom line—the FBI is not sparing any resources in this investigation," D'Antuono said in a January 8 statement.

He wasn't kidding.

In one instance, residents in a Cape Coral, Florida neighborhood watched in the early morning hours of March 12 as the FBI barricaded their street in preparation to search the home of Christopher Worrell, an alleged member of the Proud Boys. A Fort Myers television station reported that the raid involved "armed men with helmets and a tanker truck." One neighbor confirmed the agents broke down the front door of Worrell's modest home where he lives with his girlfriend. "This was a little too much when you see FBI and SWAT teams. They were taking duffel bags out," Lynn Elias told a reporter for WINK-TV.

Agents were wearing "whole outfits like [the] military" and arrived in "six or seven...big black vehicles." Worrell, however, was not home. His girlfriend connected agents with Worrell by phone. The FBI instructed Worrell to turn himself in at the Sarasota field office; Worrell refused, drove back home, and was arrested later that day. He was indicted in April on several counts including using pepper spray against law enforcement. Worrell never entered the Capitol building on January 6; he was ordered detained and transferred to the D.C. jail.

In another Florida raid a few months later, a neighbor of Olivia and Jonathan Pollock, siblings accused of assaulting police on January 6, told a local reporter he "grabbed his gun" around 5:30 a.m. on June 30 when he heard the sounds of explosive devices outside his home. The FBI had surrounded the Pollocks' rural property in Lakeland to execute a search warrant and, according to video taken by the neighbor, agents used flashbangs and bullhorns to instruct the Pollocks to "come out with your hands up." An elderly relative of the Pollocks told Tampa reporter Stacy Da Silva that she was so shaken by the hours-long raid "she could hardly talk."

As one of the few reporters covering the Capitol breach investigation, I heard stories from dozens of people about their experiences with the FBI. The fiancée of a high-profile defendant told me what happened when the FBI raided their home in March

and arrested the father of her three young children. "Twenty
agents showed up with weapons drawn to arrest him and ransack
the house. She was taken into a separate room—the couple did
not ask to have an attorney present—where she was interrogated
by three FBI agents. They asked her who they voted for and which
political party they identified with. The agents grilled her about
what news channels they watched and their views on immigration, including the border wall. She was asked if they followed
Qanon. The FBI agents asked her if she belonged to a group such
as the Oath Keepers or Three Percenters. She told me she had no
idea what they were talking about."

The woman texted me after I interviewed her to say she felt
"stupid" for talking to FBI agents without a lawyer present. "But
we're not criminals, we weren't hiding anything, [and] I knew he
did nothing wrong that day. I'd like to think I answered their
questions wisely and honestly but now I realize . . . how they turn
everything against you. Most of the questions I answered I don't
know or I can't remember. I feel so stupid!!!"

The FBI even harassed people who did nothing wrong on
January 6. In April, the FBI stormed the residence of Paul and
Marilyn Hueper. The couple runs a day spa and inn in Homer,
Alaska. While reading emails in his bedroom the morning of April
28, Paul Hueper heard a loud commotion which turned out to be
several armed FBI agents who had broken down his front door.
Paul and Marilyn immediately were handcuffed along with a few
guests including a teenager.

Investigators placed the couple in separate rooms and interrogated them for at least three hours. They refused to produce
a warrant. Marilyn was informed that she was a suspect in the
case of Nancy Pelosi's missing laptop computer. When agents
showed her photos they believed to be her inside the Capitol on
January 6, Marilyn said it wasn't her and wondered if the photos
had been photoshopped. Paul also denied that the photos were
of his wife.

Despite the invasion, the Huepers kept their humor. "We laughed a lot of the time because it was so ridiculous," Marilyn told a local radio host the day after the raid. "I could hear Paul laughing in the other room."[5]

The Huepers said they did not come "within 100 yards" of the Capitol building on January 6. It was a case of mistaken identity. Nonetheless, the FBI took electronic devices and, inexplicably, their copy of the Declaration of Independence. Agents warned Marilyn that she could be charged with perjury or obstruction if she didn't provide the correct answers.

As of September 1, the Huepers have not been charged. When Rep. James Jordan confronted FBI Director Chris Wray about the raid of the Huepers' home during a Congressional hearing in June, Wray was unfamiliar with the name. "Have I talked to who?" Wray replied after Jordan asked if he had spoken with the couple since the botched search. He evaded Jordan's follow-up questions, insisting he could not comment on open investigations.

Not everyone shared the Huepers' good nature about the FBI's intimidation tactics. Joseph Bolanos, sixty-nine, lives with his elderly mother on the Upper West Side of New York City. He was president of his block association and looked after his homebound neighbors during the pandemic shutdown.

Bolanos, a registered Democrat, took the train to Washington that morning and briefly attended Trump's speech, according to a lengthy profile in the New York Post. After it was over, Bolanos went to his hotel room to get out of the cold. He and his friends then walked to the Capitol around 2 p.m. to see what would happen with the Electoral College certification; they did not go inside the building.

Four FBI agents arrived at his home on February 3 to ask questions after a neighbor contacted the FBI tip line claiming Bolanos had boasted about his trip to Washington on January 6. He explained his story and showed photos and videos to support his account of his movements that day.

---

5   Chris Story, *Optimism and a Homeowner Raided by FBI* (On Top of the World Radio, 2021).

A few days later, Bolanos was awakened at 6 a.m. to the sound of banging on the apartment's front door. "I opened the door and there's about 10 tactical police soldiers and one is pointing a rifle at my head," Bolanos told *Post* reporter Miranda Devine. "[They had] a battering ram and a crowbar."[6] His apartment and his mother's apartment were ransacked; agents confiscated his devices.

Bolanos was interrogated inside an FBI vehicle parked outside; an NBC News crew was on the scene, tipped off by someone ahead of time. He began to feel sick around 11 a.m. and was taken by ambulance to the hospital. Bolanos had suffered a stroke.

Bolanos was never charged but the damage was done. "The neighbors he had helped all those years have turned their backs on him," Devine wrote. "One woman who cooked him a nice dinner last Thanksgiving wrote him a nasty note: 'I hope Antifa gets you.'"

Sharon Caldwell and her husband, Tom, had one of the more terrifying experiences with the FBI. The Caldwells' legal nightmare began on January 19 when they were awakened around 6 a.m. by a loudspeaker outside their Virginia farm. "Someone was shouting Tom's name," she told me by phone in July. They awoke to find what Sharon called "at least 40 SWAT officers" using a battering ram to bang down their front door.

Barefoot and still in her nightgown, Sharon was confronted by armed agents pointing rifles at her. "I had these red laser dots all over me, Tom was afraid they were going to shoot me." In a separate interview with the Caldwells in September, Tom broke down retelling the scene. "I said a prayer, 'Father, please don't let them kill my wife,'" he sobbed over the phone.[7]

Caldwell, sixty-five, a decorated military veteran with no criminal record, was then dragged through the cold January grass by his legs. He suffers from debilitating back injuries from his military service and underwent spinal surgery in 2020. "They threw me face down on the hood of the car, kicked my legs apart, put a chain around my waist and put me in handcuffs."

6   Miranda Devine, *FBI tears innocent New Yorker's life into shreds after Jan. 6* (*New York Post*, 2021).
7   Julie Kelly, *An American Horror Story* (American Greatness, 2021).

Caldwell asked several times what he was being charged with but FBI agents refused to answer. He sat in the back of a police car before he was led back toward his house. That's when he saw an FBI agent vandalizing one of his prized possessions. "I have a [collector] '63 Thunderbird in my garage as a reminder of my grandfather, a retired Army colonel. An agent kicked one of the doors open and was leaning with his battle gear up against the car, scratching it up."

Once inside, Caldwell was relieved to see Sharon "was still alive." At least twenty agents raided their home, seizing electronic devices including old computers and hard drives. One device contained a trove of downloaded pictures. "They took every family photo we have," he told me.

The Caldwells, like many other Capitol protesters, consented to speak with the FBI that day without a lawyer present. Defendants routinely told me or admitted in interviews that they "had nothing to hide." People like the Caldwells thought they were helping the FBI find the bad guys, not realizing the nation's top law enforcement agency considered *them* the bad guys.

*   *   *   *

The FBI's bad behavior isn't just related to intrusive, putative raids at the homes of trespassers or even innocent Trump supporters. Investigators, in search of a crime, swept up personal information off electronic devices using surveillance tools designed to track legitimate terrorist threats.

Cellular providers have been eager to help the government. It appears that not a single telecommunications company has put up a fight to protect their users' privacy. Subpoenas to confirm cell phone numbers, email addresses, and other personal information linked to social media accounts have been fully complied with as far as court documents show.

"In the hours and days after the Capitol riot, the FBI relied in some cases on emergency orders that do not require court authorization in order to quickly secure actual communications from people who were identified at the crime scene," an investigative report by The Intercept revealed in February. "Federal authorities have used the emergency orders in combination with signed court orders under the so-called pen/trap exception to the Stored Communications Act to try to determine who was present at the time that the Capitol was breached, the source said. In some cases, the Justice Department has used these and other 'hybrid' court orders to collect actual content from cell phones, like text messages and other communications, in building cases against the rioters."[8]

Members of Congress and congressional staff were part of the massive dragnet. So, too, were people who were in D.C. that day but did not participate in any of the events. Senator Mike Lee confronted Christopher Wray on the issue during a March 2 hearing. Lee told Wray he had heard from numerous individuals who "never got near the Capitol or any violence on January 6 who have inexplicably been contacted by the FBI by agents who apparently were aware of their presence in Washington, D.C. that day. Are you geolocating people through the FBI?"

When Wray tap danced around the question, Lee pressed forward, asking if the FBI used national security letters or the Foreign Intelligence Surveillance Court, the secret court that had improperly authorized spying on Team Trump, to secure the geolocation data.

Wray told Lee he "does not believe" national security letters or FISA warrants were part of the collection process, but confirmed that warrants were issued to get the cell data "under the legal authority we have in consultation with the department and the prosecutors."

Those warrants—Wray intentionally did not elaborate—were geofence warrants on Google, which has a much better way of tracking users than cell phone providers. An investigative report by Wired in September confirmed at least forty-five January 6 criminal

---

8   Ken Klippenstein, Eric Lichtblau, *Fbi Seized Congressional Cellphone Records Related to Capitol Attack* (The Intercept, 2021).

cases used evidence collected by a Google geofence warrant. One warrant was issued as the protest was underway on January 6.

"A geofence warrant initially seeks an anonymized list of devices tracked within a specific area at a specific time," Wired reporter Mark Harris wrote on September 30. "Investigators then use that list to focus on tracks that look suspicious, and can ask Google to widen the time or geofence boundaries on only those devices. Finally, investigators can go back to Google to unmask the real name, email, phone number, and other information of just a few account holders. But where a typical geofence fishing expedition might catch only one or two suspects, the January 6 investigation appears to have landed a netful."[9]

Since the Justice Department had categorized the Capitol complex as a "crime scene" and Wray designated the four-hour event an act of "domestic terrorism," private corporations from Verizon to Facebook undoubtedly felt it was their duty to comply.

"The collection effort has been met with little resistance from telecom providers asked to turn over voluminous data on the activity that day. 'No one wants to be on the wrong side of the insurrection,' a source involved in the collection effort told The Intercept. 'This is now the scene of the crime.'"

---

9   Mark Harris, *How a Secret Google Geofence Warrant Helped Catch the Capitol Riot Mob* (Wired, 2021).

CHAPTER NINE:

WHERE IS THE VIDEO FOOTAGE?

J UDGE TREVOR MCFADDEN was not happy.

The prosecutor handling the case of Timothy Hale-Cusanelli, the alleged "white supremacist" who was not charged with any violent crime related to January 6, informed McFadden during a July status hearing that the Justice Department would not meet its full discovery obligations until early 2022. And that date, assistant U.S. Attorney Kathryn Fifield said, was a "conservative estimate."

McFadden had twice denied Hale's release from a D.C. jail based almost exclusively on evidence proffered by the government. Hale was one of the first protesters arrested in the Justice Department's "shock and awe" campaign, which rounded up more than one hundred Americans before January 20. At the time of the July status hearing, he had spent nearly seven months behind bars. Yet prosecutors still didn't have their act together. "No system exists to wrap its arms around [all this evidence]," Fifield said.

Fifield told McFadden that because of the "incalculable" amount of evidence held by the government, she would not be prepared to go to trial in Hale's case in 2021. McFadden, a Trump appointee, scolded the government. "You would not arrest [someone] then gather evidence later," McFadden told Fifield. "That's not how this works."

But that is precisely how it works in the prosecution of January 6 defendants. The rush for scalps of guilty Trump supporters and the need to seek revenge on behalf of aggrieved politicians, including the new president, eventually caught up with the Justice Department.

"This does not feel [like] what the Constitution [and] the Speedy Trial Act envisions," McFadden continued. When Fifield tried to frame the discovery delay as important to Hale's defense, McFadden shot back, "Freedom also is important to the defendant."

McFadden, despite Fifield's admission she would not be ready, set a trial date for November 9, 2021. And by summer, McFadden wasn't the only judge admonishing the quick-triggered Justice Department over its discovery delays, particularly slow-walking the sharing of an extensive collection of video evidence.

January 6, 2021 is by any measure the most extensively recorded event in U.S. history. The trove of digital material is so massive that the public may never have a full accounting of the imagery taken that day.

The amount of video alone is mind-boggling. Federal and local government captured tens of thousands of hours of footage from the Capitol complex's extensive surveillance system and from body cameras worn by law enforcement officers. Photojournalists and independent bloggers produced their own recordings as well. And an untold number of protesters and bystanders took videos throughout the day then posted clips on numerous social media platforms.

This "avalanche" (as one prosecutor described it) of electronic evidence unquestionably poses a huge hurdle for the Justice Department. But since the government manages nearly all of the evidence, including information retrieved from confiscated personal devices, it also gives prosecutors the upper hand in court filings and shaping the storyline in the news media.

The Justice Department has an almost unchallenged advantage in charging documents, particularly in motions seeking pre-trial detention. Cherry-picked video clips and screenshots of videos only available to prosecutors comprise most of the evidence presented in court to argue that a defendant should be kept behind bars awaiting trial. Defense counsel is denied equal access to all related footage that might give the clip greater context or even include exculpatory evidence.

Early on, prosecutors sought protective orders in nearly every case in order to manage the exchange of evidence. But it became clear the government isn't just withholding electronic evidence due to the overwhelming amount of it; the Justice Department clearly wants to keep a very tight lid on all the recordings in its possession.

The Department lists ten categories of evidence considered "sensitive" or "highly sensitive" government material in its standard protective order; this includes "surveillance camera footage from the U.S. Capitol Police's extensive system of cameras on U.S. Capitol grounds." The protective orders detail very specific rules on how evidence can be viewed.

Defendants must be "supervised" by an attorney, or someone employed by the defense attorney. Materials cannot be downloaded or shared in any way. Notes taken by the defendants must omit any personal information.

In a separate filing, the general counsel for the USCP further explained why not just the public but defendants should have very limited access to more than 14,000 hours of footage recorded on January 6 by closed-circuit TV cameras situated around the Capitol grounds and inside the buildings. In an affidavit added to a March protective order in a case against two January 6 defendants, the general counsel for the USCP explained why the surveillance video from that day should be kept under wraps.[1]

Thomas DiBiase said his agency operates a "sophisticated" system of cameras "inside and outside the buildings including the U.S. Capitol itself and the other Congressional office buildings." The elaborate system is monitored live in real time by Capitol po-

---

1   USA v. McCaughey III, et al., *United States' Motion for Protective Order* (United States District Court, 2021).

lice officers twenty-four-hours-a-day, seven days a week, DiBiase confirmed. Any request to release footage must be approved by the assistant chief of police; a special form must be completed and signed by several other officials.

Although normally these recordings are automatically delet-ed after thirty days, USCP preserved the collection captured on January 6. Video recorded between noon and 8:00 p.m. on Jan-uary 6 was provided to two Congressional committees, the FBI, and the D.C. Metropolitan Police department. According to DiB-iase, the agencies agreed to keep the footage in the "legal control" of the USCP and the recordings would not be subject to Freedom of Information Act inquiries. (As part of the legislative branch, USCP is shielded from FOIA requests.)

But DiBiase said his agency has "significant concerns" about releasing the footage to January 6 defendants. "The Department is aware of efforts made before January 6, 2021, by such defen-dants and others, to gather information regarding the interior of the U.S. Capitol, including references to the tunnels below the Grounds and maps of the building's layout, which information is generally not publicly available," DiBiase wrote on March 17. That comment seemed to be an attempt to bolster the rumor some House Republicans gave "tours" to protesters the day before. "Our concern is that providing unfettered access to hours of extremely sensitive information to defendants who already have shown a de-sire to interfere in the democratic process will result in the layout, vulnerabilities, and security weaknesses in the U.S. Capitol being collected, exposed, and passed on to those who might wish to at-tack the Capitol again."

There was, however, one group that did not meet resistance by USCP: Democratic House impeachment managers overseeing Trump's second impeachment trial based on the events of January 6. DiBiase claimed the lawmakers had a right to use the footage since USCP is part of the legislative branch and the clips were used in a trial, "similar to what would be used in a court of law."

But the use of often choppy video clips produced by the government and kept away from the public eye met resistance from an unexpected source. The Press Coalition, a group of several major news organizations, petitioned the D.C. District Court to request greater access to video evidence used in court documents and hearings. The group includes the three major network news outlets: the *Associated Press*, the *New York Times*, and the *Washington Post*.

In a letter to the D.C. District Court, lawyers representing the coalition complained that journalists did not have copies of videos played in court, especially for pre-trial detention hearings. The videos, the Coalition lawyers argued, are official court exhibits and should be made available to both the media and the public. "In multiple cases, the Government and defendants have expressly relied on video evidence in support of their arguments, but those videos remain largely inaccessible," Charles Tobin, an attorney for Ballard Spahr, wrote in a May 3 letter to Chief Judge Beryl Howell.[2]

Tobin said the lack of access to video evidence in January 6 cases is "widespread" and noted the public's need for more information about the historic investigation. "While we appreciate the extraordinary workload these prosecutions present to the hard-working Judges and staff of this Court, delayed access to these historic records shuts the public out of an important part of the administration of justice."

Noting the media's "frustration" at lack of access to video evidence, Howell authorized the use of a drop box to post court-related videos for journalists to view. News outlets "will be required to file applications…to view exhibits in each individual case," Howell wrote in a May 14 order. But there are still plenty of legal loopholes. "Access to these video exhibits may be authorized after the presiding judge has the opportunity to consider the positions of the parties."

2   Charles D. Tobin, Maxwell S. Mishkin, *Letter Dated May 3, 2021 Re: Press and Public Access to Video Exhibits in the Capitol Riot Cases* (Ballard Spahr, 2021).

The ruling appeased the media, at least for a short time.

It must be noted, of course, these are the same news organizations that breathlessly promote the "insurrection" narrative on a daily basis. Photos of January 6 plastered the front pages of newspapers for months. Local, network, and cable news channels aired damning videos on a continual loop and interviewed victims of the "insurrection," including Congressional lawmakers and Capitol police.

Members of the Press Coalition also produced their own cherry-picked video montages. On January 10, ABC News posted a ten-minute video entitled "US Capitol Riot: Tracking the Insurrection," claiming several people were killed, "including an officer." Later that month, ABC aired an hour-long special on Hulu that documented the "assault on the Capitol."

Ten days after the arrest of George Tanios and Julian Khater on March 14, the *New York Times* released footage of what it described as an "attack" on Officer Brian Sicknick. The video, the reporters claimed, showed for the "first time how the U.S. Capitol Police officer who died after facing off with rioters on Jan. 6 was attacked with chemical spray." But the video was a choppy compilation of body cam footage and still images taken by another photographer that did little to prove Sicknick was sprayed by either man. There was no clear evidence Khater directly sprayed Sicknick or any officer; a brief clip showed Sicknick rinsing his eyes. But considering the copious amounts of chemical spray law enforcement used against people outside, it's impossible to know whether Sicknick was sprayed by a protester or by "friendly fire" from his own colleagues.

In June, the *Times* released a forty-minute video entitled "Day of Rage: An In-Depth Look at How a Mob Stormed the Capitol." The paper claimed it was "the most visual depiction to date" of the events of January 6. Most of the clips were obtained from since-deleted social media posts of those involved, as well as body cam footage and communications by law enforcement officials. The video, however, glossed over key events of the day including police officers using explosive devices on the crowd and the killing of Ashli Babbitt.

CNN, another member of the Press Coalition, also had its hand in airing selective video favorable to the Justice Department's narrative with a two-hour documentary special in June called "Assault on Democracy: The Roots of Trump's Insurrection." Drew Griffin, CNN's senior investigative reporter, claimed that "although the attempted coup was over in a few hours, there are still millions of Americans who believe in the propaganda messaging, that those who stormed the Capitol were right, as they hope to put Donald Trump back in office to fight their perceived enemies."

This kind of overheated rhetoric was typical of media coverage from the very beginning. Needless to say, no evidence has been shown to the public—or the press—that anything like a "coup" was being attempted.

Body cam footage that allegedly showed the assault on D.C. police officer Michael Fanone, who had become a media celebrity after January 6, was leaked to CNN in May. Fanone later told *Time* magazine that he was at a D.C. wine bar that night and asked the bartender to turn on CNN. "The bar fell silent as the body-cam footage played," Time reporter Molly Ball recounted. "And suddenly, for the first time since that day, Fanone was sobbing uncontrollably, shoulders heaving as his buddies put their arms around him."

CNN's motivation, by the way, was less about the public interest than about protecting their narrative. Prior to the release of the network's "insurrection" special, Drew Shenkman, a CNN lawyer, told Brian Stelter that the demand for more videos was to push back on the "denialism that's growing every single day."[3]

January 6 "denial" became the latest iteration of the "anti-science" charge frequently leveled at conservatives for evincing reasonable skepticism about such topics as catastrophic climate

---

3   Drew Griffin, *CNN Special Report: Assault on Democracy: The Roots of Trump's Insurrection* (CNN, 2021).

change and Covid vaccine mandates. Anyone challenging the official narrative was accused of living in an alternate universe that rejected the reality right before their eyes.

Rep. Andrew Clyde (R-Ga.) infuriated the media after he said during a House hearing that some scenes that day resembled "a normal tourist visit." Senator Ron Johnson (D-Wisc.), who early on rejected the description of January 6 as an "insurrection," told Fox News' Laura Ingraham in May that "it was peaceful protest, except for there were a number of people, basically agitators that whipped the crowd and breached the Capitol. That's really the truth of what's happening here."

Tucker Carlson openly mocked the Left on his show with a graphic titled "Insurrection Day" that would appear right before he lampooned the latest hype about January 6. "For those of you who are not good at dates or don't have calendars, this is the day that we pause to remember the white supremacist QAnon insurrection, that came so very close to toppling our government and ending this democracy forever," Carlson said on April 6.

"You saw what happened. It was carried live on television, every gruesome moment. A mob of older people from unfashionable zip codes somehow made it all the way to Washington, D.C., probably by bus. They wandered freely through the Capitol, like it was their building or something. They didn't have guns, but a lot of them had extremely dangerous ideas. They talked about the Constitution, and something called their rights. Some of them made openly seditious claims. They insisted, for example, that the last election wasn't entirely fair."

But the denial wasn't just coming from a few House Republicans and a handful of reporters on the Right. Ironically, Judge Amy Berman Jackson in July denied a request by the Press Coalition to see all the footage from Fanone's body camera. The Justice Department shrewdly circumvented using any video and instead proffered screenshots for use in the case against three men charged with assaulting Fanone.

"Entering a screenshot as an exhibit does not make the entire video from which the screenshot was taken an exhibit," prosecutors artfully objected in a motion to deny the coalition's request for the underlying video. Jackson agreed. "The Court further finds that [the] Videos are not 'judicial records' subject to public access because they were not provided to the court. Accordingly, the Application . . . is hereby DENIED."

The media encountered an uphill battle in every case where it sought access to video evidence. In June, the Press Coalition filed a motion to intervene in the case against John Anderson. The Florida resident was charged with numerous offenses including civil disorder, assaulting, resisting, or impeding certain officers, and trespassing.

A thirty-second clip captured by the USCP surveillance system had been designated, like all surveillance footage, as "highly sensitive" material in the case against Anderson. Press coalition lawyers asked the Justice Department to remove the designation and make the brief clip available to the media and the public.

Part of the reason is because Anderson was in the west terrace tunnel where so much of the violence between protesters and police occurred. Anderson, sixty-one, suffered a medical emergency on January 6 after he was sprayed with a chemical irritant. He has several pre-existing conditions including asthma and hearing loss. Anderson was arrested for trespassing that day and released; in February, the FBI arrested him at 5:30 a.m. while doing his normal outdoor exercises and charged him with a slew of new offenses including assaulting a police officer and stealing government property.[4]

Pushing back on the argument that USCP surveillance video should be kept under strict protective orders, the coalition noted that the government used the footage when it served their interests including routine postings by the FBI asking for help in identifying Capitol suspects.

4   Grand Jury, *USA v. Anderson, Complaint* (United States District Court, 2021).

Open source video taken by protesters and journalists, co-alition lawyers explained, made the government's insistence that releasing USCP recordings posed a security threat moot. "Be-cause the public already has access to an enormous amount of videos from inside the building, the Government likewise cannot demonstrate that releasing those thirty additional seconds would pose any further threat to the security of the Capitol. The Court should therefore order the Government to remove that designa-tion from the Video Clip and to make the Video Clip available to the press and the public."

The Justice Department quickly objected to the coalition's motion and asked Judge Rudolph Contreras to deny the request. Not only was the clip in question not submitted to the court by the government, assistant U.S. Attorney Robert Juman argued, it did not influence any judicial proceedings. Further, remov-ing the "highly sensitive" designation did in fact pose a security threat, Juman claimed. "[T]he Capitol Police are aware of efforts made by individuals, whether participants in the Capitol At-tack or not, to gather information about the interior of the U.S. Capitol that is generally not publicly available," Juman wrote. "Were the Court to accept this argument, it would have sweep-ing ramifications for the Capitol Police's ability to protect the U.S. Capitol."

Juman also warned that removing the "highly sensitive" label would lead to a slippery slope that "would require the government to de-designate many hours of security footage from video camer-as throughout the U.S. Capitol."

But the Press Coalition remained undeterred. Pointing to the government's release of footage in other high-profile cases, coali-tion lawyers called out the Justice Department's hypocrisy. "The Government . . . in several other riot prosecutions . . . expressly agreed to the release of such 'select video' from inside the Capitol. Indeed, in opposing the release of this Video Clip, the Govern-ment directly contradicts its own prior positions."

On July 29, Judge Contreras denied the coalition's motions but approved a similar request from Anderson's attorney, Marina Medvin. The "highly sensitive" designation on the thirty-second clip was removed and no longer subject to the protective order in the case.

Tragically, Anderson passed away in September. In a statement announcing his death at the age of sixty-one, Medvin said the video exonerated her client. "May his family find comfort and finality in knowing that John was genuinely innocent of the serious charges of which he was accused before his death. May America know that John Anderson died a wrongfully accused man who maintained his innocence until his last day."

*   *   *   *

By summer, the government started filing discovery updates explaining the delays. "The investigation and prosecution of the Capitol Breach will be the largest in American history, both in terms of the number of defendants prosecuted and the nature and volume of the evidence," Channing Phillips, the acting U.S. Attorney for the District of Columbia, the office handling every January 6 case, wrote in a pro forma July motion added to several January 6 cases.

Phillips detailed a long list of evidence the government had collected: Aside from tens of thousands of hours of USCP surveillance footage and body cam recordings, the Justice Department received more than 230,000 digital tips; radio transmissions from law enforcement agencies responding to the protest; more than one million Parler posts along with twenty terabytes of Parler data such as videos and photographs (oddly, the government did not mention the amount of Facebook or Twitter data, the two platforms that provided the most social media evidence in the investigation); location history and cell tower data from "thousands of devices" in or near the Capitol on January 6; and responses to more than 6,000 subpoenas.

"We are still collecting and assembling materials from the numerous entities who were involved in the response to the Breach, and we are still investigating—which means the amount of data (phones, devices, legal process, investigative memoranda) is growing," Phillips wrote July 30. "Producing discovery in a meaningful manner and balancing complex legal-investigative and technical difficulties takes time."

In a separate discovery update, Phillips added a two-page chart detailing video discovery requests by unnamed defense attorneys that the government still had not filled. Some of the missing materials included recordings taken inside the building from 2:50 p.m. until 3:35 p.m.; footage that showed Capitol police allowing people beyond the barriers and interacting with protesters on a friendly basis; and videos showing people walking around peacefully.

"Videos in the government's possession that filmed the interior of the capital building from approximately 2:50 PM to 3:35 PM on January 6, 2021."

"[A]ll video and/or audio footage in which Capitol Police and any other Gov't officials or agents remove barriers and/or interact with protestors who entered the Capitol or gained access to the patios or other structures connected to the Capitol building complex."

"Based on my review of the discovery thus far, there is official video surveillance and publicly sourced video footage that is exculpatory to the defendants. Many of those videos show [defendant] and other[s] peacefully walking around the Capitol. In these videos, they, like thousands of others, are doing nothing illegal with the possible exception of being present in the building, all of which is potentially exculpatory."

"Please provide notice of any decision not to produce requested photographs, video footage, or recorded communications so that a judicial decision as to production may, if warranted, be sought. Please also provide all photographs, video footage, and recorded communications relating to the Brady and Giglio requests articulated below."

A main obstacle was the fact the government waited until late May to hire a private company to create a database to house all the digital and documentary evidence. Deloitte Financial Advisory Systems was contracted on May 28 "to assist in document processing, review and production of materials related to the Capitol Breach," Phillips said. The $6.1 million contract was expected to reach $26 million, according to an analysis by Politico.[5]

The project hit a snag in July after Chief Judge Howell ruled the Justice Department could not share grand jury material with Deloitte. Employees of Deloitte are not de facto government personnel, as the government contended, even if they are working on a federal contract, Howell concluded. Grand jury material, which may include witness statements, is highly protected information. "The safeguards built into the government's contract with Deloitte therefore do not assuage the concern that bulk disclosure to this private entity will undermine the interests of grand jury secrecy, particularly in such a high-profile and historically significant investigation," Howell wrote in a fifty-four-page decision.[6]

Admitting January 6 defendants will have an "uphill battle" in seeking disclosure of grand jury material, Howell said the government's proposal would give Deloitte an advantage over the accused. "Deloitte, a private firm, would gain greater access to grand jury materials in all the Capitol attack cases than any individual defendant is entitled to receive in his own case," she wrote.

But figuring out the details of the contract was only a small part of the overall challenge. Judges became increasingly impatient as the government missed discovery deadlines. Defense lawyers complained of "discovery dumps" right before court hearings that included evidence unrelated to their client.

Howell also grew tired of the government's repeated efforts to keep Capitol surveillance footage out of court filings. In a motion filed in August related to the plea arrangement for a January 6 defendant, prosecutors again urged the court to oppose release

---

5   Josh Gerstein, Kyle Cheney, *Feds Agree to Pay $6.1M to Create Database for Capitol Riot Prosecutions* (Politico, 2021).

6   Grand Jury, *In Re Capitol Breach Grand Jury*, Memorandum Opinion (United States District Court, 2021).

of videos used in the case. The government reminded Howell several videos were under protective orders and, while admitted in discovery, were not used as exhibits.

"[T]he Videos here are particularly sensitive because they depict the interior—as opposed to the exterior—of the U.S. Capitol and thus revealing information less likely to be obtained through other means," the government wrote in an August 18 filing to Judge Howell.

This Video is part of a larger group of videos in these cases which could be aggregated to reveal non-public information about 'entry and exit points, office locations, and the relation of the crucial chambers and offices (such as the Speaker's Office or Majority Leader's Office) to other areas of the Capitol.' Where disclosure of one video may not present a significant security threat, the U.S. Capitol Police has a larger legitimate interest in restricting the disclosure of individual videos in an effort to avoid "unfettered access" to CCV [sic] that may indeed give rise to a significant threat to the building and those victimized by the events of January 6, 2021.

(The defendant, Eric Torrens, also objected to public release of the videos. His lawyer told Howell that publicity surrounding his case—he was charged with four misdemeanors—had already led to "public opprobrium" and the loss of his job.)

Howell ordered both the government and Torrens' lawyer to provide a "more fulsome explanation" as to why certain videos from the Capitol security system should not be publicly released. "[F]ootage from the Capitol Building submitted to the Court has been made publicly available in other cases," she wrote in an August 16 minute order. Howell snarked in a separate order in response to Torrens' request to keep the videos under wraps that "the risk of 'annoyance and criticism' is generally insufficient to rebut the presumption of public access to judicial proceedings.

Some in Congress were turning up the heat, too. Rep. Marjorie Taylor-Greene, a newly elected congresswoman from Georgia, sent a letter to Christopher Wray and the acting chief of the Capitol police in June demanding the public release of all January 6 footage from USCP security cameras.

"What's going on here is a massive cover-up by Pelosi and the Democrats," Rep. Devin Nunes told Fox News' Laura Ingraham on June 10. "These 14,000 hours should be shared across all of the committees and in Congress and then members of Congress should decide whether or not they should be released to the public."

In a speech at the Turning Point USA Student Action conference in Arizona, Rep. Paul Gosar asked the crowd to help him "demand the 14,000 hours of tape so that we can hold the people accountable for their wrongdoing even if it's insiders from the FBI and DOJ." Gosar was interrupted midway by loud applause.

That, of course, is not going to happen as long as Democrats control Congress. Nancy Pelosi has as much reason to keep the recordings secret as USCP or the Justice Department. Any footage that contradicts the Democrats' well-honed narrative could result in the total collapse of the notion that January 6 was an act of "domestic terror" perpetrated by white supremacist militias who savaged cops and nearly destroyed the building.

By late summer, even judges who early on gave the government all the leeway it needed started to confront prosecutors on unmet discovery obligations. Judge Amit Mehta is presiding over the multi-defendant Oath Keepers case; he denied bail to several Oath Keepers in the initial stages of the investigation. During a status hearing on August 10, a defense attorney confirmed what had been reported in Tim Hale's hearing weeks earlier—that the government would not be ready to meet its discovery obligations to defendants until early 2022.

Mehta was surprised by the comment and said he hadn't heard that. "If that's true, it's quite troubling," Mehta said. He reminded prosecutors of their obligations under the Brady rule, which requires the government to turn over all exculpatory material to the defendant in a criminal case. Kathryn Rakoczy, the lead prosecutor in the Oath Keepers case, assured Mehta that most of the discovery would be available to defense by early September.

But that was not accurate. In a written report to the court—Mehta had asked for a status report to be filed within a week—the Justice Department said the platforms, which would house both documentary and digital evidence, wouldn't be ready until early October. "The government will make productions of material to the platforms on a rolling basis."

Mehta wasn't the only judge running out of patience. Judge Emmet Sullivan warned that same week that he was considering imposing "sanctions" if the government did not have its database up and running within thirty days. The judge said he "didn't want to erect a barrier…but felt he needed to do something."

Compounding the government's delays in uploading all digital material related to January 6 was the fact the FBI continued to arrest people every week, increasing the Justice Department's caseload and expanding the overall body of evidence. In the case of the Oath Keepers, Mehta noted, prosecutors kept issuing superseding indictments, which added new defendants and new charges. Defense lawyers were still waiting on full discovery for clients who had been arrested in January; expanding the case not only delayed scheduled trial dates but prompted more delays in obtaining all the evidence in the case.

But the Justice Department and USCP still worked feverishly to deny access to Capitol surveillance footage. In response to a FOIA lawsuit filed in February by Judicial Watch, a conservative government watchdog, the government again rejected claims that the footage should be public record. "[T]he USCP is aware of no authority holding that law enforcement surveillance video footage should be considered a public record subject to mandatory disclosure," acting assistant attorney general Brian Boynton wrote in an August 2021 motion. Boynton argued the footage should remain protected since videos were being used in criminal prosecutions as well as congressional investigations.

James W. Joyce, a lawyer representing the USCP, notified Judicial Watch that the Capitol Police Board, the three-man body overseeing the agency, had [designated] footage capturing the evacuation of the House and Senate as "security information." Joyce also warned that additional footage could be declared "security information" to prevent lawmakers from sharing the recordings and "provide prospective attackers or others with a clear picture of the interior of the Capitol, including entry and exit points, office locations, and the relation of crucial chambers and offices." Any footage labeled "security information" can only be released with approval of the Capitol Police Board.

"The US Capitol Police is hiding a reported 14,000 hours of January 6 video from the American people to help Nancy Pelosi's abusive targeting of Trump supporters and other political opponents," Judicial Watch President Tom Fitton said in a press release responding to the filing. "Any other police department in America would be investigated and defunded for such abusive secrecy. The Pelosi Congress is in cover-up mode regarding January 6."

Then, another bombshell. In an investigation-wide discovery update posted in late August, the Justice Department said half the footage would not be made available to defendants or defense counsel. Channing Phillips, explaining the continued delay in uploading video evidence to an accessible platform, told defendants that the FBI was "transmitting" the Capitol surveillance footage to the system but that it would take "several weeks" to do so.

"Based on our current understanding of the technical complexities involved, we expect to start rolling productions from 7,000 hours of footage that the USCP provided the FBI within approximately the next four weeks," Phillips wrote on August 24. "An additional 7,000 hours of footage is not relevant to this case and, therefore will not be produced."

So, just like that, 7,000 hours of video taken on a day compared to the most horrific terror attacks in U.S. history will never see the light of day. And that's at minimum.

The harder the government tried to keep the videos under wraps, the more questions it raised. What, exactly, did the government not want the public, let alone defendants, to see? Would the recordings indeed show officers allowing people into the building, as plenty of open source videos showed, or reveal that most of the protesters were peaceful and unaware they were committing any crime?

By fall 2021, a slow release of government-held footage continued to erode the official narrative. Judges were becoming less agreeable to prosecutors' demands to keep clips used as evidence out of public view. In September, Chief Judge Beryl Howell rejected the Justice Department's well-worn argument that posting the footage posed a national security threat and ordered the release of several clips.

"The disclosure marks a setback for the US Capitol Police and the US attorney's office in their efforts to control how much footage from the Capitol's closed-circuit video (CCV) system gets out," BuzzFeed reporter Zoe Tillman, who covers the January 6 beat, wrote on September 21. "In the latest case, prosecutors argued that revealing the location and vantage points of more cameras could help 'bad actors' trying to plan some future assault on the building. A judge concluded that argument was too speculative, however, and that the public had a strong interest in seeing videos."[7]

The five videos released in that order, however, explained why the Justice Department is working so hard to keep the footage secret. One clip shows dozens of people casually entering an open door on the Senate wing of the building at around 2:25 p.m. as others climb through an open, perhaps previously broken, large window. Police are absent.

Three other clips show people walking around the area known as "the Crypt," a public area in the center of the building. And the last clip shows people exiting the same Senate door ten minutes later, at the direction of Capitol police, while one officer hits people outside the window with his baton.

---

7   Zoe Tillman, *Eight Months After The Capitol Riots, Thousands Of Hours Of Surveillance Footage Remain Secret* (BuzzFeed News, 2021).

After Tillman posted the first video, the one showing people peacefully walking through an open door, the clip quickly earned 3.4 million views on Twitter. It was heavily mocked. "Is this what George Bush compared to September 11th? Seriously?!" one Twitter user replied. "I can definitely see why they wanted to keep this under seal. The horror," posted another.

One entity, however, had the privilege of accessing secret surveillance video: HBO. The network's documentary, "Four Hours at the Capitol," boasted that the film contained "never-before-seen footage." Some of the footage clearly had been sourced by security cameras, recordings both Capitol police and the Justice Department insisted was quasi-classified material. A defense lawyer, after the documentary was released in October, noted in a motion that the footage "has not been previously revealed to the defense lawyers in these cases."

Secret footage for friendly propagandist filmmakers and Democratic impeachment managers? Yes. Potentially exculpatory footage for defendants and their lawyers? Not so much.

But time was running out for Biden's Justice Department to selectively edit and share surveillance video Discovery deadlines loomed and judges were ready to set trial dates. Footage used in court, both by the government and by defense counsel, would eventually show the public what happened inside and outside the building that day.

As more comes out, this narrative will continue to collapse until their dishonest machinations are fully exposed and discredited, just as in the Russia collusion hoax. Just don't expect the liberal media to cover it.

CHAPTER TEN:

INSIDE THE "DEPLORABLE" JAIL

O N JANUARY 6, MICHAEL CURZIO was one of the few protesters arrested inside the Capitol building. He was charged with unlawful entry; he paid a fine and was ordered to appear before a D.C. Court in June. "I thought that was the end of it," he told me in July.[1]

But as he drove to his Florida home after work on January 14, Curzio was unexpectedly pulled over. "Out of nowhere, police SUVs were in front, behind, and alongside my vehicle. The cops were screaming, 'get out, get out' and had their guns drawn."

He was arrested and charged with four of the most common misdemeanors applied against defendants in the Capitol probe investigation. Curzio, a convicted felon who had served almost seven years in prison for attempted first-degree murder, was denied release by a Florida judge. (Curzio was not on parole or probation at the time.)

Like hundreds of Americans inside the Capitol that day, Curzio didn't bring a weapon or assault anyone. He walked through an open doorway where, he said, officers were seated allowing people to walk in.

Curzio spent the next several weeks on a meandering journey back to the nation's capital where he would remain behind bars for

---

1   Julie Kelly, *A January 6 Detainee Speaks Out* (American Greatness, 2021).

almost six months. "I was transported from the local jail to the jail in Jacksonville," Curzio told me. "Then I was put on a 737 on a U.S. Marshall transport plane headed to Georgia. They picked up more people then we flew to Oklahoma."

He remained in general population at the Cimarron Correctional Facility for a few weeks before boarding another bus to take another plane to West Virginia. He ended up at the Northern Neck Regional Facility in Virginia, where he connected with four other January 6 defendants: Timothy Hale-Cusanelli, Jacob Lang, Patrick McCaughey, and Jeffrey Sabol. All had been arrested in mid-January on various offenses related to the Capitol protest.

After spending nearly two weeks in isolation quarantine, the five men were transported to a jail in Washington, D.C. They arrived on February 3. A section of the D.C. Correctional Treatment Facility had been converted to a political prison of sorts. Curzio, Hale, McCaughey, Lang, and Sabol were among its first detainees.

In an email to me shortly after his release, George Tanios described the jail's condition. The section dedicated to January 6 detainees is separated into two "pods" divided by metal double doors. "The pod is shaped in an L with the 4 showers in the middle of each Pod. On the top tier there is a walkway to the center with offices to the Case workers offices. The bottom tier is where the 4 Showers, 2 Flat Screen TVs are mounted on the walls. Roughly a dozen Metal pay phones are along the wall next to this little TV room that doesn't have working TV. We had a Pull-up Bar and water fountain. Inmates held Bible study in there where it is a bit quieter."

The individual cells, Tanios said, were ten feet by seven feet. "There's a toilet in the front by the door the hand sink and a little metal desk and metal stool. Beds are double-bunkbed style, all metal with a thin mattress."

Over the next several weeks, the population in the "pod," the nickname given to the jail by the inhabitants, would grow by a few dozen as the Justice Department repeatedly sought pre-trial detention for January 6 defendants, including those charged with nonviolent crimes. "Curzio does not engage in destructive or violent behavior, and does not appear to encourage or discourage disorderly conduct," government lawyers wrote in a March motion to keep him behind bars. "Curzio remains a defendant with a violent criminal history who unregretfully traveled over 900 miles to join a wild mob, unlawfully entered the Capitol, defied a police order to leave, and committed offenses that threatened the governance of the Republic."

While the government insisted the pod was the safest place for January 6 defendants under "protected custody" status, the jail was a place where Trump supporters would be punished for their involvement in the protest. The overwhelming majority had no criminal record; it was the first time they were charged with a crime let alone serve time in jail.

Detainees were kept in their cells for twenty-three hours a day for months on end. Access to family and defense counsel was nearly nonexistent. By many accounts, dinner consisted of bologna sandwiches and inedible gruel was served for breakfast at three or four in the morning. The water was black and "chunky" as one inmate described it. "Some guards were happy we were in there," Curzio said. "Some said we got screwed over. We were stuck in our cells for 23 hours a day. They just left us there. Only a few of us were let out at a time on rec time, so you could only talk to one or two people a day. Some of the guys were roughed up."

There were reports of mental and physical abuse by prison guards. Ryan Samsel, arrested on January 30 and accused of assaulting a police officer—a formal indictment was not issued until August 25—was beaten severely by prison employees in March. "Ryan had a confrontation with one of the guards about getting toilet paper. As a Marine, he wasn't one to put up with a lot of stuff. All of a sudden, they moved him to the last cell out of the sight of security cameras," Curzio said.

At some point in the middle of the night, guards entered Samsel's cell and beat him. "The next day, his eyes were swollen shut and he had bumps all over his head." Samsel was taken to a hospital in Virginia.

During a court hearing a few days after the incident, Ronald Sandlin, another detainee, told a judge he was afraid to stay in jail after what happened to Samsel. He, too, explained guards had threatened him and that "even making this statement is putting me in danger of violence and retaliation."

Steven Metcalf, Samsel's attorney at the time, detailed what happened to his client in an interview with the *Washington Post*. "Around midnight, two guards came to that cell, restrained Samsel's arms behind his back with zip-tie handcuffs and 'beat him to a bloody pulp,'" Metcalf told reporter Rachel Weiner in April. Samsel did not regain consciousness until the next day and has since suffered seizures for the first time in his life; his nose allegedly was broken and his jaw dislocated.[2]

Six months later, with his injuries left untreated, Samsel's condition had worsened. His lawyers again appealed for help. "He has been detained since [January] and spent substantial time enduring the torture of solitary confinement," Stanley Woodward and Juli Haller wrote in a September 11 emergency motion for medical treatment.

> At the time of his detention, Mr. Samsel was undergoing medical treatment for a cyst in his chest. On or about March 21, 2021, Mr. Samsel was viciously assaulted while in the custody of the District of Columbia Department of Corrections, and while detained in "administrative segregation"—the latest euphemism for solitary confinement. He was taken to Howard University Hospital the next day, on March 22, 2021, where he was admitted and treated

---

2   Rachel Weiner, *Capitol Riot Detainee Alleges Beating by D.C. Jail Guards* (*Washington Post*, 2021).

for injuries including, but not limited to head strike and loss of consciousness, bilateral eye ecchymosis, acute kidney injury, injury of the wrists, fracture of the orbital floor (right side / closed fracture), bilateral facial bilateral nasal bone fracture, and thoracic outlet syndrome. Ultimately, as a result of the brutal assault, Mr. Samsel lost vision in his right eye, has suffered seizures, and has continuing pain and suffering in relation to the thoracic outlet syndrome as well as a cystic condition (that may have been aggravated in the assault), and a general lack of follow up care, and rehabilitative care. There has been no genuine mitigation and instead, Mr. Samsel's condition appears to have grown in severity.

Officials at the Central Virginia Regional Jail, where Samsel was transferred after the attack, refused to provide requested treatments such as MRIs and ophthalmology care to his damaged eye socket. Citing case law and a violation of the Eighth Amendment, Samsel's lawyers urged the court to intervene. "It is beyond dispute that Mr. Samsel was assaulted while detained. He sustained numerous serious injuries and was treated at Howard University Hospital following the assault. This conduct is in direct contravention of Mr. Samsel's Constitutional Rights."

As one of the few reporters covering the detainee situation in the nation's capital, I heard from inmates and their family members on a regular basis. Some of the men were veterans with tours in Iraq and Afghanistan. A few, including Tim Hale and members of the Oath Keepers, were not charged with any violent crime. But what I have called the "Deplorable Jail" was a political prison the likes of which the country has never seen.

It was especially painful for the detainees after watching thousands of violent protesters and rioters escape unpunished for committing crimes during the summer of 2020. In June 2021, Jonathan Mellis, arrested in February and charged with several offenses including using a stick against officers outside the west terrace tunnel after Rosanne Boyland collapsed and died, sent me an email describing their frustrations and what was happening in the jail:

> I would like to voice my confusion as to why left-wing rioters are set free and shown mercy while being the source of hundreds of riots last year all over the country, causing billions of dollars in damage, dozens of deaths, yet the right-wing rioters from Jan. 6th are treated in the harshest terms. We are charged with every possible offense and held in the DC jail on solitary [sic] confinement and treated inhumanely. For example, a correctional officer from a different pod came to C2B screaming at us late at night on 6/1/21 because we had just sang 'God Bless America' [sic] from behind our locked doors like we do every night. Being as we are on lockdown 22 hours a day it's nice to keep morale up through patriotism. When [name omitted], my next door neighbor, informed the officer that we were just singing 'God Bless America' the officer responded by yelling, 'Fuck America!'
>
> After the officer left the pod for several minutes he came back in through the back door with another guard, walked upstairs, and opened [name omitted]'s door to go inside with him. I believe 2 other guards came up the other stairs to stand near [his] door as well,

although I could not see them. I live right next
door so I listened through the vent to the officer threaten [him], 'Shut the fuck up or I will
beat your ass!' and, 'Fuck you!'

[He] sounded like he was explaining himself and pointing out how obviously inappropriate the officer's behavior was. And acknowledging that the officer's camera was clearly
turned off.

I am concerned for the safety of myself
and my fellow Capitol rioters here in the DC
jail. We are locked down all day and threatened
with violence regularly. We all know that getting our hands tied together and being beaten
is something the DC jail officers have already
done to Capitol rioters in this pod.

Solitary Confinement and beatings. That
is our reality. When will the inhumane treatment end? I just want to let everyone know the
reality of how we are treated in this place. Left
wing rioters are not even held in jail. Much
less subjected to the harsh and inhumane treatment my fellow Capitol rioters and I have sur-
vived under so far this year.

Judge Emmet Sullivan, the same judge who attempted to
prolong the perjury case against Lt. General Michael Flynn even
after both sides requested a dismissal, refused Mellis' request to
attend his father's funeral in May. Jerry Mellis, eighty, a retired
Army general and decorated Vietnam War veteran, died on May

17. Jon Mellis' attorney asked Sullivan to allow him to go to the funeral in nearby Williamsburg, Virginia. Joe Biden's Justice Department opposed his brief release by insisting Mellis was a flight risk and a danger to the community. Sullivan concurred: "Although the Court is sensitive to the news of his father's death and expresses its condolences, the Court hereby DENIES Motion for Temporary Release."

Others reached out to me, desperate for attention to their plight:

> We have no fewer than 5 combat vets out of Rec at any one time. The problem is . . . if the other cell block breaks in and starts a massive brawl, WE would get blamed in the media. (Many are concerned guards will allow the general population of D.C. prison to mix with January 6 detainees.) We are white. They are not. We are conservative. They are not. They can do whatever they want. We can not. If they busted in here and caused problems, we would be accused of racism, 'continued violence,' and 'rioting,' and the usual lies and slander." (The author of that text is not charged with any violent crimes.)

> My son has seen and experienced some very inhumane abuse in that Jail. He has also been denied bond at least twice. While others from that day are already home waiting trial. I don't know what to do or where to turn. As his Mother I am heartbroken." (The defendant, a former Marine, is accused of stealing a riot shield and using it to break a window.)

This kid has been in lockup for over 4 months, 23 hours per day. Rapists, murderers, actual criminals are treated better than the way these political prisoners are being treated. [He] has no access to medical, anything fitness-related, proper grooming, or reasonably edible food choices. He sleeps on a cot with a 1-inch-thick mattress. His "rec" time is limited to one hour per day unless the guards have a wild hair up their [---]—then he gets NOTHING!" (The defendant, an Army reservist, is not charged with any violent crime.)

When he first arrived he was put in a cell for 96 hours straight and not allowed out. Then they moved him to the pod [with all the Capitol defendants] and into a roughly five and ten cell for 23 hours a day. He is let out for one hour a day and shackled for that hour. The new guards are very racist and politically prejudiced. Now they don't let them have the phones too much and they don't know if they'll get the tablets. (Inmates share a few electronic tablets and use a common phone to communicate with family and defense counsel.) Some people don't have family to send them any money for commissary so they can't buy extra food or personal items." (The defendant is not charged with any violent crimes.)

All that I'm saying is fact and truth . . . it can be verified by all of the Patriots . . . most of which are like me and committed no violence

and ARE HERE WITH MISDEMEANOR
OFFENSES. We are the object of ridicule all
because of leftist media pushing a false narrative. Its ironic how we are in our Nations
Capitol yet being treated as Un-American as
one can be treated.

Jacob Lang, arrested on January 15, was a primary target of
the DC jail guards. Lang, twenty-four, had been near the west terrace tunnel along with Mellis and other January 6 defendants as
police officers were attacking protesters with a noxious chemical
gas. When several protesters collapsed, including Rosanne Boyland, Lang attempted to help the victims and stop police from
further assaults.

A grand jury indicted Lang on eleven counts including civil
disorder and assaulting, resisting, or impeding officers. According
to the indictment, Lang was on the west side of the Capitol building near the tunnel from 4:10 until about 5 p.m. that day, the
same time period when Boyland died. (He reportedly told family
members that a "woman died in his arms" on January 6.) The
Justice Department sought his pre-trial detention and the D.C.
District Court concurred.

Ned Lang, Jacob's father, told me in a podcast interview a
few months after Jacob's arrest what was happening to his son. Jacob Lang, like all of the January 6 detainees, had been transported
to several prisons, including one in Oklahoma, before arriving
in Washington. "The conditions there are abhorrent and quite
alarming," Lang told Liz Sheld and me in April. The detainees
were not permitted outside for days, had no access to exercise or
religious services, or to basic hygiene needs.[3]

Ned Lang read a message he had recently received from his
son. "This is a human rights atrocity. I've been in solitary confinement for a hundred days now and not even convicted of any

---

[3]   Liz Sheld, Julie Kelly, *Ep. 53: Julie and Liz Talk About Biden's Speech and Talk to Ned Lang, Father to Jake
Lang, Who is Imprisoned for Protesting on January 6* (Blubrry Podcasting, 2021).

crime with no end in sight. The media needs to be alerted to our treatment. It's torture, mentally, physically, socially, emotionally, legally, and spiritually with no religious services. Cruel and unusual punishment. We've been stripped of all dignity and humanity. Enough of being treated like an animal."

Judges knew the conditions of the jail from news reports and court filings but did nothing to address it. They refused to release defendants they had sent to the D.C. jail. Prison officials had no incentive to change their behavior, so, in many instances, it got worse.

Lang's attorneys, Steven Metcalf and Martin Tankleff, filed another motion in August pleading for their client's release:

> Lang's physical abuse includes being dragged, shoved, denied regular shower access, and getting an entire can of mace in his face, while standing inside of a cell with photos and a bible in his hand. Lang's other abuses include sleep deprivation, verbal abuse, and being denied the right to counsel. Just recently, Lang was taken to "The Hole", where he remained for two straight months, without a single disciplinary ticket. After being taken out of "The Hole," he received a hero's welcome upon returning to the Patriot Unit. Within 14 hours of being back on the Patriot Unit, the guards opened his cell door, and maced him directly in his eyes. When Lang was maced he was standing in his cell with a bible in one hand and family photos in the other. Overall, Jake has been held in the hole in 24-hour a day solitary confinement on three separate occasions, totaling more than three months. While Jake is currently back on the Patriot Unit, the unit

with other J6 Defendants at the DC jail, he
has been and will continue to be subject to
these abuses at anytime. The retaliation and
scare tactics most likely will continue within
days of us even filing this application.

Corroborating what others reported after release, Lang had
not received "a single haircut or shave" since his arrest. As of September 15, Lang was still in jail with no trial date set.

Karl Dresch also condemned the jail's conditions after his release in August. The Michigan man was arrested on January 15 and
charged with four misdemeanors and the obstruction of an official proceeding felony. "The FBI almost knocked down my house
during the raid, they broke every door and window in my house,"
Dresch told me in an interview a few days after he was released.

Shuttled between several prisons, Dresch arrived in the D.C.
jail on March 9. Dresch confirmed the men were kept in their
cells for twenty-three hours a day for months. His last haircut
had been at the end of February. "They gave us something called
'magic shave,' a chemical for your face, that burned everyone,"
Dresch said.

Guards listened to any conversation with defense attorneys,
blatantly violating attorney-client privilege protections. Prison officials pushed hard to force the detainees to take the vaccine or
lose even the most basic privileges such as the use of nail clippers.
Anyone with a vaccine could have in-person meetings with their
lawyer; those who did not were forced back into a fourteen-day
quarantine.

"There are a lot of men still there being kept because of what
they thought or said," Dresch said. "This is not the way America
is supposed to be. Its a scary time to stand up, our rights are being
trampled on."

Dresch and Curzio had something else in common: both men
ended up pleading guilty to one count of "parading, demonstrating,

or picketing in a Capitol building." By the time they accepted the government's plea offer, Curzio and Dresch had served more than six months in jail, the maximum sentence for the misdemeanor.

While Curzio and Dresch finally went home, others languished behind. On August 24, Christopher Worrell gave an emotional interview to Newsmax's Greg Kelly. The Florida resident was accused of assaulting law enforcement with pepper spray; an FBI investigator on the case, however, could not confirm with certainty that Worrell used the spray against police officers.

Worrell, who has non-Hodgkins lymphoma, told Kelly his condition was "deteriorating daily" after 166 days behind bars with no medical treatment. "I am afraid for my life to be honest," Worrell said, his voice shaky. "We are being treated like political POWs in here."[4]

Breaking down, Worrell asked viewers to sing the "national anthem" at 9 p.m. Eastern time, a tradition the detainees started months earlier to keep up morale. "Everyone, everyone across the world...stand with us and sing our national anthem," Worrell urged through tears. The detainees also sing "God Bless America" and "Amazing Grace," Curzio told me. "It's definitely something to remember. We always got goosebumps when we were done. They are my brothers."

The plight of the January 6 detainees finally caught the attention of some Republicans in Congress. Five Republican senators sent a letter to Attorney General Merrick Garland with questions related to his department's "potential unequal justice" in the handling of Capitol protesters versus George Floyd protesters. "DOJ's apparent unwillingness to punish these individuals who allegedly committed crimes during the spring and summer 2020 protests stands in stark contrast to the harsher treatment of the individuals charged in connection with the January 6, 2021 breach of the U.S. Capitol Building in Washington, D.C.," the senators, including Ron Johnson and Ted Cruz, wrote on June 7.

---

4   Greg Kelly, *Greg Kelly Interviews January 6th Suspect from Jail: 'These are False and Fabricated Charges… They're Mistreating Me'* (Newsmax, 2021).

Noting January 6 defendants had been subjected to FBI raids, pre-trial detention orders, and solitary confinement conditions, the senators asked for similar data on 2020 "social unrest" protesters. "Americans have the constitutional right to peaceably assemble and petition the government for a redress of grievances. This constitutional right should be cherished and protected. Violence, property damage, and vandalism of any kind should not be tolerated and individuals that break the law should be prosecuted. However, the potential unequal administration of justice with respect to certain protestors is particularly concerning."

The senators asked for a reply by June 21, 2021. They did not receive one.

Several Republican House members visited the jail on July 27 in an effort to see the conditions for themselves. While they initially were let inside the building, once they walked out to speak with a supervisor, they were locked out of the facility. "What are they hiding?" Rep. Matt Gaetz tweeted.

At a press conference in front of the Justice Department building, the group confronted protesters attempting to drown out their comments. "We will not back down, we will not stop asking questions, we are looking for the truth," Rep. Marjorie Taylor Greene said amid hecklers.[5]

"How is it that those who are not even citizens get better treatment and due process at Gitmo when they don't have it here," Rep. Paul Gosar asked. He also called out groups such as Amnesty International and the ACLU for their silence on January 6 detainees.

But where January 6 was concerned, none of the old rules applied. In another irony, Meghan McCain, daughter of the late senator who for years fought Barack Obama's plan to shutter Guantanamo Bay, raged that Capitol protesters should be sent to the notorious prison. "We need to treat domestic terrorists the way we treat actual terrorists," she said on ABC's *The View* on January 11. "I'm not against sending these people to Gitmo."

---

5   Marjorie Taylor Greene, *"We will not back down. We will not stop asking questions. We are looking for the truth."* (Twitter, 2021).

McCain tweeted earlier in the day that "the MAGA terrorists should be prosecuted like any other terrorists who have attacked our homeland and be given the same severity of consequences. They should also be tried for treason. No mercy."[6]

Her wish came true. With few exceptions, the January 6 detainees were granted no mercy—by the news media, government prosecutors, federal judges, powerful politicians, or D.C. prison guards.

In September, Jon Mellis sent another letter to the American people about his ongoing plight:

> My name in Jonathan Mellis. I am a January 6 Capitol detainee being held in the DC jail.
>
> In the last 7 months I have experienced and witnessed the most inhumane and hateful treatment of my 34 years of life.
>
> The DOJ and the Biden Administration are doing everything in their power to break me.
>
> I write this from solitary confinement on September 15 with no clear explanation as to why I've been isolated or how long I will be here. I have been locked in this small concrete cell for over a month at this point. They call solitary confinement "the hole."
>
> This is totally appropriate because I feel like I have been dropped to the bottom of a deep and dark hole in the ground and forgotten. I am alone. My mind is all I have to keep me com-

6   Meghan McCain, *The MAGA Terrorists Should be Prosecuted Like Any Other Terrorists Who Have Attacked Our Homeland...* (Twitter, 2021).

pany. And that can become quite a scary thing after weeks all alone. What makes this much worse is that I'm not told exactly why I was put down here or when this lonely torture will end. Every deadline given by the policy book to the jail to explain to me why I am in solitary confinement has been totally ignored. If I were in trouble I would have been served a Disciplinary Report within 2 days. I was not. I should have been seen by the Housing Board within 7 days. I was not. I get no answers. All I get is lied to by Sergeants and Lieutenants.

This kind of isolation and disrespect is very harmful to one's mind and body. At first being locked in a small moldy cell is horrible and sad. You miss human interaction and your mind is racing. After a while this turns into desperate loneliness and frustration. You get headaches for days at a time and try to sleep all day. It has become a real depression. You feel worthless and ignored. Then as your energy starts to come back from sleeping all the time, it brings with it a ball of rage in your gut. You feel injured, angry, and helpless. You know you are being mistreated and there is nothing you can do about it. Your head hurts and your back muscles are tense. All the normal things in your life that give you stress are amplified and you are now consumed by bad and negative emotions. They are really hurting you. There is the feeling that you just want to collapse emotionally and physically. You just want to give up. The 4 walls of this concrete box are closing in on you. Your skin is crawling and you feel claustrophobic. It's a nightmare.

How long will they make me do this? I don't know. But I already know from experience that all of us January 6 detainees were held on solitary confinement until July. So I know first hand how long these monsters are willing to do this to me. This is inhumane and people think its OK because I'm a Trump supporter. I love people and I try to live a virtuous life. But because I like Trump they don't see me as human. They enjoy watching me suffer. It makes them smile. How sick is that? The pure hate within the Justice Department is obvious in their actions. They are a sadistic bunch. It's actually quite scary. There were over 500 violent riots last year. All of them were Left wing. Nobody is searching for these people. As a matter of fact, anyone who was arrested has most likely had their charges dropped. They were even encouraged by the Democrat politicians. They were applauded as they burned buildings down, destroyed businesses, killed people, and looted cities. They attacked police officers and took over police precincts. But nobody is sitting in jail for it. Much less being subjected to the inhumane treatment we Trump supporters' experience. We live in constant fear of being shackled and beaten by the correctional officers. This has already happened. Several of us have been beaten by the correctional officers. Yet nobody really cares because we are Trump supporters.

I am currently engaged in a deep spiritual battle. I will not let evil win. I am strong. But it is hard. They want to break me. I will not let them. My love for this country will never end. Please do not believe everything you read about me in the news. They are crucifying me before my trial. I was trying to help the people being crushed by police.

I also am pleading for any help you can afford (even it is just a few dollars) to help with my legal bills so I can get justice. There is no where else I can turn than to my fellow citizens. Please pray for me on the outside.

Strength and Honor,

Jonathan Mellis #376907

As of October 2021, Mellis had no trial date set. His court-appointed lawyer never filed a motion for bond, only a temporary release to attend his father's funeral, which was denied. Inmates received some encouraging news in mid-October after Judge Royce Lamberth found D.C. Jail Warden Wanda Patten and D.C. Department of Corrections Director Quincy Booth in contempt of court for failing to provide records related to the medical treatment of Chris Worrell, a non-Hodgkin's lymphoma sufferer. Worrell, who was transferred to the jail in April, broke his hand in May and still had not received the suggested surgery to repair the break.

Lamberth also referred the matter to the Justice Department "for appropriate inquiry into potential civil rights violations of January 6 defendants, as exemplified in this case."

It was unlikely the same Justice Department asking federal judges to detain January 6 defendants indefinitely in the inhumane jail would take meaningful action. Lamberth's ruling, however, provided a strong basis for detainees to pursue litigation against the government and D.C. Department of Corrections once their cases were settled.

Following a U.S. Marshals report confirming inhumane conditions in the D.C. prison system, Lamberth ordered the immediate release of Christopher Worrell on November 3, over the objections of Biden's Justice Department. Lamberth said he had "zero confidence" Worrell would receive the care he needed and expressed concern that prison guards would retaliate if he remained in the jail one more day.

In a surprise inspection conducted after Lamberth's civil rights referral, officials from the Marshals office had found numerous violations in the D.C. prison system. According to a memo sent to the director of the D.C. Department of Corrections on November 1, eight Marshals deputies inspected the facilities, including the jail set aside for January 6 defendants, and interviewed hundreds of inmates and staff members. The Marshals found standing sewage in numerous cells; evidence of drug use; evidence of untreated injuries; prison guards intimidating and antagonizing inmates; improper food storage and the withholding of food and water for "punitive reasons" among other atrocities.[7]

The Marshals service, however, claimed conditions in the section for January 6 detainees were "largely appropriate and consistent with federal prisoner detention standards," an unfathomable conclusion considering the overall situation at the main jail facility and how those complaints had been corroborated for months by January 6 detainees.

And in a briefing with a Marshals official before Worrell's hearing, officials admitted as much. Lamberth said what he was told privately did not exactly match what had been disclosed in the memo.

---

7   Lamont J. Ruffin, *U.S. Marshals Service Nov. 1 Memo to D.C. Dept. of Corrections re: D.C. Jail Inspection* (*Washington Post*, 2021).

In a separate hearing the following day, Judge Trevor McFadden reluctantly authorized the transfer of Robert Morss out of the D.C. jail to another prison in Northern Neck, Virginia. Morss' lawyer, John Kiyonaga, filed an emergency motion for transfer based on an invasive and clearly punitive strip search Morss endured after meeting with Kiyonaga the day before in preparation for the November 4 hearing.

McFadden downplayed the results of the Marshals evaluation, claiming, oddly, that most inmates in the regular D.C. jail would much rather be in the January 6 pod. McFadden further said the use of a strip search is justified after an inmate interacts with "someone on the outside," which would include a defense attorney.

Only after a sidebar where Kiyonaga privately disclosed the sexually explicit details of Morss' search did he authorize his immediate transfer.

One detainee, however, discovered a different get-out-of-jail-free card: write a letter denouncing Donald Trump and vilify his fellow detainees. Judge Amy Berman Jackson, one of the many Trump-hating judges on the D.C. District Court, released Thomas Sibick on October 27 after promising the court he had changed his political ways.

Sibick had been charged with assaulting Officer Michael Fanone, stealing his badge, and burying it in his yard. "January 6 was a disgrace to our nation that left a scar that trump (sic) is ultimately responsible for but we are strong and we will heal from it," Sibick wrote. "While many praise Trump, I loathe him, his words, and actions are nefarious and causing pain and harm to the world." He promised never to attend another political rally again in the future.

Sibick's lawyer, Stephen Brennwald, told Jackson the atmosphere in the D.C. jail was "cult-like" and explained how the detainees sing the "national anthem" every night. Jackson confronted Sibick's attorney and demanded to know where he received his news:[8] "He came here, fired up about a stolen election," Jackson

---

8   Marisa Sarnoff, *Jan. 6 Rioter Accused of Attacking Officer Michael Fanone Can Go Home, But Can't Watch Political Talk Shows: Judge* (Law & Crime, 2021).

said. "Where was he getting his information? Facebook, Twitter, just watching the news?"

"I thought it might have been OANN or Newsmax, but it wasn't. It was Fox News," Brennwald said.

"Wow," Jackson responded.

Jackson released Sibick to home confinement with a warning that he cannot watch any political programs including Fox News and MSNBC. In December, Rep. Marjorie Taylor Greene released a report describing what she saw during a November tour of two D.C. prison facilities including the jail housing January 6 detainees. "Unusually Cruel: An Eyewitness Report From Inside the DC Jail" provided a detailed account of her visit, along with Rep. Louie Gohmert, against the wishes of prison officials. Greene, Gohmert, and staff members spent nearly four hours in the facilities where they witnessed inhumane conditions for both the general population and January 6 defendants. Prison officials repeatedly attempted to end the tour but Greene and Gohmert were undeterred. "Moments after Reps. Greene and Gohmert entered the room, the inmates broke into excited yelling and triumphant shouting, astounded by a visit from two sitting Members of Congress," the report read. "The inmates were overwhelmed with emotions: some crying, almost all emotionally shaken. One inmate asked to hug Congresswoman Greene." They started chanting, "USA, USA" as Greene started asking questions about the conditions of their incarceration. After nearly an hour of speaking with the detainees and hearing their horror stories, Greene ended the visit in a group prayer. "You know who you are, a child of God, and He loves every single one of you. He made you and He formed you and He knew you before you were born, and that's the greatest gift. He's got a plan for every single one of us. You know you're not forgotten; you're appreciated. And you're loved, and your families love you. They miss you and your friends love you. And many people talk about you and pray for you. And I think if anything, we can come through this time in our country, hopefully we can all come back together, and we're not divided by that."

But there still was no relief in sight for the rest of the January 6 detainees. As trial dates slowly filled the calendar for 2022, it became more apparent that Capitol protestors had almost no chance of a fair trial in one of the most politically biased cities in America. In a town consumed with politics, and increasingly toxic comparisons between January 6 and events such as 9/11, defendants' uphill battle to prove their innocence looked nearly insurmountable.

CHAPTER ELEVEN:

WILL THE CAPITOL DEFENDANTS GET A FAIR TRIAL?

American history is littered with examples of citizens protesting inside and outside government spaces. Sometimes those protests turn violent; police officers are attacked, lawmakers are bullied, property is damaged. Public buildings are the ideal location for Americans to voice their views on any range of subjects from the environment to war policy to a dubious presidential election.

The closest comparison between January 6 and another instance of partisan activists aggresively disrupting Congressional proceedings was the confirmation of Brett Kavanaugh.

For weeks prior to the vote, the news media, Democratic lawmakers, and feminist groups made life hell for Kavanaugh and for the country. The chaos began during Kavanaugh's initial hearing on September 4, 2018. Senator Kamala Harris (D-Calif.) interrupted Chairman Charles Grassley's opening remarks, talking over him as the longtime senator tried to introduce the nominee and his family. Senator Amy Klobuchar (D-Minn.) quickly joined Harris' harangue. "Mr. Chairman, I move to adjourn," Senator Richard Blumenthal (D-Conn.) demanded.

Activists seated in the hearing room loudly cheered then started to berate Grassley and Republican members of the committee. The mayhem lasted for several minutes as protesters were removed.

It was a harbinger of how vociferously, and violently in some instances, Democrats and their allies would fight Kavanaugh's confirmation. That week, more than 200 people were arrested by U.S. Capitol Police, paid a minimal fine, and were released. Despite the uproar, Kavanaugh's confirmation seemed almost certain.

But unsubstantiated stories about Kavanaugh's behavior in high school, including accusations of sexual assault, were reported by the Washington Post and threatened to doom his ascendancy to the nation's highest court. A dramatic showdown between Kavanaugh and his chief accuser, Christine Blasey Ford, during a Senate Judiciary Committee hearing on September 27, 2018 further inflamed both sides.

The siege of government buildings escalated. Republican senators were angrily confronted in elevators and outside government buildings. Some received death threats. The outrage was heavily fueled by Democratic leaders including Senator Elizabeth Warren. "Hello resistance!" Warren shouted to a raucous crowd assembled outside on October 4. "I am angry on behalf of women who have been told to sit down and shut up one time too many. This is about hijacking our democracy."

Thousands heeded Warren's call for action. "We were planning to shut down the Capitol Building but the authorities were so scared of this #WomensWave that they shut it down for us," the official account of the Women's March tweeted that day. "1000+ women, survivors, and allies have gathered in the Hart Senate Building. Every hallway. Every floor."

When Pence announced on the afternoon of October 6, 2018 that Kavanaugh's nomination was confirmed, women shouted from the Senate gallery and were removed.

The nation was roiled by the Kavanaugh fiasco for more than a month yet activists opposed to his nomination were considered heroes, not villains, by the national news media.

Protesters who defiled government buildings or harassed elected officials or scuffled with police were not considered "domestic terrorists."

Democratic senators were not condemned as a "sedition caucus" for disrupting and delaying an official government hearing. To the contrary, theatrics by Harris and Warren elevated their public profile and helped launch their presidential bids the following year.

More than 230 people were arrested in D.C. on January 20, 2017 when protests against Donald Trump's inauguration turned violent. Activists associated with the "#DisruptJ20" movement, which organized "widespread civil resistance [in] the streets of Washington, D.C." during Trump's swearing-in festivities, set fires, vandalized businesses, and clashed with police that day. But the same office prosecuting January 6 defendants eventually dropped all cases related to the J20 rioting.

A more recent example is the hostile occupation of the Mark O. Hatfield United States Courthouse in Portland, Oregon in 2020. The government building and surrounding streets were under attack for months by leftwing activists following the death of George Floyd. The U.S. Attorney for the District of Oregon, Billy J. Williams, detailed the destruction on the one-hundred-day anniversary of the siege:

"There has been nothing civil, respectful, or positive about the nightly violent and destructive protests in Portland, Oregon," Williams wrote in a press release on September 25, 2020.

> On many nights, after peaceful demonstrations end, violent agitators have physically attacked police officers and firefighters, damaged buildings, and repeatedly attempted to set public buildings on fire. Following one of these political rallies, a man was shot and killed. Most recently, acts of violence towards law enforce-

ment and first responders include a Portland firefighter being shot in the chest with a steel ball bearing launched from an arm-mounted slingshot, a man dousing several police officers with high-powered bear deterrent spray, a man punching a female police officer in the face, and a woman striking a police officer in the head from behind with a wooden shield.

Some of the weapons confiscated during the Portland riots were the same that landed January 6 defendants behind bars and denied bail. Those items included a helmet, tasers, and chemical spray.

But a March 2021 investigation by KGW-TV, a Portland news station, revealed that at least one-third of the federal cases had been dropped, including defendants accused of assaulting federal officers or destroying government property. Half were dismissed "with prejudice," which means the case cannot be brought back to court.[1]

Some also took plea deals that only required a period of probation or a thirty-day stint in jail. One legal expert—law professor Laura Appleman of Willamette University—defended the move, explaining on KGW-TV how prosecutors needed to ask, "Is it worth using our limited time and energy to prosecute each and every of these federal misdemeanors?"

However, January 6 protesters received none of the usual protections or praise afforded to activists on the Left. Even more troubling for Trump supporters would be the ultimate judgment for their actions would be rendered in a city where only 5 percent of the residents voted for Donald Trump in 2020.

Since the "crime scene," as former acting U.S. Attorney Michael Sherwin described the Capitol building after January 6, was in Washington, D.C., every case is handled in the nation's capital—a bad omen for Trump supporters. The overwhelming number of judges and magistrates of the D.C. District Court were

---

1   Kyle Iboshi, *Feds Quietly Dismiss Dozens of Portland Protest Cases* (KGW8, 2021).

appointed by Barack Obama and Bill Clinton; only four were Trump appointees. Judges such as Amy Berman Jackson and Emmet Sullivan had been openly hostile to President Trump and his associates during his presidency.

In a forty-minute tirade from the bench in February 2020, Berman Jackson berated longtime Trump associate Roger Stone and accused him of "covering up" Trump's role in imaginary Russian election collusion. "There was nothing phony about the investigation," Berman Jackson said about Special Counsel Robert Mueller's investigation, which had already come up empty-handed.

She accused House Republicans of issuing a misleading report on Trump-Russia election collusion. "The truth still exists, the truth still matters. Roger Stone's insistence that it doesn't, his belligerence, his pride in his own lies are a threat to our most fundamental institutions. If it goes unpunished it will not be a victory for one party or another. Everyone loses." All of this was irrelevant to the matter at hand. Stone was not charged with any crime related to election collusion. But in the mind of this liberal judge, it was all about Trump and Russia.

Beryl Howell, the chief judge of the D.C. District Court, also is no fan of Donald Trump. A former Democratic Senate staffer, Howell was appointed to the bench in 2010 by Barack Obama; she became chief judge in 2016. The following year, Howell supervised Mueller's grand jury. Mueller's nineteen-lawyer team issued 2,800 subpoenas and executed at least 500 search warrants over a two-year period with Howell overseeing most of the legal proceedings.

Howell made her views of January 6 very clear at the start. "What happened on that day at the U.S. Capitol is criminal activity that is destined to go down in the history books of this country, of hundreds of Americans using force and violence against their own government to disrupt what we have been most proud of: A peaceful and Democratic transition of power," Howell said on January 29 during a detention hearing for Richard Barnett, the man photographed in Pelosi's office.

"On January 6, 2021, there was an assault on the U.S. Capitol during a joint session of Congress, certifying the 2020 presidential election results. This violence disrupted a constitutional function of Congress necessary to the presidential transition and to the functioning of our democracy. This was not a peaceful protest. During the assault on the Capitol that was intended to disrupt the peaceful transition of power to a new administration, as designed under our U.S. Constitution, five people died and many more were injured."

Howell noted Barnett "traveled all the way from his home in Arkansas to Washington, D.C. prepared for this assault on the Capitol." (He was never charged with a violent crime.) "I don't know how smart Mr. Barnett is but he is certainly a bragger," she continued.

It's important to emphasize that this was a hearing to determine whether Barnett should remain behind bars, not his actual trial. Barnett, according to Howell, was part of "a violent assault on the Capitol in which five people lost their lives"—as though Barnett personally had anything to do with that.

She denied his release. No date has been set for his trial.

Others were subjected to Howell's obvious contempt and overdramatic, and in some cases untrue, description of what happened on January 6. She seemed particularly agitated that Americans from across the country went to the nation's capital that week, as though this were somehow out of the ordinary and evidence of malign intent, even though Americans have been traveling across the country to the nation's capital for mass protests since the New Deal and civil rights eras. "Defendant accepted this invitation and traveled from his home in Kansas all the way to Washington, D.C. to take part in the assault on both the Capitol and the peaceful transition of power," Howell wrote in her February 26 ruling to deny the release of William Chrestman, a member of the Proud Boys, which she referred to repeatedly as a "gang."

Chrestman, charged with other Proud Boys for conspiracy, was a danger to the community, Howell insisted, because he had not sufficiently expressed regret for participating in the protest. "Nothing in the record suggests that he has any remorse about the events of January 6 or disclaimed the beliefs and gang membership animating his actions on that day, and thus there is no evidentiary basis to assume that defendant will refrain from similar activities, if instructed, in the future," Howell concluded. Seven months later, Chrestman remained in the D.C. jail awaiting trial.

She also did not take kindly to the appellate court's ruling that her decision to keep Eric Munchel and his mother, Lisa Eisenhart, behind bars, was in error. Howell, the D.C. Circuit concluded in April, had exaggerated their threat to the community. (As explained earlier, the government immediately withdrew its pre-trial detention motion. Both were released.) "The circuit's view is, gosh, take a taser, take some zipties, walk around the Senate chamber—not a sign of future dangerousness,'" Howell complained during a hearing in April. Her voice rich with sarcasm, Howell said she "didn't understand why everyone doesn't appeal detention rulings post-Munchel."

Howell clearly wanted the hammer to fall hard on Trump supporters. Frustrated by the volume of misdemeanors, Howell started to confront prosecutors, asking why the government wasn't bringing harsher charges against January 6 defendants as a "deterrence" measure.

She further suggested that the "parading, demonstrating, or picketing" offense should not apply to Trump supporters in the Capitol. Protesting election results, Howell said, didn't count as a legitimate excuse. "This is the puzzle for this petty offense charge. That is typically for an end. Demonstrating is typically about something. It's parading about something," Howell said to a prosecutor during a hearing in August, in a jab at the government's repeated use of the charge. Howell was suggesting that the protesters had nothing to protest since, in her opinion, the election was not "stolen" and Trump's claim to the contrary was an obvious "Big Lie."

At one point, she refused to sign a plea agreement until the defendant admitted in court he was there to support Donald Trump—as though that constituted a punishable offense in itself.

"Was your purpose in entering the Capitol building…to protest against Congress certifying the electoral college vote?" Howell asked Leonard Gruppo after he pleaded guilty to the parading count. The Texas man was inside the building for about seven minutes, according to prosecutors. He was charged with four misdemeanors. Gruppo told Howell that he "was there to support the president."

Howell, the *Washington Post* reported, "did not accept his plea until he agreed that he was in the building 'as part of a demonstration in support of President Trump.'"

Judge Amy Berman Jackson openly blasted another trespasser, Karl Dresch, during his plea hearing. "He was not a political prisoner. We are not here today because he supported former president Trump. He was arrested because he was an enthusiastic participant in an effort to subvert and undo the electoral process."

Berman Jackson mocked Dresch and other January 6 protesters. "You called yourself and the others patriots, but that's not patriotism. Patriotism is loyalty to country, loyalty to the Constitution, not loyalty to a single head of state. That's the tyranny we rejected on July 4th of 1776."

This comment stands in stark contrast to the chorus of liberal political and media figures who had claimed the year before that burning flags, smashing windows, torching police cars and pulling down public statues was "democracy in action" and an expression of "patriotic" dissent.

Throughout 2021, federal judges seated on the D.C. District Court made similar inflammatory statements about January 6 and those involved. Nor were such comments, for the most part, offered after sentencing or plea arrangement when a defendant accepted guilt. The judgments, in contradiction to the rules of impartiality, were made in pre-trial detention hearings where only the government had a chance to present evidence.

Here are just a few examples:

> "While the certification of the 2020 Presidential Election is now complete, and President Biden has taken office, the Court is not convinced that dissatisfaction and concern about the legitimacy of the election results has dissipated for all Americans. Former President Donald J. Trump continues to make forceful public comments about the 'stolen election,' chastising individuals who did not reject the supposedly illegitimate results that put the current administration in place."— Judge Emmett Sullivan

> "[T]his was a singular and chilling event in U.S. history, raising legitimate concern about the security—not only of the Capitol building—but of our democracy itself."— Judge Randolph Moss

> "[T]he proffered evidence shows that [Dominic] Pezzola came to Washington, D.C. as a key member of a broader conspiracy to effectively steal one of our Nation's crown jewels: the peaceful transfer of power. He then played a prominent role in using violence to achieve those ends by, among other things, robbing a police officer of his or her riot shield and breaking a window of the Capitol to allow

rioters to enter. Thus, the nature and circumstances of the offense show a clear disregard for the law and the Constitution. More than that, though, they show a willingness to use violence and to act in concert with others to obstruct essential functions of the United States government. And Pezzola's refusal to obey the lawful orders of law enforcement throughout the day suggest that he would not comply with conditions of release to keep the public safe."—Judge Timothy Kelly

"If somehow law enforcement had not been able to diffuse the situation and get the protesters—and I don't call these "protesters"—rioters who were screaming to hang the vice president and roaming the Capitol in search of the Speaker of the House, what would have happened if they had not been dispersed. I don't like to imagine it. It could have been really very, very bloody and very violent, and there could have been enormous losses of life, to say nothing of the threat to our rule of law and our electoral system and our democracy. I'm not generally given to hyperbole about crimes, but this one was horrifying. And I would just remind you of the officers who were in fact killed that day and officers who had heart attacks and officers who had their eyes gouged out and officers who will never be coming home to their families. This military man, who knows the chain of command, who's supposed to be respecting the Constitution and is supposed to be respecting other law enforcement officers, not only disregarded their commands but tried to hurt them, and very well could have killed one of them."—Judge Tanya Chutkan

As any fair-minded observer can see, these statements are rife with errors, myths and falsehoods. They assume facts not in evidence and in some cases seem to come straight from the fever swamps of the left's imagination. (The claim that officers had their eyes gouged out at the protest is obviously false or it would have been widely reported and the victims paraded endlessly on television.)

How—one has to wonder—can such prejudicial remarks, widely bruited in the press, not influence a prospective jury pool or assure defendants the right to a fair trial?

Some judges seemed to relish the opportunity to add to the misery of January 6 defendants. Chutkan, an Obama appointee, made no effort to conceal her contempt for the Trump-supporting defendants in her courtroom. In at least four cases, Chutkan sentenced Capitol trespassers to more jail time than even vengeful prosecutors had requested.

"There have to be consequences for participating in an attempted violent overthrow of the government, beyond sitting at home," Chutkan said to Matthew Mazzocco, a man from Texas who pleaded guilty to one count of "parading, demonstrating, or picketing" in the Capitol building. Prosecutors, crediting Mazzocco for his guilty plea, asked for home detention; Chutkan instead sentenced him to forty-five days in prison. "The country is watching to see what the consequences are for something that has not ever happened in the history of this country before, for actions and crimes that threaten to undermine the rule of law and our democracy," Chutkan lectured during his October sentencing hearing. Referring to Donald Trump, Chutkan accused Mazzocco of coming to Washington "to support one man...in total disregard of a lawfully conducted election."

Chutkan also called it a "false equivalency" to compare January 6 and the George Floyd riots. "The treatment of [Jan. 6] rioters…has been far more lenient than other defendants who frequently appear in our court," Chutkan claimed without proof. "To compare the actions of people protesting, mostly peacefully, for civil rights to those of a violent mob seeking to take over the Congress is false equivalence and ignores the very real damage the Jan. 6 riot poses to the foundation of our democracy."

Chief Judge Beryl Howell also became increasingly vitriolic as cases dragged on, scolding prosecutors for bringing light charges and excoriating Capitol defendants, even those charged with minor crimes, from the bench. In a sentencing hearing in early November, Howell also dismissed comparisons between the Floyd riots and January 6. "The goal of a lot of protests in 2020 was to hold police accountable and politicians accountable for police brutality—and murder, in George Floyd's case—and to improve our political system," Howell said during a sentencing hearing for Glenn Croy, who pleaded guilty to one misdemeanor count of "parading" in the Capitol. "What happened on Jan 6 is in a totally different category from that protest. It was to stop the government from functioning at all to stop the democratic process and it worked. They're not comparable."[2]

Given the facts on display, comments such as these by Howell and Chutkan reflect what can only be termed an astonishing triumph of narrative over logic and evidence.

Meanwhile Croy's lawyer, Kira West, blasted prosecutors for falsely portraying his involvement in the protest. "Creating a penumbra of evidence when there is none should not be tolerated by this Court. After an exhaustive, fruitless search for more ways to impugn Mr. Croy in order to give this Court a reason to incarcerate him rather than order a sentence of probation, the government now engages in creating 'maybe so's' and 'could be's' when there is no evidence supporting what the government argues. These conjectural statements by the government grow by leaps and bounds."

---

2   Josh Gerstein, Kyle Cheney, *Judge Rejects Comparison Between Jan. 6 Riot and George Floyd Unrest* (Politico, 2021).

Howell nonetheless sentenced Croy to fourteen days in a federal halfway house, ninety days of home confinement, and three years' probation.

Howell and Chutkan are not outliers. Judges, prosecutors, and journalists based in the Beltway did not view January 6 as a legitimate protest that devolved into a riot. Their comments and coverage make clear that they viewed the hundreds of thousands of Americans who traveled to their nation's capital as an invading army bristling with imaginary weapons and intent on somehow overthrowing the US government. They had no business going there in the first place and the fact that they did so was prima facie evidence of their guilt and reason enough to lock them up and throw away the key, if not execute them for treason.

Originally an unappealing swamp on the Potomac, Washington, D.C. has become the personal and professional fiefdom of the American ruling class. D.C. residents, and those who live in the surrounding suburbs, are almost all tied to the federal government in one way or another. Politics consumes every conversation; residents hang on every word uttered by the president and congressional leaders. A seamless flow exists between elected officials, top staffers, reporters, judges, Cabinet officials, lobbyists, think tank experts, and captains of industry. Over the past decade, the area had become the wealthiest in the nation; six of the ten richest counties are outside Washington, D.C.

That's why someone like Beryl Howell seemed astonished that an American would travel "all the way" from another state in the hinterlands to attend a political rally in Washington. The Capitol breach wasn't just a political or legal issue; it was personal to them. An attitude of "how dare they" permeated nearly every hearing and court motion.

Federal prosecutors also expressed their disgust. Joshua Rothstein, an assistant U.S. Attorney in the D.C. office, didn't hold back in attempting to shame Robert Reeder for going inside the Capitol on January 6. Even though Reeder turned himself in to law enforcement and was charged with no violent acts that day, Rothstein berated Reeder in the government's sentencing memo.

"The attack on the U.S. Capitol . . . was one of the only times in our history when the building was literally occupied by hostile participants," Rothstein wrote in the August filing. "The Defendant chose to be a part of the desecration of the Capitol rotunda. The Defendant stood in the center of the rotunda, where Ruther (sic) Bader Ginsburg, John Lewis, Ronald Reagan, Dwight Eisenhower, John F. Kennedy, and Abraham Lincoln, among others, lied in state. What the Defendant chose to record and celebrate at that place, at that time, was antithetical to the events that most Americans associate with the Capitol rotunda. "Indeed, his very presence in the Capitol rotunda that day was a desecration of hallowed ground." [3]

It's true: Reeder does not have a degree from an expensive Ivy League law school like Joshua Rothstein. Unlike Rothstein, Reeder, who lost his job and was cut off by family, friends, neighbors, and his own church after he was arrested on four misdemeanors, can't afford to throw himself a birthday party at a fancy D.C. restaurant attended by Beltway journalists and other insiders like former Homeland Security secretary Jeh Johnson, and have details of the soiree written up in Politico. Defendants justifiably started to suspect that their shot at a fair trial, whether bench or jury, was in serious jeopardy. In July, David Fischer, counsel for Thomas Caldwell in the Oath Keepers conspiracy case, filed a lengthy motion requesting a change of venue. It was joined by every defendant in the case.

Not only had his client, one of the first arrested in the Capitol breach investigation, been smeared by the government and in national news coverage, but everyone present that day had been branded racists and "domestic terrorists" by the most powerful people in the country. "Caldwell cannot receive a fair trial in the District because he is the victim of D.C.- based systemic race-baiting," Fischer wrote in a July motion. "The President, Attorney

---

3   Julie Kelly, *Our Representatives, Not J6 Protesters, Defile the 'Sacred' U.S. Capitol* (American Greatness, 2021).

General, Speaker of the House, prominent politicians, and media personalities have engaged in the most shameful racebaiting regarding Caldwell and other defendants. They have repeated false claims that Caldwell and others are 'white supremacists,' 'white nationalists,' and 'racists.' President Biden, in a speech ironically advertised as intended to heal America's racial divide, referred to January 6th Trump protesters as "thugs, insurrectionists, political extremists, and white supremacists."

Fischer continued:

> At his confirmation hearing, Attorney General Merrick Garland pledged to 'supervise the prosecution of white supremacists and others who stormed the Capitol on 6 January.' District-based media outlets daily run stories falsely claiming that Trump supporters at the Capitol were 'white supremacists' or 'white nationalists.' This disturbing pattern wherein politicians, media, and talking-heads make unsubstantiated claims of racism against others for crass, short-term political gain should be appalling to all civilized human beings. This systemic race-baiting is disgusting, vile, and definitely vitiates Caldwell's ability to receive a fair trial in the District. The constant false claims that Caldwell is either a white supremacist or associated with white supremacists are seared into the minds of potential D.C. jurors, who are largely predisposed to have negative impressions of right-of-center Americans.

Fischer also provided a helpful timeline of anti-Trump activity in the district during Trump's presidency:

Inauguration Day 2016 saw violent protests in the District, with anti-Trump protesters destroying businesses, cars, and other property, and attacking Trump supporters. The District is the birthplace of 'The Resistance,' which was a loosely organized movement among left-wing activists to thwart President Trump's lawful executive orders and actions. "The Resistance" was consistently hailed by local officials and lauded by the local press. Hardly a week went by during Trump's presidency, moreover, without an anti-Trump protest outside the White House, Congress, the Trump Hotel, at local universities, and other District locales. District residents, moreover, have hectored Trump-supporting Members of Congress, surrounded them in restaurants (e.g., Ted Cruz), congregated around their homes (e.g., Lindsay Graham, Josh Hawley), aggressively confronted them on the street (e.g., Rand Paul), and engaged in incessant "protests" around former Majority Leader McConnell's home. District protesters attempted to burn down historic St. John's church, vandalized millions of dollars of statues and other property, and surrounded the White House in an illegal assemblage during BLM and anti-Trump protests. An anti-Trump zealot shot up a softball practice just across the Potomac in Alexandria, nearly killing Majority Whip Steve Scalise. The level of antipathy towards Trump and his supporters in the District is off the charts and makes it impossible to find an impartial jury.

Pointing out that the overwhelming majority of D.C. residents identify as Democrats, Caldwell asked the judge to consider the likelihood of a fair trial.

> The (legal) issue is whether, in a hyper-political town populated overwhelmingly by hyper-political left-of-center residents, a jury will decide Caldwell's fate based on a dispassionate review of the facts, evidence, and the law? If past is prologue, Caldwell would likely face a District jury pool that, while highly intelligent and thoughtful, will be inclined to reach a decision based on their visceral hatred of Donald Trump and his supporters, and not on the fact.

In a follow-up motion to Judge Amit Mehta, Fischer further explained why his client's future was at risk.

> A trial at the Prettyman Courthouse would take place in the shadow of Capitol Hill. Basically, the Court would be summoning the defendants, their families, and their like-minded supporters to the very area of the District where traumatized victims work, live, and congregate. Additionally, security in the area will be provided mainly by Capitol Hill and D.C. Metro officers, including officers who were psychologically harmed on J6. The very notion that a group of defendants who allegedly caused psychological harm to hundreds in and around Capitol Hill will be ordered back to the 'scene of the crime,' running the risk of triggering additional trauma to the victims, seems insensitive.

During the motion hearing in September, however, Judge Mehta was unmoved if not offended by Fischer's arguments. The motions, Mehta said, sounded like something pulled off a "blog" instead of a serious legal document. He disputed Fischer's allegation that D.C. residents abhor "traditional values" and asked whether Fischer had some sort of poll to support his claim. Mehta insisted that in his experience on the federal bench, he found D.C. juries to be fair and impartial.

Time would tell.

CHAPTER TWELVE:

AMERICAN SHOW TRIALS: WHAT TO EXPECT IN 2022

By fall of 2021, Biden's approval rating was crashing amid the catastrophe in Afghanistan, rising inflation and consumer costs, a bleeding southern border, prolonged Covid mitigation, vaccine bullying, and questions about his overall fitness to lead. Americans are as divided, angry, and fed up as they were before Biden entered the White House, perhaps more so.

School board protests sprang up across the country. Parents enraged at perpetual mask mandates as well as plans to indoctrinate young children on critical race theory or sexual depravity berated school officials. Complaints fell on deaf ears; in some cases, parents were kicked out of public spaces and microphones were silenced.

Loudoun County, Virginia emerged as the flashpoint of parent-versus-bureaucrat control. The school board abruptly ended public comment during a raucous meeting in June where more than 200 residents showed up to express their opposition to critical race theory teachings and transgender policies. To quell the overflowing crowd, the sheriff declared the meeting an "unlawful assembly" and arrested two residents. Scott Smith, the father of a 15 year old girl reportedly raped in a school bathroom by a transgender student, was thrown to the ground by police and arrested when he attempted to publicly expose the board's cover-up of the sexual assault.

This prompted a national organization representing school boards to demand that the Biden White House warn the very same people responsible for funding local schools to sit down and shut up—or else.

"As these acts of malice, violence, and threats against public school officials have increased, the classification of these heinous actions could be the equivalent to a form of domestic terrorism and hate crimes," the president of the National School Boards Association wrote to Biden on September 29, 2021. The group demanded that the long arm of federal law enforcement, including the FBI, Department of Homeland Security, and Secret Service conduct an analysis of the perceived threat and develop a plan on how to address it. It even asked Biden to invoke the PATRIOT Act "in regards to domestic terrorism."[1]

Within days, Biden's Justice Department announced new plans to weaponize its authority against Americans daring to speak out against the Democrats' political agenda. "In recent months, there has been a disturbing spike in harassment, intimidation, and threats of violence against school administrators, board members, teachers, and staff who participate in the vital work of running our nation's public schools," Attorney General Merrick Garland said in a statement issued October 4. "While spirited debate about policy matters is protected under our Constitution, that protection does not extend to threats of violence or efforts to intimidate individuals based on their views."[2]

Garland directed the FBI to meet with local leaders and law enforcement officials to identify threats by parents and establish an approach to enforce "threat reporting, assessment, and response."

That proposal was a bridge too far even for Republican lawmakers who continued to ignore the Justice Department's abusive

---

1   National School Boards Association, *Letter Dated September 29, 2021* (NSBA, 2021).
2   Attorney General Merrick Garland, *Memorandum Re: Partnership Among Federal, State, Local, Tribal, and Territorial Law Enforcement to Address Threats Against School Administrators, Board Members, Teachers, and Staff* (Office of the Attorney General, 2021).

and punitive treatment of January 6 protesters—people who had been charged and were being held indefinitely precisely for holding the wrong views. Senator Tom Cotton, who described January 6 as an "insurrection" and has said nothing about the Justice Department's manhunt for Capitol protesters, even as he sits on the Senate committee overseeing the agency, confronted Attorney General Merrick Garland during a heated October hearing about plans to spy on disgruntled parents.

Cotton sharply grilled Garland about the department's outrageous suggestion that parents were engaged in acts of domestic terrorism if they angrily protested at a school board meeting. The Arkansas senator questioned why it was necessary to invoke the PATRIOT Act and involve federal law enforcement in local matters. "What on earth does the national security division have to do with parents expressing disagreements at school boards?" Cotton asked Garland on October 27.[3] "These are the people who are supposed to be chasing jihadists and Chinese spies." Garland, Cotton said, was "dissembling" the contents of his memo; Garland refuted Cotton's description, repeatedly insisting parental protests are protected by the First Amendment and his memo only addressed violent demonstrators.

But Cotton wasn't buying it. "This is shameful. This testimony, your directive, your performance is shameful. Thank God you are not on the Supreme Court." Cotton pointed his finger at Garland. "You should resign in disgrace, judge."

A whistleblower stepped forward a few weeks later to contradict Garland's insistence that the Justice Department intended only to address threats of violence. Internal emails sent to FBI field offices on behalf of the assistant director of the FBI's counterterrorism division and assistant director of the FBI's criminal investigative division ordered the use of a "threat tag" to identify parents suspected of making "threats specifically directed against school administrators, board members, teachers, and staff." FBI

---

3   Ronn Blitzer, "Tom Cotton to AG Garland: 'Thank God you are not on the Supreme Court'", Fox News, October 27, 2021

agents were asked to seek any "federal nexus" to political conduct, an ominous sign the Justice Department, like its handling of
January 6 cases, will use counterterrorism tools to prosecute and
punish anyone who steps out of line not just in a school board
meeting but in any communications to local school officials.

It's clear that Biden's White House and the agencies under
his control will continue to perpetuate the notion that domestic
violent extremists remained the nation's top security threat. This
doesn't just include alleged militiamen who stormed the Capitol,
unarmed, on January 6. Now the moving target includes fed-up
parents fearful for their children's future after nearly two years
of debilitating lockdowns, mandatory masking, and looming
vaccine requirements.

Then, a political earthquake. On November 2, Republican
Glenn Youngkin, an unknown, won the Virginia governor's race
over Democratic Party stalwart Terry McAuliffe. Republicans
also picked up the offices of the Virginia lietenant governor and
attorney general. The GOP also flipped the House of Delegates
from a 55-member Democratic majority to a 52-member Republican majority.

Another unknown, Jack Ciattarelli, came within one percentage point of beating Phil Murphy, the Democratic governor of New
Jersey. (Murphy declared victory on November 4 but Ciattarelli did
not concede.) Joe Biden won both states by double-digits in 2020.

In Virginia, exit polls showed education was the second
most important issue, clearly reflecting the state's battle over who
should control school curricula.

With little else to run on, Democrats have decided to fully
place their chips on January 6 as a gamble to keep control of
Congress and dissuade Trump supporters from backing his run in
2024. Nonstop headlines about guilty verdicts related to "Trump's
insurrection" could buoy their dimming hopes.

On the government side, the ongoing investigation into the
Capitol breach will continue to wreak revenge on Trump supporters. Meanwhile, Nancy Pelosi's January 6 select committee will

create an ongoing political drama aimed at vilifying anyone in Trump's orbit who can be tied to the purported "insurrection."

In August, the committee asked the National Archives to turn over a long list of materials related to the Capitol protest and the 2020 presidential election.[4] Rep. Bennie Thompson, chair of the committee, requested communications and records between Donald Trump, his family members—including his wife Melania—his top staff, legal counsel, and members of Congress dating back to April 2020.

Included in Thompson's twelve-page letter to national archivist David Ferriero is a list of Republican governors and statewide officials; former staffers; conservative activists such as Brandon Straka and Scott Presler; and media influencers including Jack Posobiec, Alex Jones, Ed Martin, and Gina Loudon.[5] The committee demanded "all documents and communications provided to Donald Trump or Mark Meadows referring to a stolen election, stealing the election, or a 'rigged' election" in addition to "all documents and communications related to the mental stability of Donald Trump or his fitness for office" between January 6 and January 20.

Pursuant to the Presidential Records Act (PCA), Ferriero notified Trump he would start producing documents to the committee; Dana Remus, Biden's White House counsel, subsequently notified Ferriero that Biden would not assert executive privilege on behalf of Trump, a move without precedent. Remus argued that the events of January 6 were so egregious that a full vetting of all presidential documents, including in-person meetings and call logs, should be conducted by Thompson's committee.

"Congress has a compelling need in service of its legislative functions to understand the circumstances that led to these horrific events," Remus wrote. "The Documents shed light on events within the White House on and about January 6 and bear on the Select Committee's need to understand the facts underlying the most serious attack on the operations of the Federal Government since the

---

4   Select Committee to Investigate the January 6th Attack on the United States Capitol, *Press Release: Select Committee Issues Sweeping Demand For Executive Branch Records* (SCIJ6AUSC, 2021).

5   Bennie G. Thompson, *Letter Dated August 25, 2021* (SCIJ6AUSC, 2021).

Civil War. These are unique and extraordinary circumstances. The constitutional protections of executive privilege should not be used to shield, from Congress or the public, information that reflects a clear and apparent effort to subvert the Constitution itself."

When Trump again asserted executive privilege for another batch of archived materials, Biden's lawyer once again would not uphold privilege for his predecessor. Trump immediately filed a lawsuit seeking injunctive relief that ended up in the courtroom of Judge Tanya Chutkan, the Obama appointee who routinely vilified January 6 defendants for their participation in the "riot" and sentenced trespassers to jail time even when Biden's prosecutors asked for home detention or probation.

Chutkan, unsurprisingly, sided with Biden and Thompson over Trump. In a typical dig, she stated the obvious—"Presidents are not kings, and Plaintiff is not President"—and concluded that Biden's view on executive privilege outweighed Trump's simply because Biden is the incumbent. Once again exceeding her role as an impartial jurist, Chutkan imagined a long list of new laws Congress could pass as a result of the committee's investigation including punishment for members of Congress who "engaged in insurrection or rebellion," boosting resources for U.S. intelligence agencies to go after "domestic threats to the security and integrity of our electoral processes," and harsher laws to "deter and punish violent conduct targeted at the institutions of democracy." Her inappropriate soliloquy continued: "These are just a few examples of potential reforms that Congress might, as a result of the Select Committee's work, conclude are necessary or appropriate to securing democratic processes, deterring violent extremism, protecting fair elections, and ensuring the peaceful transition of power."

Thompson praised Chutkan's ruling. Trump promptly filed an appeal to the D.C. Circuit court. After a lengthy hearing, a three-judge panel, each appointed by a Democratic president, upheld Chutkan's decision and denied the injunction. "On January 6, 2021, a mob professing support for then-President Trump violently attacked the United States Capitol in an effort to prevent a Joint Session of Congress from certifying the electoral college votes designating Joseph R. Biden the 46th President of the United States," Judge Patricia Millett, an Obama appointee, wrote at the beginning of the 68-page ruling. "The rampage left multiple people dead, injured more than 140 people, and inflicted millions of dollars in damage to the Capitol." The long-winded diatribe repeated a number of falsehoods and exaggerations about January 6, including the suggestion Officer Brian Sicknick died as a result of the protest; that the building was "desecrated" by regular Americans, and how workers had to "wipe away blood, and clean feces off the walls" after the protest. Repeatedly invoking the notion that the event of January 6 required special legal consideration, the panel concluded that "a rare and formidable alignment of factors supports the disclosure of the documents at issue" and lamented that "the events of January 6th exposed the fragility of those democratic institutions and traditions that we had perhaps come to take for granted."

Thompson issued his first four subpoenas in September.[6] Former Chief of Staff Mark Meadows, former communications director Dan Scavino, former chief of staff to the acting Defense Secretary Kash Patel, and Trump advisor Steve Bannon were summoned to testify before his committee and provide documents. Nothing that Thompson cited in his cover letter to the Trump aides bolstered accusations of criminal conduct—Thompson included a tweet by Scavino promoting Trump's speech on January 6 as proof of wrongdoing—but the subpoenas were a warning shot that Trump would be next. (Bannon defied the subpoena, prompting the committee to pass a resolution to cite him in contempt. The Justice Department announced in an official press release issued on November 12 that Bannon would be charged with contempt of Congress "Since my first day in office, I have promised Justice Department employees that together we would show the American people by word and deed that the department adheres to the rule of law, follows the

---

6   Select Committee to Investigate the January 6th Attack on the United States Capitol, *Press Release: Select Committee Subpoenas Individuals Tied To The Former President In The Days Surrounding January 6th* (SCI-J6AUSC, 2021).

facts and the law and pursues equal justice under the law," Garland said in the release. "Today's charges reflect the department's steadfast commitment to these principles."

Bannon pleaded not guilty.

A flurry of subpoenas followed, including for Amy Kremer, the head of Women for America First, and her daughter, both of whom organized the November, December, and January 6 pro-Trump rallies in Washington.[7] Kremer opened up for Trump on January 6; the event was permitted and more than a mile from the Capitol complex. The only reason Thompson subpoenaed Kremer and ten others tied to the event was to create the illusion that it was unlawful and somehow "incited" the chaos that unfolded that afternoon.

Another big target was Jeffrey Clark, the former acting assistant Attorney General under Trump. Clark appeared to be the only Justice Department official who justifiably believed major violations of election law took place in key states, contrary to a public statement made by William Barr to the Associated Press on December 1. Clark met with Trump in the Oval Office on December 24, according to a scathing report released in October by the majority on the Senate Judiciary Committee entitled "Subverting Justice: How the Former President and His Allies Pressured DOJ to Overturn the Election." The report accused Clark of going over the heads of his superiors to discuss election fraud with Trump and proposed sending a letter to Georgia state lawmakers urging them to delay certifying that state's electoral college slate.

As it had from the beginning, January 6 remained the excuse to criminalize objections to various aspects of the 2020 presidential election and to punish those who tried to expose and investigate them.

Rumors floated that the committee might subpoena Mike Pence. Rep. Adam Kinzinger, fresh off Illinois' Democrats elimi-

---

7   Select Committee to Investigate the January 6th Attack on the United States Capitol, *Press Press Release: Select Committee Subpoenas Organizers of Rallies and Events Preceding January 6th Insurrection* (SCIJ6AUSC, 2021).

nating his congressional district in the remap process, warned that Trump would face a subpoena as well.

The fishing expedition hopes to catch Trump and his Republican allies right as campaign season gets underway. The 2022 election will not just decide control of the House and Senate, which Republicans are projected to win, but governorships in every major state. In December, Cook Political Report flipped the senate races in Arizona, Georgia, and Nevada—all held by Democrats—from favoring Democrats to toss-ups.

But rather than ease voters' fears about the economy, crime, and border security, Democrats seem hell-bent on making January 6 a top political issue. And the media shows no sign of letting up or yielding on the narrative, with cable news outlets and major newspapers continuing to run daily features on the events of that day in the evident hope that this will finally be the means to take downnot just Donald Trump, but his supporters as well.

Will the gambit work? Or will Democratic lawmakers and voters urge their party's leadership to abandon yet another ultimately fruitless and destructive criminal pursuit of the former president?

A separate criminal trial will provide a useful and perhaps illuminating backdrop to January 6 goings-on in 2022. In March 2022, the trial of six defendants charged with federal crimes related to the "kidnapping" of Michigan Governor Gretchen Whitmer will commence, undoubtedly shedding new light on the use of informants and undercover agents that may in turn yield further parallels between that FBI-concocted plot and the Capitol protest.

The government cannot continue to withhold discovery and Brady material that will reveal how many FBI assets were involved in January 6. An October motion by one defense attorney noted that Brady material in her case revealed "information that there were FBI agents in the crowd" that day. Time will tell whether a plausible line between the Whitmer debacle and the events of January 6 might be factually drawn.

*   *   *   *

By November 2021, more than 650 protesters have been arrested and charged. At least 120 have accepted plea deals, the overwhelming majority for the misdemeanor charge of "parading" in the Capitol building. The clock is running out on the government's sketchy application of the "obstruction" charge, applied to more than 230 defendants, and prosecutors wanted to notch as many guilty pleas as possible on the felony count before it was tossed out of court by a judge or jury. At least 210 defendants face charges of "assaulting, resisting, or impeding officers or employees," according to a November update by the FBI.

As of this writing at least seventy defendants remained behind bars indefinitely. Judges continued to comply with Justice Department requests to keep some newly arrested defendants incarcerated. It was clear the nationwide manhunt for Capitol protesters has no end in sight.

Meanwhile, federal judges are pushing marquee trials far into 2022. Trials for the Oath Keepers and the Proud Boys, the alleged white supremacist militia groups charged with nonviolent crimes, will begin in the spring. In mid-October, Judge Amit Mehta, while expressing frustration that prosecutors still had no clear date as to when all discovery materials would be available, nonetheless gave the government a pass. He officially vacated the first trial date in January 2022 for detained Oath Keepers and pushed it until April 2022, which in turn pushed back all the other Oath Keepers trials.

But how will prosecutors make their case given the lack of evidence to support outlandish claims they planned an organized attempt to take over the Capitol building? What "conspiracy" aside from overheated rhetoric on group chats and the use of matching costumes as a form of political cosplay can the Justice Department prove? How much of their involvement on January 6 was organic and how much will turn out to have been instigated by federal informants or agent provocateurs, in the time-honored FBI tradition?

Further, will the flimsy "obstruction of an official proceeding" felony hold up in court? Or will even partisan jurors recognize the chilling effect it will have on future political protests?

And how desperate will prosecutors become to obtain plea deals before the government must disclose the participation of not just the FBI but perhaps other agencies including Capitol police, D.C. Metro police, and the D.C. Department of Homeland Security in prompting the chaos?

Ten months later, government prosecutors still have no "smoking gun" to show the public that January 6 was indeed an "insurrection." Most defendants have pleaded guilty to low-level offenses; nearly a year later, not a single noteworthy scalp had been captured by the Justice Department. In fact, none other than Chief Judge Beryl Howell called the government out for its "almost schizophrenic" approach to the Capitol breach prosecution.

Angry that harsher charges and sentences were not recommended by the Justice Department—while at the same time admitting that her court rarely deals with Class B misdemeanors, the most common January 6 offense—Howell blasted prosecutors for repeatedly agreeing to plea deals on trespassing charges while using inflammatory language to describe January 6. "After all that scorching rhetoric...the government goes on to describe the rioters who got through the police lines and got into the building as 'those who trespassed,' This was no mere trespass."[8]

But of course, as the government well knows, for the overwhelming majority of January 6 protesters, that's exactly what it was. And no amount of bluster or hectoring by Judge Howell or her colleagues can change it.

---

8   Kyle Cheney, Josh Gerstein, *'Almost Schizophrenic': Judge Rips DOJ Approach to Jan. 6 Prosecutions* (Politico, 2021).

*   *   *   *

Meanwhile the struggle to sustain the liberal narrative intensifies even as the prevailing groupthink steadily unravels. No one "murdered" Brian Sicknick. The only people who died on January 6 were Trump supporters, some at the hands of violent, or at least highly reckless, law enforcement officials. No one has been convicted for bringing guns into the building that day.

Damage claims have been debunked by defendants and the Justice Department itself. No one has been charged with "insurrection" or "sedition," including Donald Trump. And few thinking people still believe that the FBI had nothing to do with the Capitol protest.

Many Americans—especially as the full scope of the Russiagate hoax comes into clearer focus with shocking indictments out of Special Counsel John Durham's investigation into the origins of Crossfire Hurricane, and the FBI's illicit probe into the Trump campaign—were beginning to reconsider what they thought they saw on January 6.

The most effective challenge to the dominant liberal narrative to date has been an investigative film produced by Fox News' Tucker Carlson. On November 1, Carlson released "Patriot Purge," a three-part documentary on January 6 which accurately explained how the left is weaponizing the government in a new war on terror aimed at the political Right. Reporters Darren Beattie, attorney Joe McBride, Ali Alexander, and the Huepers among others were interviewed for the film.[9]

Reporters, Democrats, and even some Republicans including Adam Kinzinger and Liz Cheney quickly condemned the film before they even watched it.

Given Carlson's influence, the documentary couldn't help but force a re-evaluation of the supposed "known facts" about that day for many in the Republican Party who had previously gone along with the liberal media narrative. After Garland's disastrous memo on school board meetings, the public, and some Congres-

---

9   Tucker Carlson, *Patriot Purge: Part 1* (Fox News, 2021).

sional Republicans, realized how far the Biden regime would go to target their political enemies.

What else will Americans learn in 2022 about January 6? Will the FBI ever find the suspect who allegedly planted pipe bombs, prompting the first round of evacuations and fear? Will the government make its case that the "insurrection" was planned and executed by white supremacist militia groups? Will the full involvement of the FBI be revealed in public trials and media coverage? Will the Democrats pay a political price at the midterms for their unhinged fixation on January 6, the weaponization of government power against everyone from Trump to people like Paul Hodgkins and Robert Reeder, and the unleashing of the weapons of war against American citizens?

It's tempting, and politically palatable, to lament how the events of January 6 should never have occurred. But that ignores critical open-ended questions that the American people need to have resolved.

Americans deserve to see all the footage captured by security cameras and police officers on the scene that day. Americans deserve to know the full extent to which the FBI was involved before and during the ruckus. They deserve an explanation as to why Capitol protesters have been treated much more harshly than the "social justice" protesters of 2020, which inflicted far more damage than anything that happened during four hours on the afternoon of January 6. They deserve to know what happened to Rosanne Boyland; why Officer Michael Byrd still has a job; why the U.S. Capitol Police should be allowed to expand their unaccountable reach to states outside their jurisdiction; and what limits the surveillance state will honor in its new war on terror against citizens on the political Right.

Will those reasonable demands be fulfilled or ignored? As we wrap this up in late 2021, the likelihood is that all of this will be eschewed by Biden and the Democrats while keeping the heat on Trump and anyone who supported him.

But the public can only be fooled for so long. The November 2021 trial of Kyle Rittenhouse, the Illinois teenager charged with killing two and wounding one during another destructive anti-police riot in Kenosha in August 2020, showed extended video footage that disproved the media narrative that Rittenhouse recklessly and randomly shot people, including blacks, that summer evening. After watching the video for the first time, many Americans realized they again had been duped by the corporate media into believing a myth. Rittenhouse was found not guilty, forcing another reckoning between truth and lies that had festered in the public square for more than a year.

I anticipate the same sort of reckoning will eventually occur regarding January 6. When surveillance video and body-worn camera footage are released, either under court orders or during trials, I believe the American people will be shocked by images of rampant police misconduct that day. Scenes of brawls between police and protesters will make a different impression on viewers from what they've been told, and the circumstances surrounding some of the more vicious encounters will earn more scrutiny.

Meanwhile, prosecutors will fight hard to prevent defendants from telling juries about police misconduct. In advance of a February trial for Robert Gieswein, accused of attacking police with pepper spray, the Justice Department requested that Giewsein "not be able to put forth any evidence that he had a reasonable belief that his action were necessary to defend himself against the immediate use of unlawful force." Prosecutors asked the court to "exclude any testimony and evidence purporting to assert a claim of self-defense." Thomas Webster, the veteran NYPD officer who confronted police that afternoon, notified the government that he will claim self-defense and cite at least 12 minutes of body-worn camera footage from the officer he is accused of attacking to show "repeated use of excessive force" prior to Webster's altercation with a fellow brother in blue.

More evidence will support thousands of first-hand accounts that police allowed protesters into the building. Trials will expose the government's weak cases against the most heavily-charged individuals, including those accused of conspiring to "attack" the Capitol and "overthrow" the government. Proof of "white supremacist" bogeymen will never be found, nor will proof of the existence of lethal, rightwing militia groups. The FBI will also face pressure to address the still-unsolved pipe bomb scare, the threat that prompted the first set of evacuations.

As I tell many desperate victims of the Biden regime's war on terror, facts can't hide forever. And no matter how muddy and dirty the year 2021 turned out to be, 2022 holds out hope, thanks to public trials and more media scrutiny on the Right, that the truth about what really happened on January 6 will finally come to light.

ACKNOWLEDGMENTS

When 2021 began, my plan was to continue reporting on COVID hysteria, feckless Republican leadership in Washington, and the Biden regime's plans to reconfigure the economy around climate change dogma. The nonstop drama surrounding Donald Trump, I figured, would take a welcome break.

Then January 6 happened.

Since then, my coverage of the Capitol protest not only has been the most grueling and fulfilling work of my career but a personal mission, too. Fighting for the rights of January 6 defendants, especially those denied bail and held in an inhumane and punitive prison in the shadow of the U.S. Capitol building, is more than a job—it is a crusade rooted both in empathy for those entangled in this abusive investigation and a desire to protect the Constitution, rule of law, and sense of fair play that Democrats want to destroy in their bloodthirsty drive for political power.

This effort has consumed my time, both professionally and personally. So, I must first thank my husband, John, and my daughters, Victoria and Josie, for their support over the past several months. I would be lying if I said I've never worried how my very public condemnation of this government might affect my family; it's been top-of-mind since the start. Thankfully, I am blessed with a courageous, compassionate, and feisty family; we've shared tears and outrage about the fate of so many innocent Americans whose lives are being destroyed; we have celebrated on the rare occasion a detainee was released; we have laughed many times when my cell phone would ring and one daughter would ask, "Is it a prisoner?" or my husband would walk in the door and announce, "More prison mail!" There is no way I could have taken on this battle alone—their love, encouragement, and good humor is a daily blessing and source of solace.

I am so grateful for my publisher, Adam Bellow, for accepting this risky, controversial project at a time when no one wanted to touch it. He grasps what's at stake in how the Democrats and media are weaponizing January 6; he shares both my professional and personal dedication to exposing the truth and defending the voiceless. His detailed (and I mean *detailed*) edits made my initial manuscript so much stronger; without his careful attention to ensuring this account was fair and reflected the full context of what happened before, during, and after January 6, the book would have fallen far short of my purpose here.

My publisher and editors at American Greatness also have shown great fortitude; nearly every outlet on the political Right immediately echoed the groupthink of January 6. Deconstructing the alleged "insurrection" has been the third rail of political punditry. Chris Buskirk, my publisher, undoubtedly took heat early on for my reporting but never wavered; in fact, he encouraged me to write my first piece in early February on the existence of America's political prisoners when it sounded like a crackpot idea. I'm also deeply appreciative of my editors, Julie Ponzi and Ben Boychuk, and the tireless work of Deb Heine, one of the best breaking news writers in the business.

Roger Kimball, who published my first book in 2020, showed me the ropes on how to write a manuscript and, more importantly, how to prepare for an onslaught of pride-crushing edits. Roger is a dear friend and a compatriot in the fight to expose the truth about January 6. (And a fellow lover of good wine!)

Liz Sheld, my podcast partner, has become a trusted confidante and much-needed sounding board. Plus she tells me everything that's happening in the Hallmark Christmas movies.

My talented and endlessly patient publicist, Mary Diamond, juggled all media requests while encouraging me to stay on the story and occasionally holding back my torch.

I am profoundly grateful for influential media figures who have covered my reporting: Mark Levin, Tucker Carlson, Dinesh D'Souza (who, along with his wife, donated $100,000 to the Patriot Freedom Project), Dennis Prager, Dan Bongino, Megyn Kelly, Jesse Kelly, Lisa Boothe, Jack Murphy, Steve Deace, Sebastian Gorka, Darren Beattie, Greg Kelly, John Bachman, Kara McKinney, Ed Martin, Carl Jackson, Vince Coglianese, Chris Stigall, Larry O'Connor, Steve Bannon, Daniel Horowitz, Justin Hart, Tim Young, Vicki McKenna, and Michael Koolidge have been instrumental in educating the public about January 6. (If anyone is overlooked, please accept my apologies.)

Tucker's three-part documentary on January 6, available on Fox Nation, is a must-watch. The premature pearl-clutching over his eighty-four-second trailer released in late October proves he is over the target. And the highlight of 2021 was appearing on Mark Levin's "Life, Liberty, and Levin" last spring—that interview helped shift the public discourse and opened a lot of eyes.

Tom Fitton at Judicial Watch is an indefatigable warrior who does the granular investigative work that Congress and the national news media refuse to do.

Only a handful of Republican lawmakers in Washington have stood up for January 6 defendants, condemned the political prison, and demanded fair treatment under the law. They are: Senator Ron Johnson and Representatives Louie Gohmert, Marjorie Taylor Greene, Paul Gosar, Matt Gaetz, Andy Biggs, Chip Roy, and Thomas Massie—all are indispensable allies in this fight. Others who have spoken out against the new war on terror against Americans on the political right are Representatives Devin Nunes and Jim Banks. On the flip side, it's an outrage that so many Republican leaders, including House Speaker Kevin McCarthy and Senate Minority Leader Mitch McConnell, have been silent as the rights and dignity of hundreds of Americans are stripped away by Joe Biden's ruthless Justice Department. Shame on them.

Special thanks to friends and colleagues for amplifying and/ or endorsing my work: Lee Smith, David Reaboi, Mollie Hemingway, Sean Davis, Victor Davis Hanson, Miranda Devine, Benjamin Weingarten, Jordan Schachtel, Kyle Shideler, Steve Cortes, Mike Cernovich, Emerald Robinson, Nick Searcy, Darren Beattie, Jack Posobiec, Kash Patel, Jack Langer, Kurt Schlichter, Ace of Spades, Jonathan Bronitksy, Ned Ryun, and David Azerrad.

Unfortunately, few private attorneys have been willing to represent January 6 defendants; most have public defenders or court-appointed attorneys. A special shout-out to Steven Metcalf, Joseph McBride, Marina Medvin, David W. Fischer, and John Kiyonaga for working so hard on behalf of their clients and for justice.

Cynthia Hughes, a relative of a January 6 detainee and a mom with a huge heart, founded the Patriot Freedom Project to raise funds for legal costs and help alleviate the debilitating financial strain endured by so many January 6 defendants. (Most, even those accused of minor offenses, have been fired from their jobs. Detainees have lost their businesses and any means to support their families.) She is a brave fighter for the unfairly prosecuted and a beacon of hope and comfort for so many who think all is lost.

The list of defendants and family members I have connected with over the past several months is too long to list here; suffice it to say, all have been gracious and grateful despite facing life-destroying persecution by the Biden regime and libelous, vicious media coverage. I have received many personal letters filled with both heartbreak and hope. I'm especially grateful to Thomas and Sharon Caldwell, George Tanios, Richard Barnett, Michael Curzio, and Karl Dresch for directly sharing their stories with me.

Micki Witthoeft, Ashli Babbitt's mother, has not just suffered the loss of her daughter but endured the media's demonic justification of what happened to her—nonetheless, she remains optimistic for the country she loves and is a passionate defender of all January 6 defendants. I am thankful she shared her painful story with me.

As I work on this issue, I often think of my late grandparents, John and Lois Copeland, who met in the U.S. Army right before both were deployed to Europe in the waning months of World War II. They were married in the American Church of Paris in September 1945, returned to America, raised three sons including my late father, and helped build this country into what it is today. They would laugh at the idea the four-hour disturbance at the Capitol that day was an act of "war" or amounted to a terrorist attack. Further, they would be mortified at what is happening—they didn't make the sacrifices they did so the Biden regime, corrupt national news media, and desperate anti-Trump Republicans could destroy it. Their legacy and fighting spirit are always with me.

God Bless—and Save—America.

About the Author

Julie Kelly is a political commentator and senior contributor to American Greatness. Her past work can be found at The Federalist and National Review as well as guest columns in the Wall Street Journal, Chicago Tribune, The Hill, and Roll Call.

Born and raised in the suburbs of Chicago, Kelly worked as a political consultant for Republican candidates and office holders.

For more than a decade, Kelly was a full-time stay-at-home mom to her two daughters. In 2014, Kelly launched an in-home cooking class to teach other moms how to cook, which led to writing free-lance columns on food, agriculture, and biotechnology.

Her reporting on the events and aftermath of January 6 has been featured on Fox News, Newsmax, and OAN as well as on syndicated radio programs across the country.

A native of Naperville, Illinois, Kelly now lives in Orland Park, Illinois with her husband, John and daughters, Victoria and Josie. She also has two very protective German Shepherds. She graduated from Eastern Illinois University in 1990 with a bachelor of arts degree in speech communications and double minors in journalism and political science.